THE GOOD LIFE

THE GOOD LIFE

Options in Ethics

BURTON F. PORTER

ROWMAN & LITTLEFIELD PUBLISHERS, INC.
Lanham • Boulder • New York • Toronto • Plymouth, UK

Published by Rowman & Littlefield Publishers, Inc.
A wholly owned subsidiary of The Rowman & Littlefield Publishing Group, Inc.
4501 Forbes Boulevard, Suite 200, Lanham, Maryland 20706
http://www.rowmanlittlefield.com

Estover Road, Plymouth PL6 7PY, United Kingdom

British Library Cataloguing in Publication Information Available

Library of Congress Cataloging-in-Publication Data
Porter, Burton Frederick.
  The good life : options in ethics / Burton F. Porter. — 4th ed.
      p. cm.
  Includes bibliographical references and index.
  ISBN 978-0-7425-6542-5 (cloth : alk. paper) — ISBN 978-0-7425-6543-2 (pbk. : alk. paper) — ISBN 978-0-7425-6544-9 (electronic)
  1. Ethics—Textbooks. I. Title.
  BJ1012.P67 2009
  241—dc22

                                                                                    2009019893

∞™ The paper used in this publication meets the minimum requirements of American National Standard for Information Sciences—Permanence of Paper for Printed Library Materials, ANSI/NISO Z39.48-1992.

Printed in the United States of America

To William and Owen
who are entrusted with the future,
which means the future is in good hands

CONTENTS

PREFACE

People today have an unprecedented degree of freedom in deciding how they want to live, but this freedom of choice comes at a time of widespread uncertainty as to which way of life is best. The two are related, for freedom generates uncertainty as we realize the range of possibilities open to us, but our confusion goes beyond that. Deciding how to live is a problem today in ways that would not seriously have troubled our ancestors. The contours of an individual's life used to be more narrowly defined, social and religious expectations held people more firmly within acceptable limits, and there were clear standards as to what constituted a worthwhile existence. However, as we begin the twenty-first century, the traditional sources of knowledge have lost their authority and people are left somewhat bewildered, without center or direction. We have enormous latitude to choose whatever life we want, but we are not sure what life we want to choose.

In response to this condition, some people return to the ideals they absorbed as children, the values of a particular place, but such thinking becomes sentimentality and escapism unless accompanied by reflection; we cannot go home again. The only justifiable course of action is to consider the various life alternatives in an independent and critical way, thereby arriving at some viable purpose for our personal lives.

This work has been written to help the reader in this search—not to provide ready answers but to highlight possible directions. And the theories that are discussed should not be approached in an impersonal way. Rather, readers should "mix their blood" with the ideas about the good life, and try to decide which is the most defensible. For we are dealing with one of the most personal and fundamental questions of existence; namely, what is the best way for our lives to be lived.

ACKNOWLEDGMENTS

In preparing this edition of *The Good Life* I gratefully acknowledge the persistence and counsel of Ross Miller, senior editor at Rowman & Littlefield, who is both sharp-minded and kind-hearted. I also appreciate the assistance of Jonathan Sisk, editor-in-chief; Evan Wiig, editorial assistant; and Alden Perkins, senior production editor.

Burton Porter
Amherst, Massachusetts

1

THE NATURE OF ETHICS

People are not content merely to live; they feel impelled to evaluate their existence and to determine whether they are living well or badly. They try to judge the value of the goals they are pursuing and the broad purposes that motivate their actions. They want to know whether their conduct toward others is right and reasonable or whether they are being unjust, unfair, or in some way morally blameworthy. They want to justify themselves to themselves, and be assured that their life choices are not only good but are pursued in ways that are ethically right.

In short, people reflect upon their lives throughout the living of them, and measure their conduct against an ideal that strikes them with the force of an external standard. To some this is God; to others it is conscience; to still others it represents a higher self that draws them forward beyond the self of any given moment. Whatever the name assigned to this power, it operates at times of deliberation and introspection, and distinguishes human life from animal life. For animals may be conscious and the higher species even self-aware and capable of reasoning and symbolizing, but they cannot feel remorse at having ruined their lives or satisfaction at having kept their promises. No animal experiences a sense of integrity, regret, penitence, innocence, or self-reproach.

There are, then, ongoing internal dialogues within human beings that can also become disagreements when values are at variance. People are concerned to defend the principles they hold, either to others or themselves, summoning good reasons to support their choices. That is, they feel the need to enter into the realm of ethical discussion and attempt to establish strong grounds for maintaining the values fundamental to their lives.

The field of Ethics helps in reaching such decisions, exposing people to the theories of the good life that have been proposed and the critical considerations that apply in evaluating those theories. Ethics tries to determine the goal or end in living, the ideal life that human beings should live, and offers justification for thinking so. Ethicists are also concerned with conduct as well as purpose, with what is right and wrong, praiseworthy and blameworthy in the way of actions. People's character is also evaluated because outstanding actions flow from outstanding people; what we do reflects who we are. The Greek *ethos*, in fact, means character.

Ethics asks fundamental questions about existence that each person must answer as thoughtfully as possible: What type of life would be fulfilling and worthwhile? What should we live for? How can we distinguish between correct and incorrect behavior? Does right and wrong depend upon the situation or are there basic principles that apply in all circumstances? What authority can justify the values we endorse? To what extent should our pursuit of life goals be limited by obligations to other people? Ethics conducts a rational investigation into such questions, and tries to determine our purpose in living, the proper conduct of our lives, and the kind of person we should aspire to be.

A. THE PLACE OF ETHICS WITHIN PHILOSOPHY

Morals are often used interchangeably with ethics, but when a distinction is made morals refers to right and wrong, ethics to the rules that govern right and wrong. Beyond that, ethics is a branch of philosophy along with *metaphysics, epistemology, logic,* and *aesthetics,* and it involves each of these, for the fabric of philosophy is a seamless cloth. Therefore, to understand ethics more fully we need to explore the nature of these fields and how they interconnect with ethical concerns.

Metaphysics, which lies at the core of philosophy, takes as its subject matter the study of the nature of reality—its essential character, structure, and processes. To Aristotle (384–322 BCE) metaphysics is a single, comprehensive study of what is fundamental to all existence, and he categorized everything as a substance, quality, quantity, or relation.[1] This approach (although not this classification) may be taken as representative of the metaphysical approach. Metaphysicians want to comprehend the basic nature of what is real, its ultimate truths, first principles, underlying essence. They speculate on fundamental things such as the nature of the self and the external world, form and matter, causes and reasons, space and time, and they try to diagram the universe as it actually is. They inquire into the "mode of being" of mind, number, infinity, spirit, and God, and even question the powers and capacity of human beings to understand reality, piecemeal or as a whole. David Hume (1711–1776) and Immanuel Kant (1724–1804), for example, regarded the primary task of metaphysics as the determination of its own limits.

The metaphysician also wants to discover whether the universe possesses a purpose, an ultimate end such as a Day of Judgment or the maximum evolutionary development of all forms of existence. Metaphysicians ask if there is any meaning to the universe, any inherent value to life, or whether all events occur by chance, including human life on earth. Are people a part of the natural and material order of things, without a soul animating their bodies, or does the external universe resemble human beings, with a mind and a will? When one asks questions of this type one is engaged in metaphysical speculation.

Ethics touches metaphysics when issues are raised concerning the place of values in the overall scheme of reality, what is called the "ontological status" of values. Do certain ends in living have an objective foundation, and are certain principles grounded in the universe itself? If, for example, we choose to live in accordance with nature, following the rhythm of its seasons, harmonizing our spirit with its tranquility, reducing our activities to the satisfaction of elemental needs, are we then linking into the cosmos in some fundamental way? If we choose to develop our potentialities to the utmost, striving to realize our ideal selves and become all that we can be, is this in keeping with the basic function that human life is intended to serve? And when we defend the worth of freedom, compassion, justice, and honesty, are these natural and universal values, objectively defensible and real? Does the universe contain intrinsic rules of right and wrong that can be found and followed, or is it devoid of values, containing only physical matter, brute facts? Has the universe a moral dimension as part of its metaphysical reality, or do human beings invest life with meaning through free commitments, creating values rather than discovering them?

We can see by these questions how ethics and metaphysics can be intertwined. Whenever we begin wondering why certain types of actions and ways of life are preferable to others, we are inevitably led to reflect on their relation to the overall scheme of things.

Epistemology. When we reflect not on the nature of reality but on the means for knowing reality, on how to gain genuine knowledge of what is so, then we are engaged in the branch of philosophy named epistemology. Epistemologists are not so much concerned with what we know as how we know. They want to determine how genuine knowledge can be obtained, and how to differentiate between certainties, possibilities, assumptions, hypotheses, guesses, convictions, and obvious truths. They ask how one verifies historical statements, religious beliefs, and aesthetic judgments, and how that differs from proving mathematical propositions and scientific laws. Most importantly they want to know whether sense perception, reason, or intuitive awareness is the most trustworthy means of knowing the world.

Normally we are only concerned with the content of knowledge not with its basis, but occasions can arise when *how* we know becomes crucial. To take an exotic example, suppose we are traveling in the desert and see what appears to be a body of water in the distance. It is at a place off our route where, according to our map and knowledge of geology, there should not be any water, and we wonder whether it is a hallucination. We then must decide whether to trust our senses, which tell us there is water at that site, or our reason, which tells us there cannot be water there; and if we are dying of thirst it will be a critical matter. Should we conclude that seeing is believing or that the phenomenon is a mirage? Furthermore, our decision in these circumstances cannot be avoided; it is, in the phrase of William James (1842–1911), a "forced option." We must decide one way or the other, because not deciding would be deciding; we would be continuing the line of our march. Therefore, an epistemological choice is unavoidable, and we have to rely on either the evidence of our senses or our rational judgment.

Obviously, not all decisions in epistemology are matters of life and death, but the point of the example is that we must establish reliable criteria for knowledge or we will have no way of deciding what is real and what is appearance. Conflicts do occur between the various means of knowing so that the epistemological issue can be insistent, forcing us to come to terms with the question of how reality is determined.

The connection between epistemology and ethics is obvious, for in order to assert that certain values are worthwhile we are eventually required to explain how one knows this is true. That is, whenever we claim priority for particular ethical standards, we must substantiate that claim in terms of an epistemological justification. Every ethic must have its epistemic base, otherwise value assertions become mere prejudices, wishes, or dogmas. We cannot reply, "It is self-evident," when asked for the authority behind an ethical judgment, for that may mean only that it is evident to ourselves.

How do we know, for example, that the preservation of life is morally preferable to the taking of life? Presumably we cannot use our senses and see that life is better than death. We can only perceive the character of both. Do we reason, then, that being conscious is better than being unconscious? But that judgment hardly seems a rational truth like "parallel lines never meet" or "the square of the hypotenuse of a right triangle is equal to the sum of the square of the other two sides." Is it, therefore, a matter of intuitive awareness whereby we experience an immediate appreciation of the value of life over death? But intuitions are notoriously unreliable, varying enormously between individuals. How can something so subjective be taken as the foundation of moral knowledge? Can we depend upon an authority such as parental wisdom, a sacred book, or the weight of tradition? No, because we establish someone or something as an authority according to certain standards of reliability, and what constitutes a reliable standard is precisely what is in question. In fact, this epistemological predicament plagues all epistemological theories. What, then, can we take as the fundamental means of knowing in establishing our fundamental means of knowing?

Many of these objections can be met, but they are being raised here to show some of the difficulties involved in establishing an epistemological basis for ethics. Perhaps an intuitive awareness or "moral sense" plays a part in achieving ethical knowledge, particularly of first principles. But the point is that some epistemological foundation must be established to support any ethical theory.

Logic. A third branch of philosophy that is connected to ethics is logic, although the connection may not be as apparent. In order to develop our ethical ideas in a systematic, consistent, and rigorous way we must employ the rules of logic, otherwise we could have a mass of notions that are irrational or even self-contradictory.

Logic is the study of the laws of inference or the theory of proof. Correct reasoning is its chief concern, and it does not matter what is being reasoned about or even whether the conclusions of an argument are true. The logician is primarily interested in sound thinking, a system of thought that is valid in its chain of reasoning.

The logician's work is both positive and negative. He or she wants to describe the process of constructing valid arguments and detecting fallacies in reasoning. For example, it would not be sound reasoning to argue "nothing is better than a good doctor," "a bad doctor is better than nothing," therefore "a bad doctor is better than a good doctor." The logical mistake, of course, is contained in the ambiguous term "nothing." The first statement, which is called the major premise of the argument, can be paraphrased as "there is not anything which surpasses a good doctor," whereas the second statement, or the minor premise, translates into "a bad doctor is better than none at all." Once this ambiguity is made clear, the conclusion can be seen not to follow from the premises.

In constructing valid arguments there are rules of formal reasoning that must be used, and they apply to both deduction and induction. In deductive logic we reason from the general to the particular. For example, beginning with the proposition that "all fish have gills" we can argue that if "tuna are fish" then "tuna have gills." This is a typical deductive syllogism. In inductive logic we reason from the particular to the general, so that if we examine a substantial number of green plants and finds that each one forms starch in the presence of light, we can conclude that all green plants form starch in the presence of light. The conclusion is not certain because we cannot examine all green plants, and the degree of probability depends upon the adequacy of the survey. If the generalization is based upon the observation of two cases it is naturally much weaker than if several thousand cases were chosen, and from different climates, elevations, ecologies, and so forth. The randomness of the sample is a significant factor.

Ethics, like all other disciplines, must adhere to the rules of logic in developing systems of ideas. It is possible to reach sound conclusions using an illogical argument, but then the conclusions are true by chance and not by logic. For example, one could argue that since dancing makes people happy, and there are protections against self-incrimination, therefore the earth turns on its axis. The conclusion happens to be true but only by chance; there is no rational inference that makes the conclusion true. If we use a logical argument, we are much more likely to reach a sound conclusion. In fact, if the premises of a deductive argument are true and the form of the argument is valid, then the conclusion is necessarily true. It is advantageous, therefore, for anyone interested in building a viable theory of ethics, to pay attention to the validity of the reasoning process.

Aesthetics is the fourth branch of philosophy and it is very often grouped with ethics under the common heading of value theory or axiology. This field of philosophy deals principally with standards in judging art, and with the various theories that have been developed as to what makes good art good. Aestheticians are also concerned with the relationships between the arts, how to differentiate art from other things (non-art), the aesthetic experience, the process of creation, and so forth. Beauty is also studied by the aesthetician, although in the contemporary world most artists do not try to create beauty. A work of art may he moving, offensive, witty, profound, disturbing, uplifting, and so forth rather than attractive.

Aesthetics and ethics are often grouped under the same heading of axiology because evaluating a work of art and evaluating an action or ideal is similar. We can ask, for example, whether there exists an objective basis for determining value, and to what extent our judgment reflects our society or our personality; in art the question is whether beauty is in the eye of the beholder, and in ethics whether right and wrong are only a matter of taste. Another common question relates to the degree to which people can live privately, indulging their own interests, versus the obligations that are owed to society at large. For example, can artists, in clear conscience, foster art for art's sake without considering the moral impact of their work on viewers?

As this last question indicates, aesthetics and ethics also touch on the issue of obscenity. Some philosophers feel that a genuine work of art, by its very nature, cannot be obscene since beauty and goodness are one. For art to be beautiful and degrading would be an internal contradiction. However, others believe that a work of art can be aesthetically good but morally bad, degrading society to by its sensual content; the writings of Jean Genet (1910–1986) and the Marquis de Sade (1740–1814), for example, have sometimes been placed in this category.

And if genuine works of art can be corrupting, then the moral question of censorship arises. Should that which is obscene be prohibited, or should people be free to demean themselves if they so choose, provided that they do not force the experience on others? Which takes precedence in the case of obscene art: the aesthetic importance of the work or its moral impact? Is it more important for people to have access to the art or to be protected from corruption?

One way to evade the problem is to claim that although art may be obscene, it should be available to the general public because it does no real damage; no one was ever harmed by a book. But if art never harms anyone, then it never helps them either. It is irrelevant to life and does not affect people's attitudes or behavior one way or the other. That claim is obviously false and certainly would not be held by anyone who takes art seriously. Most artists assume that what they create has some influence on society; otherwise they would stop working. It would be the rare exception for an artist to create art only for himself, writing poetry in the morning and burning his work at night. Artists generally want to move others, and this influence can be for good or ill. Therefore the question of censorship for the sake of the public welfare is a real one.

One final point of contact between ethics and aesthetics might be mentioned. From time to time a proposal has been made to judge the quality of a person's life in terms of its aesthetic character. According to this approach, what is done is not nearly so important as how it is done; the style of an action is significant, not its content, its manner, not its matter. If a person lives in charming ways, with great spirit and grace, if he or she has a harmonious personality and sensitivity to others and to the variety and depth of experience, then it becomes irrelevant what actions have been chosen. It is the way the person's life is conducted that counts, not the particular conduct, for all actions that flow from such a person are imbued with beauty.

There are serious problems in accepting this theory, of course, when one considers whether graceful assassins are exonerated because of their style. Nevertheless it holds considerable appeal and deserves mention as an identification of aesthetics and ethics. The aesthetically refined life is here the standard of excellence. In a sense we have returned to the idea that what is beautiful is good, not only in art but in a human life itself, which has become a work of art.

Political Philosophy. Metaphysics, epistemology, logic, and aesthetics each has a place in the construction of ethical theories, and these four areas together with ethics make up the main fields of philosophy.

But brief mention should also be made of *political philosophy* which, although not one of the five principal areas of philosophy, is nevertheless important and intimately connected with ethics. Broadly defined, political philosophy deals with theories concerning the ideal form of government, with the nature and purpose of the state, and with the ultimate justification of its authority over individuals. In speculating on how the state should be constituted so as to bring about the maximum good for its citizens, the political philosopher relies upon a base of ethics to determine what the good life might be, both individually and collectively. Aristotle, for example, conceived of his *Nicomachean Ethics* as a necessary complement to his *Politics;* they were in fact, two halves of a single work. And Plato in *The Republic* began with a discussion of virtue and justice in the individual, and then developed his famous theory of the just state as an analogue. To Plato, the state is the individual "writ large," and the nature and ideal functioning of the one directly corresponds to that of the other. Although most philosophers would not identify the state and the individual quite so closely, there is a logical connection between the two, and anyone concerned with the welfare of human beings would want to understand which political structure would promote human flourishing. Conversely, in order to form a theory of a political utopia, one must first know what it is that constitutes human welfare. Thus political philosophy and ethics are necessarily interrelated.

Ethics itself has been defined throughout the chapter, but it might be useful to describe its scope more precisely. As a branch of philosophy, ethics consists of an inquiry into the nature of the right and the good. *Right* refers to actions, conduct, and behavior, and here the ethicist is concerned with judging the morality of acts such as stealing, promise-keeping, killing, and truth-telling, and concepts such as self-deception, integrity, exploitation, and compassion. This part of ethics also deals with duties and obligations, the relations between "right" and "ought," means and ends, excuses and responsibility. *Good,* on the other hand, applies to the ends, goals, or purpose of existence, the fundamental reasons for living rather than particular portions of conduct. One refers to someone having lived well or badly, and in this sense the ethicist or moral philosopher considers the question of the good life. What goals should people pursue in order to lead personally successful lives? What constitutes a valid reason for living, and what purposes should motivate people in their life choices? Good also refers to people's character, and what makes a person commendable and worthy of being admired.

It is the latter part of ethics which forms the subject matter of this book. We are almost exclusively concerned here with the examination and evaluation of the various theories of the good life offered by moral philosophers, the alternative proposals and complementary conceptions as to the purpose of human existence. Questions of right are only dealt with insofar as they contribute to our understanding and evaluation of some life purpose.

The problem of the good life is not, of course, the exclusive domain of professional ethicists, for everyone speculates on the best way to live. But moral philosophers tend to explore the question more systematically and rigorously, with knowledge of the various alternatives that have been proposed throughout human history. They bring to the issue a certain expertise in assessing rival claims and in developing a personal system of thought.

At the same time, because of the universality of the issues involved, we can identify with the moral philosophers' theories and appreciate their efforts. These theories are not beyond us, and we too want to assess the meaning and value placed upon the various lives we live, the basic aims and principles around which human activities are organized. Everyone is concerned with the best way to exist. It is more than an academic matter, therefore, to investigate what some outstanding minds have thought to be good reasons for being in the world.

B. ETHICAL ISSUES AND THEIR RESOLUTION

But how is it possible for ethical positions to be justified? Disputes about scientific facts can be settled by using objective empirical tests, which help confirm or refute claims about the physical world. The proof takes the form of the reaction of gases, the color of litmus paper, or the appearance of organisms under a microscope. But how can one resolve the question of whether duty to others or personal development is more important, or whether loyalty overrides the value of honesty? It would seem that ethical disputes cannot be resolved with any certainty but merely show differences in taste and attitude between people. Perhaps values, by their very nature, are impossible to verify, and the ethical positions people take only reveal the societal or parental norms they have assimilated. When a person says, "Promises should be kept," this may be only an autobiographical comment which reveals more about the psychology of the person than about the nature of promises.

Such a conclusion is extremely tempting when one is faced with the difficulties of justifying values but it does not hold up well under scrutiny; in a sense, it is not a conclusion at all but a throwing up of one's hands, a cry of exasperation. People who say that value judgments cannot be validated usually mean that they are puzzled as to how to validate them. But not knowing how to justify values is not the same as knowing that values cannot be justified.

It is certainly true that ethical problems are not solved in scientific ways, that is, by means of the types of observation and experimentation common to the physical or social sciences; nevertheless standards do exist for determining which ethical ideals are more likely to be correct. Although empiricism is not the principal method used in ethics, that does not mean no criteria are available to separate better and worse values or that all ethical judgments merely reflect our socio-psychological background.

The Standard of Reasonableness

One criterion that can be employed in ethics is that of reasonableness, whereby that theory most in accord with reason is judged to be true. More specifically, the standard of reasonableness means that an ethical theory must: (1) be consistent within itself and with regard to its implications; (2) take the relevant facts into account and not contradict those facts; and (3) provide the most probable interpretation of human experience. Each of these criteria requires elaboration.

Consistency. First, we should strive for consistency in our position and especially avoid self-contradiction. This is true in ethics as well as in philosophy in general. That is, we cannot say something *is* and *is not* at the same time. The sky cannot be both blue and not blue, an action cannot be both kind and unkind, a surface cannot be rough and smooth. If we refer to a square circle or a married bachelor we are talking nonsense. This rule of thought was first articulated by Aristotle who said that X cannot be affirmed and denied simultaneously. Of course, a statement can be true in one respect but not true in another respect (a pin drop is soft to a person but loud to a gnat), but something cannot be both true and false in the same way. In *A Tale of Two Cities* Dickens wrote, "It was the best of times, it was the worst of times, it was the age of wisdom, it was the age of foolishness," but he is not contradicting himself; some aspects were wonderful, others terrible, and there was a mix of good sense and nonsense.

In this connection there are *seeming* contradictions called oxymorons as in jumbo shrimp, deafening silence, and make haste slowly; humorous oxymorons include pretty ugly, British cuisine, pop culture, and military intelligence! Strictly speaking, these are not self-contradictory because they make sense; we know what is meant, we understand the irony.

Genuine inconsistencies and self-contradictions would include, "It is absolutely true that everything is relative"; "There is an exception to every rule" (which is itself a rule, with exceptions); "I would kill for the Nobel Peace Prize"; "Everything people say is nonsense"; "I am giving up on altruism; it just doesn't pay;" and "Procrastinate Now!" The comedian Oscar Levant wrote a book called *Memoirs of an Amnesiac*.

In addition, proverbs can contradict one another, as in "Absence makes the heart grow fonder" but "Out of sight, out of mind"; "You can't teach an old dog new tricks" but "It's never too late to learn"; Too many cooks spoil the broth" but "Many hands make light work"; and "If it's not broken don't fix it" but "A stitch in time saves nine."

It would also be contradictory to claim that virtue is always rewarded (that what goes around comes around) and that nice guys finish last. Equally contradictory is the view that people who are raised in a slum should not be blamed for committing crimes (we ought not to punish the victim) but people who pull themselves up by their bootstraps should be praised. Similarly, we cannot believe that everything happens according to fate and that people are free and responsible for what they do. An inconsistent position of this last kind was taken at various points in intellectual history by theologians such as St. Augustine (354–430), Martin Luther (1483–1546), and Sören Kierkegaard (1813–1855), who tried to explain it away by calling it a mystery.[2] But if all events are preordained, this must include human actions as well. When people cannot do other than what they did, then they have no freedom of choice and cannot be held accountable. "I could not help it" is a complete excuse.

Such inconsistencies represent the type of muddled thinking that should be avoided if we are to arrive at a sound philosophic position. One should not give credence to the incredible any more than one should doubt the indubitable.

Take the Relevant Facts into Account. To illustrate this second point, we could look at the issue of race and crime in the United States. Just less than 40 percent of the prison population is black, although blacks constitute only 12 to 13 percent of the population at large. That fact cannot be ignored—although its implications might be debated. Does that show that a disproportionate number of blacks are committing crimes, or that blacks are more likely to be arrested, tried, convicted, and jailed? Does it only show prejudice in the criminal justice system? If, after allowing for racial bias, we still conclude that blacks commit proportionately more crimes, is that a function of their relatively lower income and, ultimately, discrimination? Whatever conclusion we reach, we cannot pretend the prison population is not heavily black.

Another instance in which factual information should be taken into account is in discussing the ethics of homosexuality. One source of AIDS is sexual contact between homosexual partners—although there are other sources as well; drug addicts who use dirty needles are at high risk. Again, this does not settle the issue but it is relevant to it. We might conclude that, since AIDS is a public health problem, homosexual contact should be condemned as morally and legally wrong. However, we could also argue that homosexuals, as well as heterosexuals, should practice safe sex. If condoms are used, the danger is minimized or eliminated.

Knowing when a fact is relevant can be problematic. For example, if adultery can be proven, that is often taken as grounds for divorce. But a marriage could break down even if adultery has not occurred, and there might be adultery in a basically sound marriage. Perhaps the important issue is whether the marriage is hopelessly broken and that should be the basis for divorce, regardless of whether adultery has taken place.

Another example of uncertainty as to whether a fact is relevant can be drawn from the early American pioneers. Some of them bypassed the Great Plains in their search for fertile farmland. They reasoned that since the land did not grow tall trees, it would not grow strong crops. They traveled on to wooded land, felled and cleared the trees, then planted their fields. If they had realized that that fact is not relevant, they could have saved themselves a great deal of labor.

Although the above example is not drawn from ethics, the same questions arise in ethical matters. We know we cannot recommend that someone do something if, in fact, the person cannot do it. To tell someone who is in a wheelchair that they should save a child from a speeding car makes no sense; they then have no moral obligation.

A philosophic example can be found in the ancient Greek philosopher Plato (428–347 BCE). As part of his ethical theory Plato held that virtue is knowledge. This cryptic phrase has been variously interpreted but one meaning is that moral behavior is the result of knowledge concerning the nature of goodness, and wrong acts can be attributed to ignorance about the good. It was Plato's view that no one who knows what is good would deliberately do what is bad. All wrongdoing, therefore, is due to people mistaking what is good, rather like a child who foolishly eats too much dessert not realizing that a stomachache will follow. With understanding, one naturally makes sensible and worthwhile choices. Moral education, then, is a prerequisite for moral behavior, for whoever knows the good will automatically act in accordance with it.

To our minds, steeped in psychological knowledge, this seems a naive assumption. A modern thinker would never believe that people always act rationally, in accordance with what they know to be good for others or themselves. Psychologists have demonstrated that people sometimes act in self-destructive ways, even after they realize that what they are doing is wrong. Out of frustration, guilt, compulsion, fear, aggression, anxiety, and so forth, people will repeatedly commit harmful acts despite their realization of the damage they cause. In fact, the concepts of guilt and sin presuppose awareness by the person of his or her wrongdoing, and moralists have expended a great deal of energy attempting to fortify not the weak-minded but the weak-willed against temptation. Even among the Greeks the concept of *akrasia* existed, and it was defined by Aristotle as knowing what one ought to do but still not doing it. This undermines the claim that virtue is knowledge. Any ethical theory that fails to consider facts of this degree of significance can be criticized as having a serious gap; a sin of omission can be as important as a sin of commission.

The Most Probable Interpretation of Human Experience. Just as we want to incorporate relevant facts, we want the most plausible interpretation of experience. In the late twentieth century some people argued that hats caused baldness because a high incidence of baldness was observed in men who wore hats. However, this was not a good interpretation. The causation was actually the reverse: bald men tend to wear hats to cover their baldness.

Similarly it has been asserted that Arizona and New Mexico have poor air quality, despite the fact that they are desert states without much industry. This assertion was made because a high percentage of the population have respiratory illnesses such as bronchitis, asthma, and tuberculosis. But statistics can be misleading. In reality, Arizona and New Mexico attract a large number of people with respiratory illnesses because of their dry climate and clean air.

In the same way, children might think that flapping flags cause the wind to blow, and that winter is brought on by birds flying south; they might think summer would stay if the birds could be caught. It is not a sign of animal intelligence that deer will cross at deer crossings, and eating rare steak does not make people aggressive, although aggressive people tend to eat their steak rare. It is not uncanny that the Pilgrims left Plymouth, England and landed exactly on Plymouth Rock; we should not be amazed at the odds or at their navigational skill. Pre-technological people might believe that a rain dance can cause rain when, in fact, timing has a great deal to do with the success of a rain dance.

To take a more serious example, people sometimes feel that their wrongdoings are known and punished by a hidden but just power governing the world. Usually this power is identified as God, but it need not be. An impersonal moral force or a mechanical system of rewards and punishments could also be thought responsible for all joy and suffering, as in the Hindu and Buddhist concept of karma. Whatever the attribution, people may believe that they reap what they sow, that when disaster strikes it is the result of some transgression on their part. "What have I done to deserve this?" is a familiar cry when sickness occurs or when people find themselves the victims of some natural catastrophe. It is the cry of Job in the Bible, an upright and God-fearing man who suffered a multitude of misfortunes, and the cry of all those who feel themselves oppressed by calamities and try to discover the sins that have brought such punishment down on their heads.[3] We say, "Why me?" and by that phrase we mean not only to search our own souls but the soul of the universe, wondering whether fairness and justice exist and whether our pain is deserved.

When we question the justification for our suffering, we can be led to doubt the entire idea of the universe functioning in a retributive way. For the scheme of rewards and punishments is strangely askew. People who are essentially good can experience one tragedy after another, while some awful people enjoy amazing luck, getting through life virtually unscathed. Not only is the distribution of suffering askew but the degree of suffering does not correspond to the severity of people's offenses. In a court of law we may strive for justice but in the natural world the punishment rarely fits the crime.

Simply stated, the universe is not necessarily fair, at least this side of the grave. Our experience does not support the notion that immoral people are visited with natural evils in their earthly life and moral people are blessed with happiness. The rain seems to fall on the just and the unjust alike.

A more probable explanation as to why certain people are the victims of a catastrophe is that they happened to be at that place on earth where the event occurred, whether a hurricane, an earthquake, or a volcanic eruption. Similarly, the reason some people contract poliomyelitis or leukemia has to do with microscopic forms of life that happen to be present in their bodies. It does not seem to correlate at all with their moral character.

These three criteria, then, constitute the standard of reasonableness that an ethical theory must satisfy if it is to be taken seriously. This means that the mode of ethical justification differs from that of scientific verification, but not in being subjective; it is an equally objective and rational matter. Therefore, one person's opinion is not necessarily as good as another's, for, as we have seen, ethical theories vary in the degree to which they are rationally defensible. As Voltaire remarked, "Men will continue to commit atrocities as long as they continue to believe absurdities"; reason can help us avoid the absurd and destructive ideas.

From the foregoing it should not be inferred, of course, that science does not operate rationally as well as empirically. In fact, we label a field as science not because of its subject matter but because of its systematic and rigorous method of dealing with empirical phenomena. Both astronomy and astrology concern the stars but only one is a science; the same is true of alchemy and chemistry. It is scientific method that distinguishes science, and that is a highly rational activity involving the formulation of a hypothesis, experimentation, observation, statistical analysis, and the testing of the predictive power of the hypothesis.

Justifying the Use of Reason

It could be objected here that the standard of reasonableness used by ethics, in all of its individual criteria, depends upon an acceptance of reason as the yardstick for measuring truth, and that such an acceptance is biased and arbitrary. Why should reason be privileged in deciding truth and falsity?

This charge appears plausible but is really rather odd because it uses reason in questioning the reliance upon reason. It presupposes the need for reasonable argument by attacking reason rationally. The individual who refuses to reason about reason is in a stronger position, but few people are satisfied with a refutation of silence (or slaps, as in Zen Buddhism). And the moment one enters into rational debate about the validity of reason one gives the game away, for one affirms rationality in the very act of denying it.

Usually a criticism is launched against reason whenever a person dislikes the conclusion to which he or she is forced by a rational argument. But this is rather like kicking over the chessboard when one's opponent says checkmate. Or as one philosopher puts it, when reason goes against people, people tend to go against reason. Such a reaction shows a weakness in the person, not in rationality.

In all fairness it should be pointed out that, although one cannot rationally argue against the use of reason, it may be equally absurd to argue in favor of reason by marshaling rational arguments to support that choice. For one is then begging the question; that is, assuming the efficacy of reason, which is precisely the point at issue. But here we have reached our ultimate "epistemological" level, our fundamental tautology as to how reliable knowledge is obtained. One cannot support reason by referring to its reasonableness, and if one refers to any other type of proof such as intuition or experience, then reason is no longer being considered as the basic means of knowing.

But although calling reason reasonable does not really lend support, it is preferable to the self-contradiction involved in attacking reason rationally. Furthermore, there are considerations that justify our rejecting the non-rational approach, the main one being the implications that are involved.

If we reject reason as a standard, we could then readily indulge our wishes, whims, and passions, unrestrained by considerations of fairness, logicality, coherence, or even sanity. We could convict innocent people of capital crimes because we disliked their appearance; believe that inanimate objects possess spirits; eat sawdust for nourishment and salt to allay our thirst; accept a political system that calls slavery freedom; and maintain that an object is both large and small, and wet and dry. Once we abandon the authority of reason, there is no criterion for separating good sense from nonsense, the meaningful from the meaningless. The irrationality of a theory would not deter us from accepting it. The potential for deception and harm in such an approach is overwhelming, and constitutes strong evidence against it. For if the implications of a position are impossible, this reflects upon the worth of the position itself. It does not seem justified, then, to cut the rational ground from under our feet but rather to use the standard of reasonableness as a way of ascertaining truth. The theologian and mathematician Blaise Pascal (1623–1662) wrote "*Le coeur a ses raisons que la raison ne connait pas*" ("The heart has its reasons which reason does not know"),[4] but we need our minds to determine whether it has good reasons.

C. ETHICS AND SCIENCE

In the field of ethics, reason is especially valuable because, as was previously noted, the empirical method of science cannot be used in deciding ethical issues. Ethics, however, cannot use reason alone; scientific facts are also important. We saw this under the second criteria for reasonableness, namely that the relevant facts must be taken into account in reaching sound conclusions. In short, scientific facts can be germane to ethics but cannot provide the basis for an ethical judgment. Science is essentially a descriptive and explanatory discipline, whereas ethics is concerned with evaluation and prescription. That is, science deals with the physical world, and through the use of observation and experimentation attempts to explain the functioning of that world. Ethics inhabits an intangible world of right and wrong, good and bad. It is not so much interested in what is the case as with what should be the case, not the area of factual assertions but that of value judgments. Science can provide the means for satisfying our desires but ethics can judge whether one desire is better than another. For example, chemists can tell us that strychnine kills people and streptomycin cures certain diseases, but they cannot tell us whether to use the strychnine or the streptomycin. *Qua* chemists, they are disqualified from judging a moral question such as whether to assassinate a tyrant; their expertise extends only to the behavior of chemical substances.

In the same way, sociologists can determine whether the high divorce rate in the United States is due primarily to the decline of religion and the loss of belief in the sanctity of marriage, but they cannot, as sociologists, make any moral judgment as to whether marriage itself is worth preserving. In other words, they can provide an explanation of the causes, function, and structure of the institution but not an evaluation of whether marriage is a contribution or an impediment to the good life. Even if the sociologist were to point out that the marital relationship lends stability and security to human existence, that still would not tell us whether marriage is worthwhile, for the values of stability and security remain to be judged against considerations of personal growth, openness, and freedom. On a question of this kind sociologists are necessarily mute, confined as they are to descriptions of social institutions and social relationships.

Similarly, biologist may tell us that a vast majority of animals are "un-faithful" to their mates, but whether there should be monogamy or open marriages cannot be decided by statistics. The biologist might also point out that many animals are carnivores, but that does not justify our eating meat; vegetarians argue that we know better and should not kill animals for food when we could survive on vegetables.

In short, scientific information cannot establish ethical value. How the world operates is beside the point in deciding which principles we ought to hold; it leaves the question of right and wrong fundamentally untouched. From the fact that nature is "red in tooth and claw" we cannot conclude that warfare is permissible and that it is acceptable for one person to kill another. To decide on the ethics of a war we should consider whether it is carried out as self-defense, whether the cause is just, whether it is the last resort, and so forth.

The Naturalistic Fallacy

This point is labeled "the naturalistic fallacy," which is the mistake of deriving values from facts, an "ought" from an "is," evaluation from description. The discussion of why it is a mistake has been associated principally with the British philosophers David Hume and G. E. Moore (1873–1958),[5] although the latter gave it an unusually wide meaning. According to the standard version, the naturalistic fallacy is committed whenever an argument asserts that, because of certain facts concerning human behavior or the physical world, certain values therefore follow as a consequence. This is a fallacy in terms of formal logic because the conclusion of a valid deductive argument cannot contain anything that is not present in the premises. One cannot begin with oranges and reach conclusions about apples. It is a *naturalistic* fallacy because it denies that values can follow from any natural facts.

Not all philosophers, of course, accept the naturalistic fallacy as a genuine mistake in thinking; some claim that to call the views of one's opponent a fallacy is merely a cheap rhetorical device.[6] But the logic is difficult to combat, and there is a definite usefulness in separating the realm of description from that of evaluation.

To take one more example, people often make the mistake of assuming that what one desires (descriptive fact) is *ipso facto* desirable (value judgment), and that whatever a person likes is acceptable by virtue of the fact that he or she likes it. But what is desired is not necessarily worth desiring, and what someone likes does not automatically become worthy of being liked. People can pursue superficial or harmful goals, and their pursuit of them does not render them good. A poor purpose for living cannot be transformed into a worthwhile one simply by choosing it, any more than something trivial can be made important by taking it seriously. The life of a galley slave is pretty dismal, even if the galley slave consents to it.

In brief, the naturalistic fallacy reminds us that no account of what people do has any bearing on what people ought to do. And that brings us back to the point that ethics, which deals with values, cannot be based on science, which is concerned with the description and explanation of phenomena.

D. ETHICS AND RELIGION

Another field often erroneously identified with ethics is that of religion, and the difference between the two should also be made clear.

Religion obviously differs from ethics in that it deals with beliefs and practices related to the spiritual or transcendent, especially faith in a supernatural being; but this is not the area of confusion. Frequently people make the mistake of thinking that ethical positions must ultimately be based on religious convictions, that religion is the foundation of ethics. This is a time-honored notion and widely prevalent, but its truth can be questioned.

Historically, philosophy was sometimes considered to be conscripted in the service of religion, and ethics along with it. This view was especially prevalent during the Middle Ages when philosophy was thought "the handmaid of theology." Philosophic reasoning was used whenever possible to demonstrate the truths which had been imparted by God through scripture, miracles, and divine revelation. But whenever philosophy conflicted with revealed truth, it was philosophy that had to give way; the intellect was fallible whereas God's word, as contained in the Bible, was the infallible source of knowledge. If reason and faith collide, then so much the worse for reason; Athens must not take precedence over Jerusalem. Philosophy could lend support to theology, as St. Thomas Aquinas (1225?–1274) showed in his famous five proofs for the existence of God,[7] but it could not challenge church doctrine with rational arguments. But the Middle Ages were not labeled the "dark ages" without some justification. The contemporary view is that philosophy is independent of religion and does not function to confirm revealed points of doctrine. Philosophic reasoning is now used by theologians to separate apparent from authentic revelations, to differentiate between the valuable parts of scripture and those that are the product of superstition and primitive thinking, and to decide which of the competing interpretations of God's will is closest to the truth. Even if God is considered to be infallible, we can never assume that we are interpreting his will infallibly.

Philosophic reasoning is also used by the nonreligious as an analytic instrument to probe the foundations of belief and to support skepticism. Just as Socrates (469?–399 BCE) maintained that the unexamined life is not worth living, the unexamined faith is not worth holding. If religion can withstand critical scrutiny, then we may be justified in believing it; if it fails to meet critical standards, then perhaps the faith, not the philosophy, should be called into question.

Plato's Euthyphro

Ethics is separate from religion today, together with the rest of philosophy, and is usually regarded as autonomous. The specific reason for its independence can be found in a logical distinction made in ancient Greece. It occurs in a Platonic dialogue called the *Euthyphro* and is uncovered by Socrates during one of his inquiries, in this case into the nature of piety.

All of Plato's writings are cast in dialogue form, in which Socrates is usually the principal spokesman (and gets the better of the argument). In this particular dialogue Socrates is questioning a man named Euthyphro in order to educe from him a sound definition of piety. Socrates professes to be interested in knowing so that he can defend himself against charges of impiety that have been brought against him by citizens in the city-state of Athens. Euthyphro appears to be the person to ask, Socrates tells him, because he is bringing charges against his own father for causing the death of a slave. Anyone who can accuse his father of impiety before a court of law, Socrates reasons, must surely know what pious action consists of, and Socrates could do no better than to become his pupil.

Euthyphro rises to the bait and declares, "What all the gods love is pious and holy, and the opposite which they all hate, impious."[8] But Socrates finds this definition unsatisfactory and says, "The point which I should first wish to understand is whether the pious or holy is beloved by the gods because it is holy, or holy because it is beloved of the gods."[9] In other words, Socrates asks whether God approves of actions because they are right or whether actions become right by being approved by God.

This distinction may appear trivial but it carries enormous implications. For if one affirms the first and says that God loves conduct that is right in itself, then morality is independent of religion; rightness and wrongness do not depend upon God's approval and disapproval. If, however, one affirms the second, then God is declared the creator of morals, and conduct becomes right insofar as it is willed by God. On this reading, morality is derived from religion, for it is God who confers value upon actions.

In the dialogue, Socrates forces Euthyphro to admit that the pious is loved by God because it is pious; it is not pious because it is loved. For God cannot make actions right or wrong; he can only recognize their intrinsic moral quality. He cannot, for example, make cruelty praiseworthy by approving of it or compassion blameworthy by condemning it. Even though he is God, he is precluded from inverting moral value, turning it inside out like a glove. Some actions are right, others are wrong by their very nature, and God issues his commands for that reason; he does not will things arbitrarily.

Religion, therefore, does not furnish the basis for ethics. Even if religion disappeared from our culture, and the concept of God along with it, there would still be ethical principles. Right conduct would remain right regardless of whether God existed. The decline of religion, therefore, need not entail any corresponding decline in moral behavior. There may be a psychological connection between ethics and religion, but no logical connection exists.

As the philosopher Brand Blanshard has put it,

> The conviction that the ultimate ground for duty is the will of God . . . is questionable, first, because it implies, regarding Deity, that he does what he does, not because it is right but because he wants to, which imputes to him a character below our own; and secondly, because it implies that if he willed that we should commit murder, that would make it right, which seems clearly untrue. The moral law is an immutable and objective law, which holds because the good is really good and the bad, bad; and only a morality so based is safe. The person who accepts it because it is the will of God will all too naturally conclude, if he loses his belief, that he has lost all reason for morality also.[10]

A common objection to this argument is that if God is the Creator, as he is considered to be in Western religion, then he also created moral values and can change them if he so chooses. God *would* not make cruelty right and compassion wrong, but that is not to say he *could* not do so. As the supreme being, maker of heaven and earth, he also established the moral standards of the human race.

But theologians never assume that God can do anything. He cannot, for example, both forgive sinners and not forgive them, perform a miracle and fail to perform it, create the world and not create the world simultaneously. He could erase his actions and begin again but each fresh start would involve him in the same limitation. In short, God cannot do what is logically self-contradictory.

This is the answer, incidentally, to the old philosophic chestnut of whether an almighty God can create a rock so large that he cannot lift it. Replying yes or no is equally nonsensical, but one can escape the dilemma by realizing that even God cannot do what is self-contradictory; he is constrained by what is logically possible.

Just as God can be limited by logic, he might also be limited in his capacity to dictate moral values. The fact that he cannot make awful actions into virtuous ones by divine decree does not militate against his perfection, at least according to theologians. Therefore, even if one is a believer, one can still maintain that ethics is autonomous. Besides, to say that God would not make cruelty right and compassion wrong means that he recognizes their independent moral nature and would act accordingly.

E. ETHICS AND PSYCHOLOGY

According to the American Psychological Association, psychology can be defined as "the scientific study of the behavior of individuals and their mental processes." Psychologists analyze perception, cognition, personality, emotion, and behavior, and when they look at behavior they are usually interested in the motivation behind it, the basic causal factors. They are trying to understand the individual, and actions are important insofar as they are indicative of the underlying person. "What made Mary react that way? Why did she respond with such embarrassment or hostility or distress in that situation?" The fundamental springs of conduct are of paramount interest.

If the psychologists are oriented toward Sigmund Freud (1856–1939) they will want to understand the person's mind, the defenses of the ego, the extent to which the superego has repressed the impulses of the id, and so forth. If they are behaviorists, they may deny the person has a mind, and look for the stimulus-response pattern, the structure of conditioning. If they are cognitive psychologists they will study the higher mental processes of people, the phenomenon of consciousness, language use, perception, and problem solving. In all cases, the concern of the psychologist is why people act as they do.

The ethicist, on the other hand, does not want to know the causes of action but the reasons for action, not the motivation but the justification for various types of behavior. In ethics one looks for good reasons for choosing one mode of conduct over another, and the fact that someone may have been affected by childhood abuse or maternal deprivation does not excuse the behavior. Unless the person is underage, abnormal, or legally insane, and acting under compulsion or ignorance of right and wrong, the ethical judgment is unaffected by the psychological causes involved. People do not escape blame for a blameworthy act because of their psychology, any more than we withhold praise for praiseworthy actions because of the psychological forces that prompted it. To show the motivation behind action is irrelevant to determining its worth.

In a case of killing, for example, the psychologist may find that the killer's motivation included rebellion against an oppressive father with whom the victim was identified, the assertion of manliness due to anxiety about homosexual tendencies, the need to combat basic feelings of inadequacy and inferiority, and so forth. However, if we were to attempt to justify the killing ethically, we might argue that the person accidentally fired the gun, or that it was a case of self-defense, or that he was forced to kill because his wife and children were being held hostage. It is the second set of factors, not the first, that could exonerate the person from a charge of murder.

Ethics and psychology, therefore, do not have the same subject matter by any means, and questions about the moral nature of actions are not answered in terms of what prompted a person to act as he or she did. As the American philosopher William James (1842–1911) put it: "The only logical position is to judge an idea not according to its motivation but according to its content. . . . By their fruits ye shall know them, not by their roots."[11]

The Genetic Fallacy

To evaluate conduct in terms of its origins is, in fact, to commit a logical mistake that has been variously labeled the genetic fallacy or the biographical fallacy. It has also been called an *argumentum ad hominem* (argument to the person) because it judges the person who makes a statement rather than the statement itself, who said it rather than what was said. Like the naturalistic fallacy, it is the confusion of fact and value but, more specifically, it judges an idea or an action in terms of its source. Examples of this fallacy would be to dismiss the theories of Sigmund Freud because of his use of cocaine, to ridicule the philosophy of Friedrich Nietzsche (1844–1900) because he ended life in a mental institution, or to reject the nationalist movement in Ireland because its leader Charles Parnell (1846–1891) was an adulterer. The fallacy would also be committed if we approved of actions or ideas because we admired the person behind them, accepting vegetarianism because we respect Gandhi, or believing in Christian Science because of the charisma of Mary Baker Eddy (1821–1910).

If we think about it, we realize that the authority of an individual does not establish the worth of what he or she says; rather it is the worth of what is said that establishes the authority of the person. The quality of an idea is what counts, its intrinsic quality, irrespective of where it originated.

In terms of our discussion of psychology and ethics, since we do not evaluate moral issues in terms of their source, then psychology, which deals with the springs of behavior, cannot be identified with ethics, which is concerned with evaluation.

Psychological Egoism

We cannot explore the complete relation between ethics and psychology, but we should discuss one psychological position that acts as a stumbling block to ethics. This is the doctrine of *psychological egoism*, which maintains that human beings are so constituted that they always act in terms of their self-interest.

In support of this position, the egoist sometimes points to "the pleasure principle" according to which people must seek the satisfaction of their desires and avoid pain and discomfort. We are simply made this way, the egoist claims; it is the nature of the beast, and we have to function within that context of self-interest. We always pursue our own advantage above that of others, acting selfishly rather than altruistically. When we have a choice between helping someone else and helping ourselves, we will naturally choose ourselves first.

To the psychological egoist, then, unselfish acts are either extremely rare or a myth altogether because every supposedly generous act can be analyzed down to a selfish motive. We may pretend to ourselves that our actions are founded on noble purposes and humanitarian ideals, but this is only self-deception—a pretext for self-interest. We may even perform actions that are helpful to others, but only as a means of benefiting ourselves, for if helping another person should conflict with our welfare, then that behavior soon ceases. We are generous only in cases where helping others and helping ourselves happen to coincide, which shows that our behavior was selfish all along. We were performing altruistic actions for egoistic reasons.

To the objection that military heroes are admired for their sacrifice and dedication to their country, the psychological egoist answers that heroes are characteristically people who desire honor and glory; individual recognition is the motive behind their actions. And if we should point to acts of charity, the psychological egoist explains these away by saying that philanthropists want praise for their generosity; they seldom cast their bread upon the waters. They also want to have a sense of superiority over those they have helped and the personal satisfaction of knowing they are good people. Even martyrdom is accounted for by the egoist as designed for posthumous fame, perhaps canonization as a saint. Martyrs would rather live a brief, spectacular life, crowned by a moment of greatness, than have the unrecognized life of the average citizen. Their martyrdom, therefore, is not for God or humankind but for the perpetuation of their name; it is essentially egocentric.

A theory called *ethical egoism* is sometimes based upon this psychological interpretation of human nature. The *ethical egoist* argues that not only do people act for themselves but they ought to do so. The fact of selfishness is said to constitute good reason for accepting selfishness as a valid mode of behavior. In short, the psychological findings are taken as justification for an ethic of self-interest.

This argument is sometimes used in business contexts to try to justify unethical actions such as using insider information, manufacturing unsafe products, or practicing deceptive advertising. The fact that companies do harm others in order to help themselves is offered as proof; business is business.

It is apparent that this type of reasoning violates the naturalistic fallacy. The fact that people may act selfishly is irrelevant to the question of how people ought to behave; it is an extraneous consideration in deciding which type of behavior is morally preferable. Not all ethical egoism is based on psychological egoism, but when it is, the logical mistake has been committed of deriving values from facts.

However, the question remains as to whether psychological egoism is correct. Psychological egoism cannot furnish the grounds for ethical egoism but, if it were true, it could preclude recommending any ethic of generosity. If we cannot help but behave selfishly, then there is no point in recommending that we should behave with concern, care, or consideration for others. Every altruistic ethic would then become pointless. Fortunately, psychological egoism does not seem to be a strong theory.

To take the main criticism, the psychological egoist dismisses cases of apparent altruism by showing the benefits that the person derived as a *result* of his or her action. But the fact that people receive benefits for doing something right does not mean that they performed the action for the sake of obtaining those benefits. In the same way, people can feel pride at sacrificing their own interests and helping another human being, but that does not mean they helped someone else in order to feel proud of themselves. The consequences of an action should not be confused with the motive. Personal satisfaction can be an effect rather than the end for which the action was done, a byproduct rather than the intention behind it. To view some actions as generous, then, can be a more reasonable analysis.

To put the point somewhat differently, people perform actions out of desire, including the desire to help others, and not for the benefits expected. Perhaps people only do what they want to do, but that can include wanting to be generous.

For these reasons, psychological egoism is not generally considered a threat to ethics. It is an exaggeration, and only seems persuasive at times when we feel jaded and disillusioned with the behavior of our fellow man.

REVIEW QUESTIONS

1. Describe the difference between epistemology and metaphysics, and give illustrations of the fields of logic and aesthetics. How do they all relate to ethics?
2. Explain the standard of reasonableness with illustrations of the three criteria that comprise it.
3. Differentiate between ethics and science. How does the naturalistic fallacy confuse the two realms?
4. With regard to the difference between ethics and religion, what does Socrates mean by asking whether "the pious or holy is beloved by the gods because it is holy, or holy because it is beloved of the gods"?
5. What is the relation between ethics and psychology? In what way can psychological egoism be criticized?

2

FREE WILL AND DETERMINISM

In attempting to establish values, either of right conduct or good ends, we soon confront two theories that have been problematic for ethics since its inception: *determinism* and *relativism*. These theories are obstacles because each in its own way casts doubt on the authenticity of ethics; each opposes the assumption that genuine values can be established.

The determinist claims that all our thoughts and actions, including those of an ethical nature, are the result of prior factors. Laws of nature govern all happenings, including personal ones, and they admit no exceptions. We think and act the way we do as a direct consequence of heredity times environment, and all our moral values can be traced to some combination of these determinants. It is a delusion, therefore, to believe that we can arrive at sound values after due deliberation or that we can freely choose to act in accordance with our ethical judgments. To the determinist it is also a mistake to preach or recommend any values, for doing so presupposes people's ability to freely change their minds and behave differently. As Immanuel Kant said, "ought implies can." There is no point in telling people they *ought* to do something unless they *can* do it. Determinism denies that people can do what they are told they ought to do; they can only do what they must.

Relativists are equally challenging in their theory, for they maintain that values do not possess any objective moral quality but are relative to the person or group from which they emanate. What is right in one society is wrong in another, and what Mary praises, John condemns. Nothing can be said to have intrinsic worth; rather, each group establishes values relative to itself. These values are not arguable since right and wrong and good and bad mean different things to different people. Whatever is thought valuable *is* valuable to the group that believes it so, and no objective standard exists against which it can be measured.

Each of these positions must be carefully analyzed because of their powerful effect on all theories of ethics, and although we have touched on them previously,[1] we should explore further to see if they constitute genuine threats or are paper tigers. In this chapter we undertake the examination of determinism; Chapter 3 deals with relativism.

A. DO WE HAVE FREE CHOICE?

As mentioned above, the *determinist* maintains that all ideas, attitudes, and values are the necessary products of prior forces. Our allegedly independent decisions in favor of one set of beliefs over another, or for a particular mode of conduct, are only the consequences of causal factors and are beyond our control. Equally mistaken is the assumption that we are free to act in accordance with our ethical ideals. To the determinist, all our actions are inevitable responses to given conditions, the strict effects of antecedent causes. People cannot do other than they do and are not responsible for their actions. This means that both praise and blame are inappropriate; people should neither be rewarded nor punished for what they have done because it was beyond their power to do otherwise.

Opposed to the determinist view is that of the *libertarians*, who affirm the freedom of the will. They believe that human beings are in control of their lives, and that their decisions proceed from themselves as autonomous entities. Libertarians do not assert that all ideas and actions are free, since people can be manipulated and controlled unconsciously, but they do say that human beings, excluding children and the mentally ill, have the potential to think and act freely. Determinists, on the other hand, deny free will and maintain that choices are never self-initiated; to the determinist, free will is a product of our pride, the need to feel in charge.

Although it is not strictly followed, a distinction is sometimes made by libertarians between having *free will* and exercising our *freedom*. Free will means being free to choose what to do; freedom is being free to do what we choose. Someone in prison may have free will while being denied freedom. The one is the ability to decide internally, the other the power to carry out our decisions.

Fatalism and Predestination

An earlier form of determinism is actually a pre-determinism, which claims that *fate* or destiny rules all events in the world, including human behavior. This fatalistic view is sometimes linked to providence, a predestination by God who is the author of the Book of Fate, or it can be based on a general concept of a universe permeated with ineluctable forces; these cosmic powers control the movement of stars and people and nations. In either case, the pre-determinist affirms a fatalistic view in which everything happens according to spiritual mandates that predestine its occurrence. Human beings are thought simply to respond to the inevitable events that are their lot in life; they have no choice in the matter.

Arabs use the term "*kismet*" and believe that whatever occurs is preordained; "*Inchallah*," they say, meaning "it is Allah's will." The ancient Greeks called it *moira*, which was not the will of the gods but a more encompassing destiny embracing the lives of both mortal and immortal beings; the gods too were governed by fate. The Greek dramatists, especially Sophocles and Euripides, depicted the ways in which the machinery of fate operates to bring about some inevitable, tragic end. Oedipus, for example, cannot escape fulfilling the prophecy that he would one day murder his father and marry his mother. And because the events are predestined, they can be foreseen by the seer Tiresias in the same way that Cassandra and the Hebrew prophets could foretell disaster. The Romans too accepted predestination as part of the Stoic philosophy prevalent at the time; they thought that practicing poise and equanimity even in the face of tragedy was the wisest way to live. The Spanish say *que sera sera* (what will be, will be), and mean that the future is as fixed as the past. The French have the expression *C' était écrit*, which literally translates to "this was written," and the Germans speak about *seinem Schicksal entgegengehen*, or "going to one's fate." Almost every nation has the doctrine of pre-determinism as part of its cultural heritage—although considerable differences exist in the extent to which the theory is followed today.

Most people in the Western world have now abandoned pre-determinism and regard it merely as a historical curiosity. The only times we feel sympathy for fatalistic views are when events are out of our control or when we try to escape responsibility for our actions and need some psychological defense. For example, people who smoke heavily might claim that if they were meant to die at forty they will die at that time, and smoking cigarettes will not make any difference. Or a soldier on a battlefield might feel that if his "number is up," then he will be killed, but otherwise he will be safe even in a hail of bullets. Nevertheless our customary attitude today is to reject belief in destiny as a general description of the way in which the universe operates. Pre-determinism is largely an archaic view which has not been refuted so much as abandoned. Not all theories in intellectual history die as a result of philosophic attack; some die of neglect.

The following passage from Shakespeare's *King Lear* might be a fitting epitaph:

> This is the excellent foppery of the world, that when we are sick in fortune, often the surfeit of our own behaviour, we make guilty of our disasters the sun, the moon, and the stars; as if we were villains of necessity; fools by heavenly compulsion; knaves, thieves, and treachers, by spherical predominance; drunkards, liars, and adulterers, by an enforc'd obedience of planetary influences; and all that we are evil in, by a divine thrusting on—an admirable evasion of whoremaster man, to lay his goatish disposition to the charge of a star![2]

B. SOCIAL SCIENTIFIC DETERMINISM

The contemporary form of determinism has a social and biological character, as opposed to the cosmic overtones of pre-determinism. The modern determinist maintains that people's character, conduct, ideas, attitudes, and so forth are the product of hereditary and environmental factors. We think and act as we do because of our genetic inheritance as well as the various psychological, political, educational, cultural, and economic forces that play upon us. According to the contemporary determinist, we harbor the illusion that we are free to decide in favor of one alternative or the other but in actuality all of our decisions are made for us. For example, if a student opts to attend college it may seem to be a free choice in that he or she was able to choose otherwise; but the determinist would say that, upon analysis, various external factors can be seen to be responsible for the decision. The expectations and socioeconomic level of the student's parents would have played a major role, as would peer pressure, prior educational experiences, the student's I.Q., the drive to achieve, and so forth. These are the operative elements that caused the decision; it was not a voluntary act of choosing one option over another; in retrospect, the student could hardly do anything else.

The determinist is here denying that human beings possess free will—the ability to make free choices. It is a mistake to think that people can autonomously decide which behavior or beliefs they will select. All of our decisions, it is claimed, are the result of determinants beyond our control, and although we may say we are the masters of our fate and the captains of our souls, that is simply to boost our egos; cool, objective, scientific analysis proves otherwise. When contemporary determinists are asked to specify the factors behind people's thoughts and actions, they will usually draw up a list of determinants including many or all of the following: genetic endowment, climate and geography, social and cultural influences, and psychological background. We will consider each of these here.

The Compelling Factors

Genetic Endowment. The chemical, anatomical, and physiological characteristics we inherit make an enormous difference in the kind of person we become. These traits include our skeletal structure, nervous system, glandular activity, gender, height, intelligence (that is, our IQ or *g* factor), sense organs and internal organs, secondary sexual characteristics, chemical metabolism, and so forth. It also includes body type or physique which, according to the classification by W. H. Sheldon, can be divided into ectomorph, a slender, angular, fragile, light body build; endomorph, a round, soft body with a tendency toward fat; and mesomorph, a muscular, large-boned body.[3]

Accordingly, an ectomorphic female who is short, with a slight build and little muscle mass, poor motor coordination, an underactive thyroid and a sluggish metabolism (resulting in low energy) is extremely unlikely to become a professional football player. In the same way, someone with an endomorphic male body, with slow reflexes, a low IQ, and poor hearing and eyesight has a slim chance of becoming an astronaut. Not only would these individuals be barred from the respective fields by the qualifications but, more importantly, they would be unlikely to choose anything contrary to their capabilities. Only those fields compatible with their biological makeup would hold any appeal, which means that their "decisions" would have been made already. In this sense, biology is destiny.

Climate and Geography. Laypeople and scholars alike have recognized the influence of climate and geography on human activities and individual personalities, and historians have sometimes taken a closer look at their effects.

In this they are following the seminal theory of Arnold Toynbee (1889–1975), who maintained that people in cool climates are characteristically serious and industrious, and have highly developed social, economic, and political systems; they tend to be brisk, organized, and efficient. In warm climates, on the other hand, there is a tendency for people to be phlegmatic, to value pleasure over accomplishment, to live sensuously rather than intellectually, and "to relax, submit, enjoy." (One may think, perhaps, of North America as opposed to South America, Germany in contrast to Italy, or northern France in contrast to southern France.)

Toynbee, in fact, proposed as a theory of history that the world's work is done by people in the northern temperate zone, and that the main contributions to civilization have come from the northern latitudes of Asia, Europe, and America.[4] The climate cannot be too harsh, for arctic conditions can stifle progress, but an equatorial climate, on the other hand, does not offer enough challenge. According to Toynbee, soft conditions produce soft people, while hardy conditions produce hardy souls who are stimulated to achieve; the latter, transform stumbling blocks into stepping stones, having just enough stimulation to mobilize their energy.[5]

Other climatic conditions are said to operate in a like manner: A rainy climate drives people toward indoor activities, a sunny climate inclines them to enjoy an outdoor life. Hot, humid conditions produce lethargy, whereas cool, dry weather is invigorating and results in energetic action.

It has been similarly proposed that the geographical area in which one lives partly determines the kind of person one becomes. People in mountainous regions are said to be more independent and self-reliant, quiet, strong, and introspective, whereas those in the plains tend to be more gregarious, extroverted, and mutually dependent. People in landlocked areas are inclined toward isolationism, conservatism, and extreme patriotism, to be ingrown in their attitudes. Those living along the seacoast are thought to be more open-minded, sophisticated, and liberal in their thinking; they have been exposed to a variety of people and different perspectives.

In analyzing the effects of climate and geography, determinists do not declare that every person, say, from Brazil is apathetic and lethargic; rather, they are generalizing and perceiving differences in national character between peoples living under different climatic and geographical conditions.

Whatever nation we inhabit, then, will unconsciously affect us by its size, shape, outline, and location, as well as by its climate and weather. Also operative are such social geographical factors as density of population, age distribution, male-to-female ratio, and principal occupations. Pastoral or agricultural people are different from those who are the product of an urban, postindustrial society.

Although climate and geography do have an undeniable effect on conduct, Toynbee's particular analysis is largely in disrepute. His claims are far too sweeping and Eurocentric; indeed, they have been criticized as racist. Africa has certainly contributed to world culture, for example, in art, music, dance, and sculpture; human beings, in fact, originated on that continent.

The Tigris-Euphrates Valley does not lie in a temperate zone; neither does Egypt, Greece, or Rome, but civilization first flourished there.

Society and Culture. No one lives in a vacuum or a watertight box; rather, each person is part of an identifiable social group with particular beliefs, traditions, and language, common interests and institutions, artifacts and activities, patterns of behavior and standards of conduct. This means that our society circumscribes the range of ideas and actions that will appear as viable options to the individual.

For example, someone raised in India as a Hindu, speaking Urdu and living in a rural village with a tradition of inherited occupation, would probably not consider following the Protestant ethic and becoming an entrepreneur. Similarly, a person brought up as "lace curtain" Irish, in a working-class district of Dublin, with a parochial education and blue-collar values, would hardly be tempted to retreat to the desert and follow Islam. What one regards as a real choice is severely limited by one's cultural background. As anthropologist Ruth Benedict (1897–1948) wrote:

> No man ever looks at the world with pristine eyes. He sees it edited by a definite set of customs and institutions and ways of thinking. . . . The life history of the individual is first and foremost an accommodation to the patterns and standards traditionally handed down in this community. From the moment of his birth the customs into which he is born shape his experience and behavior. By the time he can talk, he is the little creature of his culture, and by the time he is grown and able to take part in its activities, its habits are his habits, its beliefs his beliefs, its impossibilities his impossibilities. Every child that is born into his group will share them with him, and no child born into one on the opposite side of the globe can ever achieve the thousandth part.[6]

Thus each individual is culturally determined in such factors as dress, image of beauty, recreation, ornamentation, moral code, religion, temperament, political convictions, speech, family concept, and so forth. There are also secondary effects such as those emanating from language, for all languages possess built-in values and attitudes toward the world that will shape the minds of their users. Certain ideas that would be temptations of thought in English are almost unthinkable in Chinese. In fact, a theory has been proposed called the *Sapir-Whorf hypothesis*, which maintains that language determines thought much more than thought determines language.[7] Ludwig Wittgenstein (1889–1951), one of the founders of the contemporary philosophic movement of linguistic analysis, went so far as to claim that language traps us into making intellectual mistakes; the task of philosophy, he believed, is to show "the fly the way out of the fly-bottle."[8] That is, philosophy should help us escape from the conceptual mistakes induced by linguistic confusions.

The effects of education should also be pointed out in this context because that too is part of the social baggage we carry with us. It makes a considerable difference whether one attends a village school in Afghanistan or a lyceé in Paris, or if one is a graduate of a technical training institute in Nairobi or of a major American university. Informal education also forms the person, for the books and magazines we read, the films, videos, and television programs we watch, the friends and relatives we listen to—all affect the type of individual we become.

Thus culture and society, together with biological factors, climate, and geography help to determine people's identity and conduct. The determinist is not stating anything radical here, but reminding us that the effect of a person's social environment and upbringing cannot be denied.[9]

Psychology. Several schools of psychology lend support to the determinist position, the most notable being that of *behaviorism,* which is associated with the names Ivan Pavlov (1849–1936), J. B. Watson (1878–1958), and B. F. Skinner (1904–1990).[10] The behavioral psychologist sees human conduct in terms of physiological responses to external conditions (stimuli). The human organism responds to stimuli in the environment and is "conditioned" to repeat stimulus-response patterns. In a famous experiment, Pavlov conditioned a dog to salivate at the stimulus of a bell that was rung before each meal. In the same way, people may be conditioned to stop at red lights, clap their hands together at performances, eat their food with a fork, help others in trouble, endorse a democratic form of government, and so forth. To understand human psychology, then, we should study not the operations of the will or hidden motives buried in the unconscious but the overt structure of habits and abilities that constitutes a person's system of responses. To the behaviorist, an individual's psychology is nothing but his or her observable behavior and not some mysterious entity called "mind" that lies behind behavior. There is, in fact, no "ghost in the machine," no such thing as a mind, soul, or spirit, any more than there are things called emotion, memory, or imagination contained within us. Emotion is nothing more than muscular and glandular activity, memory is the ability to "recall to use," and imagination can only be determined by the visible evidence of its functioning. Even intelligence cannot be regarded as some intangible mental capacity but an index of the ways in which problems are confronted and solved. According to the behaviorist, we should therefore turn away from "mind-gazing" and concentrate on the stimulus-response relationships that characterize people; then we will understand their psychology.

The bearing of this position upon the theory of determinism is not difficult to see. The behaviorist is claiming that our thoughts and actions are nothing but conditioned responses to given stimuli. We do not decide what to think or do after conscious reflection; we are reactive organisms whose behavior is triggered by environmental stimuli, and the strongest stimulus always wins. We do not voluntarily choose among various options, or freely decide which course of action we will follow; in fact, we do not act at all but only react to stimuli. The same holds true in the sphere of morality. People function as machines do, and one mode of conduct will follow from pressing one button and another from pressing a different button. That is, given one set of stimuli and habitual responses, a particular moral behavior will result; with different physical stimuli another type of morality will be produced. Once an individual's stimulus-response pattern is known, that individual's behavior, including moral behavior, can be predicted.

C. THE LIBERTARIAN REPLY

Social scientific determinism is an extremely strong position, relying on undeniable facts of physical and social science. However, the libertarian who defends free will claims that, despite the numerous forces impinging on people, we still have the freedom to decide between alternatives. The libertarian argues that these forces are *influences and not determinants*, and people are always free to choose their influences. Once we are aware of the various forces operating on our lives, these forces do not compel us; we are then able to decide which influences to accept and which to reject. Influences are only determinants when we are unconscious of them and the way in which they affect us; once we are aware of them, we are empowered and free of their control.

For example, people raised in a city would be inclined to continue living an urban life, but they need not do so. They could reject this influence and decide they want a country life. Or people raised in a religious household would be inclined to remain religious, but at some point of reflection they might assess their faith and conclude that atheism has stronger arguments. Someone raised communist could choose capitalism; a New Englander might decide to live in Hawaii; someone whose parents are Democrats might join the Republican Party; and a person who learns that he or she has a predisposition toward heart disease could choose a healthy diet and regular exercise. In these cases, awareness would ensure that these prior factors did not control their lives.

People would also be free if they decided to follow certain tendencies rather than opposing them. The significant factor is that a conscious decision is made. For example, individuals raised in cultured homes might choose to continue their involvement with art, music, and literature as part of a satisfying life. In this case, they would be deciding freely even though they were following their upbringing. Instead of reacting against their background, they would freely appropriate the cultural values as their own. Teenagers who do something, despite the fact that their parents want them to, are being their own person.

In this way, southerners can decide to resist or yield to the lethargy of a warm climate, mountaineers can be unsocial or not, and mesomorphs can choose whether or not to enter fields that call for physical power: a woman from Alabama might become CEO of a Fortune 500 company, and a strong man might decide to become an accountant rather than a weight lifter.

As these examples illustrate, libertarians do not deny the importance of climate, psychology, geography, biology, and so forth in affirming a free will position; rather, they agree with the social scientist that these influences are present. What the libertarian denies is that these factors compel our behavior, that they determine our ideas and actions. The libertarian is not being unscientific but is questioning the logical connection between prior factors and human behavior. If libertarians are unscientific at all, it is by postulating the existence of an autonomous self, known through introspection and reflection.

In brief, libertarians claim that genuine actions are possible once we know the forces that affect us. A large part of the function of education, therefore, is to make us knowledgeable about the influences operating upon us and, because of this understanding, to act according to our own lights. As the psychologist Erich Fromm put it, "As man approaches maturity he gradually frees himself from instinctive and compulsive behavior and he develops his powers of self-reliance and choice."

From still another vantage point, the libertarian is asserting that there can be *reasons* for actions, not just *causes*. Having reasons implies some process of deliberation whereby a person weighs the conflicting claims and freely decides between the various alternatives. To speak of cause and effect, on the other hand, presupposes a strict mechanical system of interlocking gears with no room allowed for self-initiated acts of human beings—acts that are not the result of prior causes. According to the libertarian, people's actions are not necessarily the effects of antecedent causes;

only physical matter operates that way. People can justify what they do. Instinct causes a bird to build a nest but human beings have a purpose in building a home; they are making a deliberate choice, and they could just as well decide not to do so.

Viewed in this light, criminals cannot claim that, given their disadvantaged backgrounds, they could not help but commit their crimes. Even if they are members of a minority group and suffered unjustly because of discrimination, they are not compelled to pursue a life of crime. Becoming a criminal is not unavoidable, although circumstances can make it much more difficult to obey the law.

Arguments for Free Will

Human Behavior is Not Predictable. More specifically, the libertarian charges that the determinist position seems plausible only because it argues backwards. The real test of a theory is its ability to predict the future: if gravity is a valid theory, then a rock should fall to the ground when released. But suppose that a girl named Janet, whose mother is a doctor, decided to attend medical school. The determinist would attribute this decision to Janet's admiration of her mother. If, however, Janet should decide to study law, the determinist might say the cause was a family friend who is a prominent attorney. Even if Janet became a high school dropout, turned pantheist, and joined a religious cult in New Mexico, the determinist would see this as the inevitable result of prior factors: she was rebelling against her privileged background and American capitalist values. In other words, any decision Janet makes can be made to fit.

But this kind of analysis appears strained; whatever causes are mentioned are made to apply, but they are selected after the fact to suit the case. Determinists would be much more impressive if they could predict with certainty what Janet *will do* given her "determinants." Otherwise it seems more reasonable to conclude that, given a set of influences, Janet could choose any combination of them. She could freely decide which aspect of herself she wished to develop. In other words, if human actions are governed by the same mechanical system as falling stones, then the determinist should be able to predict those actions with the same degree of certainty. The fact that the determinist cannot do so suggests that the two cases are not alike and that human conduct is not mechanistic. In short, the libertarian argues, it suggests that people possess free will.

The determinist's answer to this charge is that, since the scientific study of human behavior is virtually in its infancy, all the factors that determine behavior are not yet known. The social scientist has had a certain degree of success in predicting how people will act, and as more knowledge is acquired about the determinants of behavior, there will be greater predictability. People do not act capriciously but according to natural law, and the prediction of human behavior will become increasingly accurate as more variables are known and laws are formulated.

But, the libertarian replies, human conduct is of a different kind, and the behavior of individuals will never be predictable no matter how much information is acquired about the factors operating upon them. It is not just a matter of gaining greater knowledge of people but of a theoretical difference between people and natural objects. Human beings can come to understand the forces that move them and decide which forces they want to be moved by; people can choose in a way that birds and stones cannot. The libertarian is not saying that human behavior is independent of all prior factors but that the particular factors brought into play are decided by the person who is aware of them. Therefore, the accurate prediction of human behavior is theoretically impossible and will not come about at some distant point in the future. Regardless of the increase in knowledge, there will never be complete predictability, because human beings are always free to choose.

Temporal Versus Causal Sequences. A second objection raised by the libertarian is related to the previous ones but has a specifically logical character. The libertarian accuses the determinist of committing the logical fallacy of *post hoc, ergo propter hoc*, which literally means "after this, therefore caused by this." It is the mistake of assuming that when one event follows another, the prior event caused the subsequent one. For example, the fallacy would be committed if we thought that voodoo caused an illness because a voodoo rite preceded the illness, or that day causes night because night follows day. Quite obviously, a temporal sequence is different than a causal one, and a subsequent event is not necessarily a consequent one.

As applied to the determinist thesis, the libertarian argues that prior factors of geography, biology, psychology, and so forth cannot be assumed to be the causes of a person's conduct. The determinist must prove that this temporal sequence is a necessary causal connection such that, given conditions A, B, and C, action X must follow. The determinists have not done this but have shown only that certain conditions preceded a person's action. They have not proven that, given these conditions, it would be impossible for a person to act differently.

The burden of proof falls on the determinist to prove a compulsion behind human behavior, otherwise we are justified in crediting our customary view, which is that people are free to kick a stone or not kick a stone, just as they will. If a theory is proposed that contradicts the common-sense view, the advocates of that theory are required to prove their point. The burden of proof lies with them rather than on the person who holds the ordinary position.

Sometimes the extraordinary view is proven, as when the earth was shown to be in motion when common sense believed it to be still, but the point is that the unusual claim must be established, not the ordinary one. The determinist, then, who says that all our actions are forced, that antecedent conditions are causal determinants, must prove that or have the case thrown out of court. In the absence of proof of causation, we are justified in maintaining the common-sense view that our decisions are free, that prior factors do not determine our conduct but form the ground for free choice.

The Inconsistency of Determinism. As a final point, the libertarian sees a basic inconsistency in the determinist position, for if all ideas are the necessary products of prior causes, this must include the idea of determinism. Those who believe in the determinist position have been determined to do so. They have not freely decided that determinism is a valid theory but simply believe it because they are forced to; they cannot do otherwise. And if that is so, then their position does not have to be taken seriously.

Or, as C. S. Lewis stated, the determinist argues rationally for his claim, but the claim is that all ideas come from non-rational forces and not rational argument, thus undermining itself.

In the same way, if determinists are to be consistent with their position, they must believe that the libertarian has been determined to affirm free will just as they were forced to affirm determinism. Any argument between the two, then, is pointless because each must think as he or she does. The only reasonable course for the determinist is to remain silent and not argue the virtues of determinism.

But determinists do try to convince libertarians to change their minds, and in doing so they give the game away. For they thereby presuppose that people are free to think differently regardless of their social upbringing, biology, and so forth, that a good idea could be accepted on its merits, and that people are not determined in what they think. Therefore, the more the determinist tries to convince others of the truth of determinism, the more convinced they become that determinism cannot be true.

The only rebuttal determinism offers to this self-contradiction is to say that the arguments in favor of determinism can be determinants forcing us to accept the theory. But the acceptance of a good argument because it is good constitutes a reason, not a cause, and is consistent with the libertarian, not the determinist, model of human behavior.

Determinists, then, have not proven their case by any means. Perhaps we are not the products of our society, biological inheritance, psychological background, and so forth. And if we are free in our ideas, attitudes, and behavior, then we cannot claim we are not responsible for our actions despite the nexus of preceding conditions. In contemporary terms, the boy raised in a slum need not become a criminal, and people can be praised for becoming outstanding individuals. We are essentially free to choose our own path, and we bear a burden of personal responsibility for the path we choose.

D. HARD AND SOFT DETERMINISM

A technical distinction is usually made within philosophy between *hard* and *soft determinism*, which sheds light on the controversy. *Hard determinism* (hard-headed, hard-edged) maintains that, since all our actions are caused by social factors, physiological events in the brain (neural impulses), or mental events (such as early experiences which produced certain desires), we do not have free will. To speak of freedom and personal responsibility when all our actions are part of a necessary causal chain makes no sense. Newtonian physics also claims that, once the initial conditions of the universe are established, everything follows inevitably.

Soft determinism (also called compatibilism and self-determinism) holds that, although all actions are caused, nevertheless people are free because they participate as causes of their actions. If an act proceeds from the individual's personality or character, rather than from external forces, then the act is free. It is the nature of the individual plus the circumstances that cause actions to occur.

Soft determinists, therefore, maintain that free will is compatible with determinism, since the person has the power to originate causes. On this reading, the universe is a system of physical laws embracing all things, including human beings, but people can be free agents within that system. Their actions can initiate a causal train and are the result of their character.

Of course, the hard determinist argues that external forces shape a person's character. Perhaps we can do what we like, but we cannot decide what we like; our actions may follow from our character, but our character is already determined.

The Autonomous Self

The *libertarian*, by contrast, claims that free will is incompatible with any kind of determinism since it places people within an iron chain of physical causes and effects; given certain events, no other outcomes are possible. According to the libertarian, human beings are exempt from the determinism of matter. They postulate an autonomous self, outside causation, and hold people responsible for their choices. People are not dominoes, or even the flick of the first domino, but observers who act independent of the game.

Ethicists tend to affirm free will, endorsing either soft determinism or libertarianism. They believe we can choose among alternative ways of living, using reasonable arguments as justification. And these ethical options can be recommended to others who are free to accept or reject them on their merits.[11]

REVIEW QUESTIONS

1. Differentiate between determinism and belief in destiny (pre-determinism). How does the social scientific determinist differ from the libertarian? How can free will be distinguished from freedom?
2. Explain how people are affected by their genetic endowment, by climate and geography, and by their nation. Do you agree that these factors are determinants?
3. In what way does behavioral psychology support the determinist position?
4. Explain what the libertarian means by claiming that outside forces are influences, not determinants, and that people perform actions for a reason, not as a result of causes.
5. According to the libertarian, how is the theory of determinism inconsistent? In what way does the determinist argue backwards?

3

THE CHALLENGE OF RELATIVISM

A. ARE VALUES RELATIVE TO ONE'S CULTURE?

Another source of skepticism about the general validity of ethics comes from the doctrine of relativism, which is an ancient theory that has recently assumed a modern form, like old wine poured into new wineskins. Cognitive relativism claims all knowledge is a social construct, and ethical relativism maintains that values too are a function of a person's culture. The two are interconnected but we will focus principally on the ethical form.

According to this type of relativism, all moral judgments merely reflect our own or society's views. We may think that values have an objective foundation but, at bottom, they merely express the attitudes that surround us. For example, when people say that polygamy is wrong and monogamy is right, this judgment only represents the mores that are a part of their culture. Likewise, when people assert that using drugs is wrong, that depends upon the society: in Holland it is acceptable; in Turkey it carries the death penalty. Therefore, nothing is intrinsically right or wrong; all judgments depend on the context.

The Society and the Individual

Different types of ethical relativism should be distinguished. According to *cultural relativism*, different societies form different standards for the satisfaction of their particular needs and there is no universally right way of behaving; the correct way to conduct ourselves depends upon our culture. "Immoral," a classic sociologist wrote, "never means anything but contrary to the mores of the time and place . . . there is no permanent and uni-

42

versal standard by which right and wrong can be established and different folkways compared and criticized."[1] To the ancient Egyptians incest was acceptable; to the European in the Middle Ages sickness should be treated by exorcism; and among Islamic extremists today it is noble to commit terrorist acts for a holy cause.

Subjectivism is a subset of relativism that also denies any objective basis for value judgments. Rather than focusing on the unit of society as the basis of values, the subjectivist claims that moral judgments spring from our personal likes and dislikes, our predilections and aversions. Morality is a matter of individual attitudes, and as such, it is unarguable. As the Romans said, *De gustibus non est disputandum* (Taste cannot be disputed or refuted). To the subjectivist, what is right to one person may be wrong to another. Opinions vary, and even if people take opposing views, they are both right to themselves. There exists no absolute standard against which our preferences can be measured, and whatever judgment we make would no longer be true if our personality were different. "There is nothing either good or bad," Hamlet says, "but thinking makes it so."[2]

Opposed to relativism is *objectivism,* which claims that values have an independent basis apart from either personal or societal beliefs. (Absolutism takes it a step further, claiming that genuine values are universal.) For example, people who say "Rape is wrong" may be identifying something reprehensible about the act that makes it wrong: it involves force rather than consent. They are not merely reflecting the disapproval of the culture or venting a personal dislike but saying that rape is sexual assault, which is wrong no matter where or when it occurs. Both individuals and cultures can be mistaken in their values, just as someone can make mistakes in arithmetic. Thinking does not make it so, and the earth is not flat, whatever some ancient culture might believe.

According to objectivism, then, societies can be criticized for holding values that are contrary to objective moral standards. There is an external and independent basis for moral knowledge apart from the attitudes instilled by any given society. This position also maintains that subjectivism is misguided in believing that each person creates his or her own moral standards, that what is right for one person may be wrong for another. According to the objectivist, if something is right for one person, then it is right for another. We do not invent moral values but discover the principles of right and wrong that should govern human conduct. People do not create standards to follow by choosing them, but realize the types of conduct that are prohibited or required. And if one speaks about discovering rather than inventing, or realizing rather than creating, this makes ethics an objective matter. It does not change with each society's preference or each individual's taste.

B. SOURCES OF RELATIVISM

The general fashion today, at least among students, is to endorse a relativist or subjectivist view, and in academic circles it is implied by the modern theory of deconstruction or postmodernism.[3] The contemporary view is that whatever a culture or person regards as right is right for that culture or person, and there are no ideal standards of behavior that can be used as a yardstick. Everyone forms standards that are adequate for themselves, and no one outside a society's framework or an individual's skin can presume to judge their behavior. By and large, psychologists, sociologists, and anthropologists tend toward this view, holding that there are no better or worse values, only those that serve specific needs. These will be the values selected in social evolution, and, if they prevail, they become *ipso facto* right. Any allegedly objective evaluation only reflects the opinion of the evaluator. No single model of behavior fits all.

Social Science and Multiculturalism

Relativism can be an attractive theory for a variety of reasons. For one thing, it promotes *tolerance* for the values of others in our multicultural society. The United States today contains diverse nationalities, ethnicities, and races, people with different customs, religions, politics, and sexual orientations. We are a pluralistic society, and people are encouraged to retain their national origins within an American identity. Rather than thinking of our nation as a melting pot, it is more a tossed salad, and we should respect differences between peoples.

Along with this, it is sometimes argued that no culture within the nation can be judged as better or worse than any other. No culture's values should be excluded or "privileged" for inclusion, whether in choosing the canon of good literature or deciding what to include in a history or geography course. In other words, the values of different cultures are relative, and all cultures should be equally respected.

Relativism also supports the *freedom of the individual*, at least in its subjective form, because people are free to create their own moral standards. What's right for me may not be right for you; different strokes for different folks. Sexual abstinence is all right for some people but not others; the same holds true for drinking, attending church, smoking marijuana, eating meat, or having an abortion. We should not impose our morality on others but give people the space to develop their own values; any other approach is oppressive and arrogant.

In addition, relativism arises from our *uncertainty* today as to which actions are truly valuable. Prior to the twentieth century, people had greater confidence in the principles and ideals they held, believing they were rooted in reality itself. Now that we have greater exposure to different cultures, and have experienced rapid changes in the values held within our own culture, we question whether we know what is best. An ethical relativism seems appropriate, humility rather than certainty. We ask ourselves "Who is to say?", "How can we judge?", because there is a multiplicity of values in the world and opinions change with unnerving speed.

But relativism also draws support from academic sources, especially the fields of sociology and anthropology, the ramifications of Freudian psychology, and the ideas of Marxism as expressed in the *Communist Manifesto*. We should examine each of these sources, in their classic renderings. Each supports the same conclusion: that values do not have any objective basis but are simply relative to the time and the place from which they spring.

To begin with *the evidence of sociology and anthropology*, the book *Folkways*[4] by William Graham Sumner (1840–1910) can be taken as representative of the relativist position. According to Sumner's theory, all ethical ideals concerning the nature of goodness and all conceptions of what is right are derived from the folkways or customary usages societies have developed to satisfy their needs. Whenever any customs become necessary for the well-being of a society, they become part of the mores of that society. These mores do not consist of principles of ethics that are identified as being right but instead are developed in response to the essential requirements of the culture; they are functional and pragmatic means for securing the general welfare of a people. As conditions change and different responses are called for, the mores change correspondingly, and no mores remain fixed over a long period of time (as one might expect if they were objectively based). The mores are not rational or consistent but are shaped by the needs of and the external circumstances surrounding the people who espouse them. Furthermore, the mores can run counter to the group's welfare through the phenomenon known as "cultural lag." A society will gradually change its mores to those most beneficial to it, but a lapse of time may occur between the recognition of the inadequacy of the old mores and the change to a more efficient system.

In this analysis Sumner is not only accounting for the way our ethical values arise, that is, as the necessary mores of a culture, but also dismissing any kind of absolute standards. Because mores change, we can see they are not eternal; and because they change in accordance with needs and circumstances, we can see their true base, viz, the needs that exist at a particular time and place. Each culture, therefore, has the norms it requires. A conflict that occurs between cultures cannot be settled by referring to any rational basis of behavior but must be resolved through negotiation or by force. There is no universal standard that cultures can recognize and accept for the adjudication of their differences.

Within a culture, actions are judged to be right when they follow the time-honored customs and wrong when they are opposed to these customs. And it is impossible for an individual to get outside the confines of a culture and make any independent moral judgment. There simply is no external standard that can be found, and even if there were, people are so socialized within a particular tradition that they would not accept a different value system. Whatever a society regards as right becomes the standard for every member of the group, and whatever is considered wrong becomes taboo. Even social rebels demonstrate the force of cultural values by the strength of their rebellions; they are trying to overcome enormous resistance.

Vilfredo Pareto (1848–1923) in his book *Mind and Society*[5] echoes this relativistic point of view, and emphasizes especially the subjective character of our values. To Pareto, our ethical judgments are not logically based but emerge from the non-logical parts of our personality. Our judgments are functions of our instincts, sentiments, and emotions, so that whenever we say our actions are right we are only saying "We like to behave this way and we wish others did too." To approve of an action is merely to express one's personal taste and the desire that such an action become generally accepted. According to Pareto's interpretation, the word "right" is a term of approval that has persuasive power by virtue of its connotation. If people claim that it is more than a positively charged term, this claim is hypocritical, delusional, or mistaken. When people use value-laden words, they usually know they are employing emotive language to persuade others to their own points of view.

The social anthropologist Ruth Benedict also argued in the book *Patterns of Culture*[6] that cultural differences account for the way people think and behave, including their ideals and notion of proper conduct. To illustrate her thesis, she described the customs and institutions of three cultures: the Zuni Indians of the American Southwest, the Dobuans who live on Dobu Island off eastern New Guinea, and the Kwakiutl Indians of the northwestern region of the United States. Each is radically different from the others in the values that permeate the culture.

The Zuni Indians are deeply religious—a sober, hard-working, peaceful people. They are strongly concerned with building a harmonious relationship between human beings, nature, and the gods. Their whole purpose in life is to achieve balance and integration between themselves and their natural environment. The Dobu culture, in contrast, prizes vigilance against evil forces that surround and threaten them. If people maintain an attitude of suspicion and defensiveness, and approach others with caution, then one is living cleverly and rightly. The Kwakiutl culture differs from that of both the Zuni and the Dobu by having a highly competitive character; personal success, prestige, and pride are of paramount importance, not just reaching the heights but being able to look down on those beneath you. The way a Kwakiutl is made to feel big is to make others look small. In general, the competitive and aggressive person is considered worthy of admiration and emulation.

Because of the great diversity in standards of conduct between these three cultures, Benedict concludes that there are no absolute moral principles accepted by all people; rather, each culture develops values relative to itself. And what is right in one culture can be foolish or shameful in another. A Dobuan male who acted aggressively would be respected by his culture but Zunis would disapprove of him and Kwakiutls might regard his conduct with disdain. If an individual in the Kwakiutl culture should succeed in making himself important, this would be considered unseemly by Zunis and regarded as rather childish by Dobuans. And the Zuni approach to life—the attitude of achieving tranquility, harmony, and peace—would be looked at as absurd by the Dobuan and Kwakiutl.

The implication of this diversity of ethical standards seems to be that all values are relative to a person's culture. One cannot find ethical beliefs that are universally held, and one cultural pattern is as legitimate as another. It is not that a pattern of culture *seems* worthwhile to each culture; in point of fact it *is* valuable. For the word "valuable" means nothing other than that which is socially approved.

It is worth mentioning that the philosophic counterpart of this sociological and anthropological position was expressed by the eighteenth-century empiricist David Hume.[7] Hume argued that moral judgments are not based on reason. Reason is confined to judgments of truth and falsity, which apply only to statements of fact ("the cat is on the mat") and relations of ideas ("bachelors are unmarried males"). To approve of conduct, on the other hand, means to have positive feelings about it. By and large, if an action tends to bring happiness to significant people in our lives, we treat it with approval. The judgment that behavior is right indicates only that people in our society generally favor it, that the behavior meets with the majority's approval. But, to Hume, these feelings cannot be argued about, for it would be absurd to try to prove or disprove a feeling. Rational argumentation, then, is inappropriate to morals, and Hume goes so far as to say that, if by flicking a finger, the entire human race could be saved or destroyed, the one choice would not be any more rational than the other—although we might have strong feelings about the matter.

Hume is saying in effect that we merely vent feelings toward types of actions when we call them right or wrong—as another philosopher put it, shouting "hurrah" for one and "boo" at the other. Argument can legitimately occur over whether certain conduct will produce the goals we like, but there can be no rational arguments over the value of the goals themselves; that is strictly a question of attitude.

Freudian psychology also offers theoretical support to the relativist and, more particularly, the subjectivist critique of universally valid ethical systems.[8]

According to Sigmund Freud, the conscious mind constitutes only a small portion of the entire psyche. In the analogy used by psychoanalysts, it resembles the tip of an iceberg whose main bulk lies hidden beneath the surface. The greater and more powerful part of the mind is termed the *unconscious*—that dynamic energy system of the psyche that lies below the level of awareness; it is only glimpsed occasionally through slips of the tongue, dissociated acts, or dreams. The unconscious is a seething cauldron of desires that are elemental in nature and basic to every individual, whether we admit it or not.

The unconscious is not an undifferentiated, amorphous whole, however, but has three divisions, each of which plays a part in the decisions and actions we take; together these parts are responsible for whatever we do, even though we might delude ourselves into believing that we make conscious choices.

The *id* exercises demands upon each of us that are primarily sexual in nature, totally selfish, primitive, insatiable, and without social or moral restraint. All of our forbidden desires, lusts, and sexual passions come moiling up from the id seeking expression and satisfaction.

The *superego* checks the id, keeping it from wholly controlling our actions. This is the force of social rules and prohibitions that we have internalized, and which we call conscience; it is the general voice of society, instilled in us by and large by parents and teachers who are society's surrogates. They impose the culture's standards upon us. The superego applies strong controls over all of us, imposing a rigid and puritanical social ethic; its tyranny matches that of the id in strength. The superego opposes the desires of the id, especially the main thrust toward unlimited sexual gratification. A general warfare then takes place inside each individual, with the id on the one hand demanding expression and the superego on the other repressing these desires with the weight of conscience.

Mediating between the demands of the id and the superego is the *ego*, which attempts to reconcile the conflicting forces in a way that will produce the least anxiety for the individual. Unless the ego can bring about a satisfactory adjustment between these twin tyrants (which are the mirror images of each other), mental disorder will result.

Enlisted in the battle is another agent that Freud termed the *censor*. Standing at the gateway to consciousness, the censor only allows us to be aware of those thoughts and emotions that do not violate general moral standards. It filters and selects those appetites that are socially acceptable and excludes from consciousness the large body of desires swirling up from the id. Most wants are too obscene and threatening to be passed by the censor. Nevertheless, they remain operative within each person and their repression can lead to obsession, hysteria, and depression.

The ego in its efforts at conciliation uses various psychological expedients to bring us some peace of mind. It uses the device of *rationalization*, for one, which consists in finding plausible reasons for doing what we want to do. Rationalization is often employed to make it seem that action done from a base motive is motivated by some noble intention. We can be at peace with ourselves if we think that our awful desires are really pure; our conscience is satisfied even as the impulses of the id are being expressed. Another ploy used by the ego is called *projection*, whereby we find excuses outside ourselves for the mistakes we make; in this way responsibility is evaded. We pretend we are not to blame for immoral actions, but that the factors were beyond our control. Still another device used by the ego is *sublimation*, in which the desires emanating from the id are rechanneled in ways that are socially acceptable. If a surgeon uses his scalpel he is not condemned as a criminal even though, from a Freudian point of view, he is expressing aggression by attacking someone with a knife. Since he does this with a license, in an operating room, for socially approved reasons, he receives a great deal of money and high status, whereas an ordinary person who stabs another on the street is jailed for assault with a deadly weapon.

The relevance of Freudian psychology to ethical relativism is simply that conduct is interpreted as the product of the battle between the id, the ego, and the superego, rather than the result of reflection on right and wrong. It is these forces that form our concept of ethics and they are wholly amoral and irrational. Our conduct is always an appeasement of the powers in the unconscious mind. Any attempt at rational or objective judgment regarding values is only a pretext for the unconscious wishes, defenses, inhibitions, rationalizations, projections, and sublimations of our psyche. There are no valid reasons behind actions, only a veneer of excuses given by the conscious mind for the dictates of the unconscious.

The theory of Freudian psychology lends itself to determinism as well as relativism and subjectivism. Our conscious mind must hold the values it does because unconscious forces determine its entire content; that is, values are relative to the social controls of the superego and the subjective desires surging up from the id. The individual is at the mercy of these forces, a puppet of the unconscious rather than an autonomous entity that consciously decides which values are worthy of being chosen.

Relativism and subjectivism also gain strength from the nineteenth- and twentieth-century theories of *Marxism*, which has as its cornerstone Karl Marx's *Capital* and *The Communist Manifesto*.[9]

Karl Marx (1818–1883) was preeminently a revolutionary who, in the words of his co-author, Friedrich Engels (1820–1895), strove "to contribute in one way or another to the overthrow of capitalist society." Or as Marx himself put it, "the philosophers have interpreted the world in various ways; the point, however, is to change it."[10] But in order to effect a change, the laws governing the inner workings of nations had to be scientifically analyzed. This Marx did through a long period of research at the British Museum, and his conclusions were that the structure and history of nations are determined by economic forces.

The "modes of production" constitute the economic foundations of society and produce all social, political, religious, and intellectual forms and institutions. In traditional economic theory the modes or factors of production are usually listed as land, labor, and capital, but Marx analyzed them as materials (resources), labor (purposive activity), and instruments (techniques). In any case, corresponding to these modes of production are "property relations," a concept that refers to the forms of ownership. Property relations are relatively stable through time, whereas modes of production change more rapidly, and this differential produces tension and eventual conflict. The modes of production inevitably win the contest and new property relations must be established that are appropriate to them. In this way, new historical realities come into existence, epochs in the progress of society, which Marx referred to by such labels as "the asiatic," "the ancient," "the feudal," and the "modern capitalist."

The final struggle, Marx believed, is now occurring in our capitalist era between the property relation of bourgeois ownership and the mode of production in which proletarian labor is intolerably exploited. As the bourgeois power becomes concentrated in the hands of a small number of increasingly wealthy capitalists, and the proletariat become poorer and more numerous, a polarization occurs which erupts into violent class conflict. A revolution ensues in which the bourgeois capitalists are necessarily overthrown and the economic ownership passes into the hands of the proletarian workers. On the political level, after a brief period of proletarian dictatorship a golden age comes into being—the era of a "classless society" and the "withering away" of the state.

Marx believed that the process of historical change takes place in a "dialectic" or triadic pattern whereby a historic movement is introduced, which is then opposed by another movement contrary to it, and eventually the finest elements of each are carried forward to form a new (and superior) historical reality. The best parts of the previous movements have become *aufgehoben*, meaning conserved, overcome, transformed, exalted.

The appearance of a historical movement Marx called the *thesis*; he designated the counter-movement, the *antithesis*, and he called the resolution of their antagonism the *synthesis*. In the continuous unfolding of the dialectic process, the synthesis subsequently becomes a new thesis, which generates its own antithesis, and leads to the formation of a still more encompassing synthesis. The triadic pattern has been repeated innumerable times as history has proceeded, leading to higher and higher stages of development that will culminate in a final, absolute synthesis.

The dialectic process not only forms the pattern for movements in history but also characterizes the development of ideas and even the growth of biological organisms.[11] There is no "either/or" in the dialectic but only a "both/and"—a synthesis of apparently contradictory elements that find ultimate resolution. No compromise occurs; rather, an organic growth takes place with the healthy, vital parts of the thesis and the antithesis combined in a dynamic fusion to produce a greater whole.

In Marx's analysis, all social development and structure depends upon the existing economic base, which determines society's politics, art forms, religious institutions, social classes, and so forth, all of which constitute the superstructure of society. What is important for our purposes is that Marx regarded ethics also as part of the superstructure, containing those values consonant with the economic system of the society; with each change in the economic base, the values will change correspondingly. There is a direct correlation between economics and ethics, such that values will follow the existing economic forms. This accounts for the variations in moral codes between nations. By and large, a similarity in ethical views will exist among nations with parallel economic structures, and vast ethical differences will correspond to major economic differences between societies.

An example Marx uses is that of Christian ethics, which he believed to conform to the capitalist economy. A great deal has been written about the way in which the Protestant ethic, especially in its Calvinist form, harmonizes with the American capitalist system. The Calvinist ethic maintains that the degree of financial success attained in this life indicates the extent to which we are favored by God and deserve spiritual rewards in the next life. Our economic achievement is an index of our religiosity and the grace that God has given us.[12]

Marx also stressed another aspect of Christianity: its concentration on values such as meekness, humility, acceptance, selflessness, and nonviolence, all of which Marx believed keep workers in a state of subjection to the capitalist owners. The Christian emphasis on the meek inheriting the earth, its insistence that we must not lay up treasures for moths and dust to corrupt, that God favors the humble over the proud, and that the earth is a vale of tears, a testing ground for the life to come—all this undermines the rebellious spirit of the exploited and oppressed. Instead of revolting against the bourgeoisie, we are to accept our abject state as part of the suffering we must endure as the lot of human beings on earth. After Adam and Eve's fall and their expulsion from paradise, we have to live on an earth filled with pain. For this reason Marx called Christianity "parson power" and "the barking dog of capitalism," thinking that it serves capitalism perfectly in maintaining the privileged in power.[13] In Marx's famous phrase, "religion is the opiate of the masses," (in the way that opiates today are the religion of the masses).

The point is that, according to Marx, ethical values are relative to the economic system of a society, whether stemming from Christianity in league with capitalism or flowing from another source.

C. OBJECTIVISM

In the light of this brief survey, we can see that the relativist doctrine has very strong support from a number of different sources as well as being a popular belief today, but the question still remains whether it gives an accurate picture of ethics. Popularity does not guarantee the truth of an idea, for it is not a democratic matter, any more we should vote on which paintings should be in the museum. Neither is it determined by the authority of its advocates, even if the pronouncement comes from a Freud or a Marx. Relativism must be analyzed in terms of its own worth to see whether it is the most reasonable doctrine to hold.

The Counter Arguments

1. One criticism against relativism is that it contradicts itself. For relativists maintain that all our ideas are reflections of our personal beliefs or of the culture in which we find ourselves, and if that is so, then the idea that all our values are relative must also be a relative idea. It cannot be true in any objective sense because, according to the theory, there is no objective truth.

   In other words, to call relativism true presupposes that certain ideas are actually true, which contradicts relativism itself. To be consistent, the theory of relativism can only be relatively true; that is, true for specific cultures or particular individuals. No argument can be offered for the position without assuming that which is denied; namely, that there are objective grounds for assessing truth. It would be very odd to have a theory that no one can claim to be true without thereby proving it false.

   Thus, the idea of Ruth Benedict (and Pareto and Sumner), that beliefs are relative to one's cultural pattern, is only relative to her own cultural pattern. If Freud is correct and all ideas arise from the unconscious rather than our rational understanding, then so does the Freudian theory of psychology. And if, according to Marx, all intellectual ideas are relative to economic circumstances, this must include the Marxist sociopolitical philosophy. It would be inconsistent for any of these thinkers to maintain that their ideas are actually true.[14]

   As stated under the standard of reasonableness, there are certain statements one cannot sensibly make. A person cannot write that all writers are liars, because it would mean he or she is lying when writing it. Or the claim that all generalizations are false would have to include the generalization that all generalizations are false, in which case it is false to say that all generalizations are false, and so on. Or the person who says "I am not speaking" contradicts himself or herself in the very act of stating it. (Albert Camus [1913–1960] expressed this logical point when he wrote, "The moment you say that everything is nonsense you express something meaningful.")

The subjectivist and relativist are in precisely this position when they claim their theories are objectively true.[15]

2. The Greek version of this self-contradiction was stated by Plato in a dialogue called the *Theaetetus*. Protagoras here presents his well-known doctrine that "man is the measure of all things," and means to assert by this that the individual is the yardstick of truth and goodness. Socrates criticizes this subjectivist position at some length, and then concludes, "and the best of the joke is that he acknowledges the truth of their opinions who believe his own opinion to be false for he admits that the opinions of all men are true."[16] In other words, if each person creates truth for himself or herself, the individual who opposes that doctrine of personal truth would be correct in believing the doctrine to be false. If each person's opinion is right, then the person who regards subjectivism as wrong would be right in thinking so.

In essence, Socrates is pointing out that the subjectivist position leads to the paradoxical situation in which contradictory ideas are each true. This is logically absurd because of the *law of non-contradiction*, which states that we cannot affirm X and deny X at the same time. That is, it would be nonsense to claim that something exists and does not exist, is tangible and intangible, or is black and white all over. Something can appear to have one set of qualities from one perspective and another from a different point of view, but an object cannot possess contradictory qualities in the same respect. But this is precisely the position in which the subjectivist finds himself, claiming that contradictory ideas are both true if the people believe them to be true.

Plato attacked relativism in a different way in a famous passage in the *Republic*. Thrasymachus here argues that justice only means "the interests of the stronger,"[17] claiming, in effect, that whatever values are held by the dominant forces in society become the values people accept as correct. And these values are always devised by the rulers, not in accordance with any universal principles but only as expressions of the will of the powerful. Every leader enacts laws in terms of his or her own welfare, to maintain their domination and advantage. Justice is not the product of rational reflection or the codification of God's commands but the arbitrary and self-serving rules imposed on the weaker by the stronger.

In reply to this extreme cynicism, Socrates first makes a distinction. He asks whether Thrasymachus means that justice is what the stronger enforce, or what is to the advantage of the stronger. If it is the first, then the stronger might be enforcing that which is not to their advantage; they may, unwittingly, be doing that which is detrimental to them. If, however, they are legislating to their own advantage, then they are recognizing that which, objectively, would be advantageous and enacting laws in terms of it.

Thrasymachus chooses the first as his meaning, and this enables Socrates to draw out the implications between what a person wills and what is good. In other words, what a government compels an individual to accept may be different than what is advantageous—for the leaders or for anyone else. So what is just does not depend upon the state's decrees; rather, the state's decrees can be judged in terms of what truly is just. Ethics, therefore, is not a function of power and the powerful; it must have an independent basis. Might does not make right.

3. A further defect in the logic of relativism is that it can be at variance with its subset of subjectivism. In other words, although relativism and subjectivism are allegedly in the same camp, they could be in opposition. An African-American, for example, could feel that segregation is demeaning and unconscionable at a time when southern society regards it as perfectly proper. Furthermore, not only can there be differences between individual and group morals, but various groups can disagree in their values, and it would be impossible, on relativist grounds, to resolve the dispute. Republicans and Democrats have very different positions on welfare, homosexuality, and crime, and the Catholic community and advocates of women's rights have opposite views on abortion. If values are relative to what a social group believes, which group determines what is right? And since everyone belongs to several different groups, people would be divided within themselves, which is obviously an intolerable situation. It is impossible to maintain, as the relativist theory would imply, that an act is right insofar as one is a soldier but wrong to citizens, right insofar as one is a conservationist but wrong to hunters, right for consumers but not retailers. The same act cannot be both right and wrong.

4. A further charge against relativism is that it does not account for moral progress in history nearly as adequately as the assumption of objectivism. Societies have changed throughout the centuries in ways that constitute not just differences but improvements. And these improvements can be explained mainly in terms of

a progressive recognition of superior values. If our conceptions of right and wrong were nothing other than a function of our society's ideas, then it would be difficult to account for the advances of our civilization. Change can be explained in terms of different historical conditions to which societies respond but progress requires a different explanation. It would seem to be not just a chance happening that societies have become morally better but a matter of people realizing more humane ways of treating one another.

It can, of course, be questioned whether human society has improved. Some people might claim that we are not any kinder today than yesterday, but simply more refined and subtle in our cruelty. Instead of the thumbscrew and the rack, we now have economic oppression, toxic chemicals, racial discrimination, and environmental degradation.

Although this point of view may appeal momentarily to our tendencies toward pessimism, it hardly seems tenable. By almost any standard, we are more humane now than in previous times. Civilization does constitute progress from a barbaric state, and the civilization of recent centuries is generally higher in ethical charac-ter than that of earlier ages. Rules of war, for example, have been formulated so that when one nation conquers another the women and children are not slaughtered or taken as spoils. Slavery has been virtually abolished, whereas prior to the nineteenth century it was commonplace. The conditions of our jails and mental hospitals have improved immeasurably, and our standards of health and housing have become progressively higher. Countless other examples could be cited, but the point does not require much proof; the evidence is all about us, and the contrary view seems unjustifiably skeptical.

Assuming that the ethical character of society has progressed, it would appear that the improvement is due to people questioning whether the prevailing standards are right, and changing the status quo in accordance with their vision of a superior society. We are always able to ask "Is this worthwhile?" or "Will that be better?" when presented with social standards. If society were the measure of those standards, this would not be possible. Americans, for example, have always restlessly explored goals in living and ques-tioned what a better life for themselves might be. And in seeking a worthwhile life, Americans are tacitly acknowledging the good as an objective standard against which they can measure the ideals of their own or any society. Values, then, are not assumed to be good or right because society says so; rather, society may be correct or incorrect in identifying which values are worthwhile.

5. Perhaps the strongest criticism leveled against relativism is that it contradicts our moral experience. That is, we feel the power of certain obligations that strike us from without, certain "oughts" or "shoulds" that we are forced to acknowledge. For example, that we should value human life cannot be regarded as merely subjective because it would run counter to our most basic feelings. To preserve a life seems valuable, and such sentiments will not go out of style. Similarly, showing respect for people; being honest and not lying, cheating, or stealing; alleviating suffering where we can; helping the young and the elderly; playing fair—all seem valuable in themselves. On the other hand we condemn "pride killing," in which a woman who has been raped is killed for bringing shame on the family; enslaving people for prostitution, farm labor, or in sweat shops; denying women the right to education, employment, or participation in government; having child soldiers who are forced to fight in wars—none of these practices seem justified. Also prominent in our thinking today is the wrongness of discrimination, terrorism, and genocide, and we have no sense of being ethnocentric in opposing them.

As mentioned previously, those who adopt an unusual position carry the burden of proof, otherwise ideas that are in keeping with common experience can be assumed to be true. We generally recognize morals as binding upon us, as basic rules of conduct that transcend particular opinions or mores; therefore, it is up to the relativist to prove that this is not so. Judging by the sources we have examined, the relativist has done so; in fact, the argument seems very much the other way. The evidence of Benedict, Sumner, Marx, and others does not entail the conclusion that values are relative. In the absence of proof for the relativity of values, the commonsense view should prevail: that values are discovered not invented, that they are a matter of insight rather than convention.[18]

D. ARE SOME ACTIONS INTRINSICALLY VALUABLE?

Many people fear that objectivists are dogmatic in the values they hold, that they are self-righteous and try to force their values on others, thereby limiting their freedom. However, this need not be the case. Although objectivists think there are intrinsic values, they do not assume that they know precisely what those values are or that they have the authority to instruct others in the truth. As objectivists, they simply presuppose that values are there to be known. They believe we have a more accurate sense of right and wrong today than when we were homo erectus, but they never assume that anyone's knowledge is complete. That is, even though there may be absolute values, the objectivists do not claim to know them absolutely.

Since we are never certain that our beliefs correspond to what is right, our commitment to any particular value system must always be tentative. Having confidence that there are genuine values gives direction to our search, but it should not make us arrogant that we ourselves hold the true values. We can never be sure that our moral insights are correct, but it seems reasonable to assume that there are correct insights.

In this respect, the position of the objectivist is essentially that of the scientist. Scientists never assume that they know the whole of reality, but they do assume there is a reality to be known, and that by careful and patient effort we can come to understand more of it. Scientists do not think they are creating truth in the laboratory but that they understand an increasingly greater portion of the physical world. When scientists today say that the earth orbits the sun, or that atoms are in motion around a nucleus, they do not believe these facts are relative to our time. They feel confident that anyone who investigates these phenomena carefully, systematically, and objectively will reach the same conclusion; the results are public and reproducible. They will allow for disagreement in scientific findings since data, approaches, and methods differ, but they feel there is an objective truth that we might be able to grasp. Objectivists in ethics are basically in the same position and have much the same attitude. They too assume that there is a reality and believe that it encompasses moral values. Disagreements about moral truths are attributed to a clearer or dimmer understanding at different historical periods. Objectivists hope that, although a universal consensus may never be reached, there will be an increasingly greater realization as to how human beings can thrive.

A final word about multiculturalism. Although multiculturalism is a commendable aim, and functions to include people rather than exclude them from the American mainstream, it need not entail moral relativism. The movement asks for a sympathetic understanding of other cultures and for the varied perspective that different peoples bring to political, social, or cultural issues. And we should consider multiple points of view in reaching decisions rather than just the white, Anglo-Saxon, Protestant perspective.

That does not imply, however, that we live in a moral anarchy in which all values are equal and no behavior is ever condemned.

If a culture should practice wife-beating as a part of a manly image, this practice should not be considered acceptable just because it is accepted by a culture. We can still differentiate between conduct that is worthwhile and that which is worthless, regardless of the context in which it occurs. That is, multiculturalism does not mean the suspension of all moral judgments, but instead means being open to the positive values a culture can add to American life.[19]

In the light of our discussion, therefore, ethicists assume that there are better and worse values, and that people can be morally right or wrong in their choice of actions. Some types of behavior seems praiseworthy, others blameworthy, and perhaps we can come to know the difference. Actions should be chosen because they are right; they are not right because they are chosen. Moral philosophers believe they are engaged in a serious search for both right conduct and a good reason for living.

The Universal Declaration of Human Rights

In 1998 the United Nations celebrated the fiftieth anniversary of the Declaration of Human Rights—a document that specified the minimum standards that nations should uphold for their citizens:

Article 1. All human beings are born free and equal in dignity and rights. They are endowed with reason and conscience and should act toward one another in a spirit of brotherhood.

Article 2. Everyone is entitled to all the rights and freedoms set forth in this Declaration, without distinction of any kind, such as race, colour, sex, language, religion, political or other opinion, national or social origin, property, birth, or other status. . .

Article 3. Everyone has the right to life, liberty, and security of person.

Article 4. No one shall be held in slavery or servitude; slavery and the slave trade shall be prohibited in all their forms.

Article 5. No one shall be subjected to torture or to cruel, inhuman or degrading treatment or punishment.

Article 7. All are equal before the law and are entitled without any discrimination to equal protection of the law.

Article 9. No one shall be subjected to arbitrary arrest, detention or exile. . .

Article 12. No one shall be subjected to arbitrary interference with his privacy, family, home or correspondence, nor to attacks upon his honour and reputation. . .

Article 13. (1) Everyone has the right to freedom of movement and residence. . .

Article 16. (1) Men and women of full age, without any limitation due to race, nationality or religion, have a right to marry and to found a family. . .

Article 17. (1) Everyone has a right to own property alone as well as in association with others. (2) No one shall be arbitrarily deprived of his property.

Article 18. Everyone has the right to freedom of thought, conscience and religion. . .

Article 20. (1) Everyone has the right to freedom of peaceful assembly.

Article 23. (1) Everyone has the right to work, to free choice of employment, to just and favourable conditions of work and to protection against unemployment. (2) Everyone, without any discrimination, has the right to equal pay for equal work.

Article 24. Everyone has the right to rest and leisure, including reasonable limitation of working hours and periodic holidays with pay.

Article 25. Everyone has the right to a standard of living adequate for the health and well-being of himself and of his family, including food, clothing, housing, and medical care. . .

Article 26. Everyone has the right to education. Education shall be free, at least in the elementary and fundamental stages. Elementary education shall be compulsory. . .

In making this declaration, the U.N. assumes an objectivist position, identifying basic rights that belong to all peoples. Perhaps these values appeal to us because we have been conditioned by Western democracy, or by our economic position, or by rationalization or sublimation. On the other hand, perhaps such conditions do, in fact, enable people to flourish. Rather than being provincial or quaint, values such as these could be important in themselves and worth supporting for human good.

REVIEW QUESTIONS

1. Discuss the sociological and anthropological foundations of relativism. How does the philosopher David Hume support this view?

2. Explain the relevance of Freudian psychology to the theory of relativism. What does Freud mean by the id, ego, and superego?
3. Explain the relevance of Marxism to the theory of relativism. What does Marx mean that morality arises from socioeconomic class?
4. Explain how relativism is self-contradictory, including in the criticisms of the Greeks.
5. Why is it hard to accept all values as relative? Provide an example of a proposed objective value drawn from the U.N. Declaration of Human Rights.

4

HEDONISM AS THE GOOD

W hen people ask themselves what they hope to gain from life, most will reply that they just want to be happy, meaning that they want to maximize the enjoyment in their lives overall. This is the most common and natural way of thinking because from our earliest days we tend to identify the pleasant life with the good life, an enjoyable experience with a desirable one. When children say "The candy is good," they mean that it is delicious to taste, thereby making the equation between that which is pleasurable and that which is good. We use "good" in the same way when we refer to a good vacation, a good concert, or simply a good time (although there are different meanings to a good friend, a good car, good health, or good fishing).

Furthermore, as philosophers have pointed out, happiness or pleasure is an ultimate end, rather than a means toward the satisfaction of some other goal. We do many things in order to be happy, but we are not happy in order to attain anything else. It would be odd to ask people why they want to be happy, or what they hope to gain from it, because happiness is never a way of attaining something more ultimate; rather, it is that goal for which a great many things are done. As Aristotle pointed out, happiness is self-sufficient. Once we have attained happiness, we do not need anything else. It is whole, complete, without gaps. If someone lacks something, that person is not wholly happy; if someone is completely happy, he or she lacks nothing. Since happiness is self-sufficient, that seems to qualify it as the ultimate good in life.[1]

Other considerations also incline us to accept the idea of pleasure or happiness as our end in living. For one thing, both pleasure and pain are regarded as simple feelings, incapable of being reduced to more basic psychological terms. In addition, the individual who experiences pleasure considers it to be good, while the person who experiences pain regards it as unequivocally bad. Some good things may come from suffering but that does not make the suffering itself good; we would just as soon have a pleasant means to that end, the positive without the negative. Finally, it seems that all acts considered good have some element of pleasure connected with them. If pleasure is a common denominator, it would appear to be our fundamental goal.

These are some of the reasons philosophers and laypeople use to justify their commitment to happiness or pleasure. But in a more basic sense, most people take it as a "given," that is, something so self-evident it hardly requires justification; it is simply assumed that a happy life is a good life.

A. PURSUING PLEASURE OR HAPPINESS

This affirmation of pleasure or happiness as the goal in life is called *hedonism*, and it is one of the oldest theories in the history of ethics. During its long development, various distinctions and classifications have been made.

Psychological hedonism is the doctrine that human nature is so constituted that people necessarily pursue pleasure and avoid pain. Psychological hedonists do not concern themselves with what people ought to do but with what people actually do, not what should be desired but what in fact is desired, and that is pleasure.

As a theory of human behavior it is not, strictly speaking, a part of ethics but a description which has implications for ethics. In any case, the psychological hedonist claims that all animals, including human beings, automatically seek pleasure and avoid pain. This, it is claimed, is a universal law of nature which admits no exceptions. Pleasure is the prime motivator of all human activities, and people who claim they act for any other reason are only rationalizing. To the psychological hedonist, all alleged altruism is basically the pursuit of personal enjoyment, even if the agent will not admit that fact.

Psychological hedonists claim to see through the pretensions of human conduct. They claim to see that the person who gives a beggar a dollar is motivated not by any concern for the beggar's state but by the satisfaction they themselves will receive from this outwardly generous act. This interpretation is reinforced by the thought that few philanthropic acts are unknown to other people; most generosity is paraded before an audience for approval, thereby increasing the selfish pleasure of the agent. For example, a college donation usually bears the name of the donor, whether the gift is for a building, the scholarship funds, or an endowed chair. In the case of giving to beggars, the psychological hedonist will further claim that the contributors will also be increasing their peace of mind. They will think of themselves as superior to those they have helped, and the fact that the beggars are now under some obligation to them only increases their self-satisfaction. In general, the gift of money has increased their pleasure and diminished their pain, and it was because they anticipated this result that they responded as they did to the beggar. To give is not only more blessed than to receive, it is much more gratifying.

To the psychological hedonist, all actions that claim to be performed for the public good can be explained in a similar way. Doctors do not enter their profession from humanitarian motives but because of the personal and financial rewards they hope to derive from it. Parents who sacrifice to promote the welfare of their children do so because of the pride they will have in their children's accomplishments. Religious people do not seek to serve God but hope to gain the respect of their neighbors as well as divine protection for themselves—in this life and in the life to come.

We need not spend very long on this theory since it parallels the position of psychological egoism dealt with in chapter 1, and the criticisms are very much the same. Experience indicates that many activities are carried out without any desire for pleasure. We often act out of habit or distraction, or, more importantly, for the attainment of certain goals or values. It is true that pleasure may be the consequence of these activities, but the result cannot automatically be considered the motive. Those people who give a dollar to a beggar may derive satisfaction from their generosity, but it is doubtful whether they helped the beggar with the intention of increasing their own satisfaction. The psychological hedonist may claim that firefighters who risk their lives to rescue a child, or martyrs who die at the stake, or soldiers who volunteer for a dangerous mission are motivated by their ultimate enjoyment, but there is little proof of this. In fact, the evidence seems strong in the opposite direction. A person driving a car who has a choice between crashing into a tree or hitting a child in the road often chooses the tree, and thus deliberately risks his or her own life in order to protect the child. The driver could not have given any thought to the pleasure to be gained from the decision.

To look at the matter slightly differently, people seek various goals, and when they reach them they feel a certain pleasure. But the pleasure is not what they seek. The pleasure is an accompaniment or a byproduct of the achievement of their goal. Pleasure might be an emotional tone that accompanies the achievement of a purpose, rather than what all people seek.

When we want something, we are pleased when we get it, but that is not to say that we wanted to be pleased.. It is a mistake, therefore, to say that human beings are motivated by pleasure, much more that they are never motivated by anything else.

B. ETHICAL HEDONISM

Ethical hedonism is far more interesting and relevant to our concerns. This type of hedonism does not maintain that people must pursue pleasure, that it is a law of human behavior or a description of conduct, but claims that we *ought* to seek pleasure. Ethical hedonists are not interested in describing what people do but in prescribing what they ought to do. To their minds, pleasure or happiness should be the goal in life.

Ethical hedonism is sometimes based upon psychological hedonism in the sense that pleasure is considered to be natural and consequently desirable for human beings. What people should do coincides with what they must do, and seems to gain its strength from that source. In other words, ethical hedonists will sometimes claim that since people automatically pursue pleasure, they are therefore justified in doing so. However, this position not only violates the naturalistic fallacy described in chapter 1 but is basically irrational. For it makes no sense to advise people to do that which they cannot help but do. We never suggest that people breathe since they necessarily must breathe, and it is equally pointless to prescribe the pursuit of pleasure if pleasure is all people can pursue. We might be glad about it or sorry about it, but we cannot recommend it.

But ethical hedonism need not be founded on psychological grounds. Ethical hedonists can say that, regardless of whether people *do* pursue pleasure, they *should* pursue pleasure as the good in life. Even if people are capable of seeking other goals, pleasure is the preferred one. It is this ethical doctrine that constitutes the dominant form of hedonism and is the one worth exploring.

C. INDIVIDUALISTIC OR UNIVERSALISTIC HEDONISM

One important distinction which can be made within ethical hedonism is between individualistic and universalistic versions. The *individualistic hedonist* maintains that pleasure or happiness should be sought for the agent performing the action. Trying to bring enjoyment to others is never justifiable, either practically or theoretically. It is impractical because we never really know what will satisfy other people; it is difficult enough to determine what will please ourselves. Human desires are so strange and various that it is impossible to predict someone else's taste. If we offer a man a glass of wine, we may find that he is Muslim and we have caused offense. If we offer a guest a soft bed for the night, we may discover that he is an Indian fakir and would have preferred a bed of nails. And if a man opens a door for a woman, she may turn out to be a feminist who regards the gesture as patronizing.

But even if we could determine what would bring pleasure to other people, the individualistic hedonist sees no reason why we should. Our sole concern ought to be receiving pleasure for ourselves. If we forfeit our own pleasure for the sake of someone else, we will have missed life's greatest blessing, and there is no reason for us to make that kind of sacrifice. If each person takes care of himself or herself, society as a whole will be enriched; if we meddle in each other's affairs, we will make each other miserable. This is reflected in the laissez-faire doctrine of the economist Adam Smith who thought that an "invisible hand" regulates the marketplace, so as individuals pursue their private gain the entire economy will prosper in a free-enterprise system.

Universalistic hedonism stands in sharp contrast to this individualistic theory. Rather than advocating that individuals pursue their own pleasure, universalistic hedonists affirm an altruistic doctrine, claiming that we should pursue pleasure or happiness for society as a whole.

All of our actions should be directed toward the maximization of pleasure for everyone rather than just ourselves. Our own pleasure is to count as much as any other person affected by our actions, no more and no less. We should consider ourselves as one and no more than one in the moral equation, neither benefitting personally nor sacrificing our welfare. If bringing happiness to others increases our happiness, then so be it, but that is not our purpose. Universalistic hedonists believe neither in the selfless-ness of Christianity nor in the selfishness of individualism. Their concern is with the well-being of humanity, with each person considered as an equally valuable part of the whole. Our attitude toward action should always be "Will this increase the total amount of pleasure for everyone?"

Overtly it is difficult to differentiate between the individualistic and the universalistic hedonist because both will help other people. But the mo-tive for individualistic hedonists is to increase their own pleasure through helping others; their generosity is basically a means toward increasing their personal happiness. The universalistic hedonist, on the other hand, helps others for *their* sake. Since the motives that lie behind actions are invisible, it is hard to tell when we are in the presence of the one or the other. But one way of differentiating between the two is to see whether the person would continue bringing pleasure to others even if it brought displeasure to themselves. Those who persist would be universalistic, not allowing the reduction of their own pleasure to keep them from pursuing pleasure for others. Those who stopped at precisely that point at which giving pleasure to others conflicted with receiving pleasure should be considered individualistic.

An important point to stress is that both the individualistic and the universalistic hedonist are ethical hedonists. They both think that we should seek pleasure or happiness; they differ only in their answer to the question "for whom?" The individualist declares "for oneself"; the universalist declares "for everyone affected by my action."

The Cyrenaics

From a historical perspective, Aristippus (435–356 BCE) was probably the first hedonist, and he studied under Socrates in Athens before diverging from his master's sober rationalism. Subsequently, he started a school at a Greek colony called Cyrene on the coast of North Africa, and his followers were consequently referred to as the *Cyrenaics*.[2]

Aristippus held that all good is determined by pleasure, and more specifically, that the pleasures that can be enjoyed in the present are far superior to any pleasures we remember or anticipate. The pleasures of the past or the future are pale compared to the pleasures we can enjoy at this knife-edge instant of now. In one of his surviving fragments, Aristippus wrote "[the moral good] has nothing to do with the recollection of past enjoyments or with the hope of future ones."

Aristippus and the Cyrenaics felt not only that momentary pleasures are best but, as a corollary, that we need not pay much attention to the duration of pleasures. The fact that our enjoyment might be transitory, fleeting, or brief does not detract from its worth, and our life aim should be to have as many pleasurable moments as we can in the time allotted to us. Furthermore, they argued, we should strive for maximum intensity in our pleasurable experiences. The stronger the experience, the more desirable for the individual. Tranquil, sedentary, passive enjoyment was thought to be weak compared to the intense satisfactions available to the human animal. In addition to feeling that immediate pleasures of a brief and intense kind will produce the best life, the Cyrenaics also maintained that the pleasures of the body or senses are more desirable than those of the mind. In other words, pleasures such as eating rich food, drinking full-bodied wine, making love, and enjoying the beach, the sea, and the sun are preferable to intellectual understanding, the pleasures of conversation, and mellow, aesthetic enjoyment. Aristippus made no distinction with regard to better or worse pleasures; he was solely concerned with how intense, physical, immediate, and brief our experiences were. One experience was not superior to another, only fuller in the amount of pleasure it provided.

This is essentially a *carpe diem* philosophy, an "eat, drink, and be merry" approach to life that recognizes some self-restraint but is essentially uninhibited. Enjoy what you can today and do not dwell on a golden past or hope for a brighter future; live life to the full, wringing from the present all the joy it can yield. And the more intense and physical your pleasure, the more satisfying your time on earth will be.

The Persian poet Omar Khayyam, although not a Cyrenaic, expressed the Cyrenaic philosophy in his poem the *Rubaiyat*:

> Come, fill the Cup, and in the fire of Spring
> Your Winter-garment of Repentance fling:
> The Bird of Time has but a little way
> To flutter—and the Bird is on the Wing . . .
>
> A Book of Verses underneath the Bough
> A jug of Wine, a Loaf of Bread—and Thou
> Beside me singing in the Wilderness—
> Oh, Wilderness were Paradise enow! . . .
>
> Ah, make the most of what we yet may spend,
> Before we too into the Dust descend;
> Dust into Dust, and under the Dust to lie,
> Sans Wine, sans Song, sans Singer and—sans End!

Or as Edna St. Vincent Millay put it centuries later,

> My candle burns at both ends
> It will not last the night;
> But ah, my foes, and oh, my friends—
> It gives a lovely light.

But certain embarrassing difficulties emerged that constitute a practical criticism of the Cyrenaic philosophy. First, if we simply look for the pleasures of the moment and do not look ahead at what might happen later, we might enjoy ourselves today and pay dearly for it tomorrow. For example, if we want to maximize our pleasure in drinking, to intensify the experience as much as possible, we will find ourselves miserable the next morning. Or if we want to indulge ourselves in the joys of eating, gorging ourselves whenever we can, we will find ourselves with an overweight, unwieldy, and unhealthy body.

Then there is the reverse problem of refusing to undergo any momentary discomfort for the sake of future comfort, which can be equally self-defeating. There is a story about a Greek boy who was carrying a bag of gold and, because it was heavy, threw it away. Most probably, he would come to regret his impulse in later life. Wisdom dictates that sometimes we have to put up with a certain amount of discomfort in order to have a future that is enjoyable. If we are shortsighted and decide in haste, we will repent at leisure.

In short, we cannot ignore consequences in deciding how we should act. Some immediate pleasure ought to be rejected because it will lead to subsequent pain, and some immediate pain should be undergone because of the rewards it will bring in the future.

In addition, intensity might not be wholly good in terms of what might follow from it. For the more we increase the intensity of our pleasure, the more likely that an opposite state will follow. The higher the wave, the deeper the trough; the higher the mountain, the deeper the valley and "slough of despond."

For example, suppose a man wants to increase his enjoyment of speeding in a car and drives at 90 miles per hour, then 100, then 120. The dangers of having an accident are increased proportionally; the faster he drives, the more likely the accident. Or imagine trying to maximize the experience of sky-diving by opening the parachute later and later; the longer we wait, the greater the thrill—and the danger. The same holds true for the drug experience. If a man progresses from marijuana to heroin or crack cocaine, he will certainly increase the "high," but he runs a corresponding risk of addiction, of ruining his life and dying an early death. Thus, as we heighten intensity, we multiply the likelihood of pain, whereas if we lead a more moderate life, the consequences tend to be more tranquil.

And if intensity is not necessarily worthwhile, the value of brevity is also undermined, for the Cyrenaics only accept brevity in order to maximize intensity. One cannot have a long, intense experience but only a brief, intense one, so brevity is the price the Cyrenaics are willing to pay for maximum intensity. But if intensity is not necessarily desirable, we need not put up with a brief experience; all things being equal, we would prefer having pleasures extended as long as possible.

Finally, we can challenge the notion that the pleasures of the senses are the most satisfying kind. It is sometimes argued that mental enjoyment is richer, deeper, and more fulfilling than momentary sensual pleasures. As one critic wrote, "It really shouldn't surprise us that the pleasures of the moment are only momentary pleasures." The enjoyment of mental states and activities might be preferable to those of the senses, which can be viewed as ephemeral, superficial, and animalistic.

The Epicureans

Because of these problems, a series of modifications were made to the Cyrenaic theory which culminated in a separate brand of hedonism altogether, called the *Epicurean* school.[3] The philosopher Epicurus (342–270 BCE), who founded the movement and gave it his name, lived in Athens in the years following the death of Aristotle. We know that Epicurus studied Plato's system and the ideas of Democritus. We also know that he taught in Asia Minor before he founded his institute of philosophy in Athens where he conducted classes in a walled garden. The garden of Epicurus became as famous in its time as the Academy of Plato or the Lyceum of Aristotle.

Epicurus took as his goal in life the serenity or tranquility of the mind and the comfort of the body. Anything that disturbed an individual's peaceful state of being had to be avoided. In fact, Epicurus thought it was more important to avoid pain than to pursue pleasure. To his mind, a neutral state is desirable: "the absence of pain in the body and of trouble in the soul." The overall aim is to keep ourselves in a state of ideal serenity. The Epicureans criticized the Cyrenaics not only for pursuing exciting pleasures but for concentrating only on immediate experience instead of the total amount of happiness overall. If we are only concerned with specific, current pleasures, we may find that our lives are miserable in general. There should be a long-term balance of pleasures over pains, and this involves a good deal of deliberation, intelligence, foresight, and reasoning. We have to assess pleasures to see which would not be contradicted by subsequent pains, and which pains are worth enduring for the sake of subsequent pleasures. The rational approach to experience is therefore necessary to direct our activities, to temper our passions, and to look for the good in life as a whole.

Because of this emphasis on rational control, the Epicureans began to stress the happiness the mind can provide over the pleasures the senses can yield. It is the intellect that is most important, both in controlling our activities and receiving higher enjoyment. By seeking mental happiness, we avoid intensity and look for peacefulness, which is much less risky in the long run. We not only avoid the temptations of immediate pleasure, that is, the pleasures near at hand, but we also avoid the temptation of choosing the intense experience over the more serene, harmonious one. These pleasures can be of long duration rather than having to be brief, and because they are extended, they can be richly satisfying. What we seek is a pleasurable consciousness.

As noted, Epicurus regarded pleasure basically as the absence of pain. To him, the good life consists in avoiding pain insofar as possible and not seeking positive pleasures in an active way. If we can maintain ourselves in a condition that is not painful but essentially comfortable, we can say we are in a pleasurable condition. When we are in this state of mind and body we are serene.

The walled garden of Epicurus has always been taken as an appropriate symbol for the philosophy that he advocated because it was a shelter, refuge, or retreat where people could escape from the struggles and vicissitudes of the world and live undisturbed. Walls, of course, are ambiguous: They keep things in and keep things out, and it is a matter of emphasis as to which is their primary function. Epicurus's garden wall was clearly intended to keep the sufferings of the world safely outside.

There was something of the monk about Epicurus rather than the saint or martyr, for he did not dedicate himself to others but led a secluded life in the service of an ideal. For a hedonist, his life was unusually ascetic and scrupulously modulated, and he encouraged his followers to practice an equally austere and disciplined existence. Sumptuous food, intemperance, and riotous living were all condemned, and a diet of bread and water was thought sufficient sustenance, with a moderate amount of wine on feast days. A person's residence was to be modest and economically furnished to satisfy basic needs, and the daily routine was simplified to include only essential activities. Epicurus affirmed the value of friendship for the self-gratification it would bring rather than for the sake of the friend, and sharing mealtimes with others was encouraged for the same reason. Dining alone was less than human: "To feed without a friend is the life of a lion and a wolf," he wrote. The body too had to be cultivated, not for sensuous refinements of taste and feeling but to maintain the health of the organism; sickness must not disrupt our tranquility. Exercise and proper rest were essential, but not a regimen of athletic training to win honor at the Olympic Games. Only enough care of the body was required to keep it from plaguing us.

The Epicurean way of living, then, favored moderation throughout, the regulation of sexual passion, the control of bodily hungers, and the continual monitoring of the desire for sense experience. Epicurus strove to move the center of our being from body to mind, from excitement to quiescence, from active to passive modes, and from thrilling moments to lasting contentment.

It would seem as though the Epicurean type of hedonism is an advance over the Cyrenaic variety, and yet it cannot be judged as unequivocally good. By seeking to avoid pain rather than increase pleasure, Epicurus and his disciples adopted an essentially negative attitude toward life. In essence, they were withdrawing from the world, turning inward and choosing a comfortable and uninvolved existence. This attitude can be characteristic of old age when people want to be left in peace; they no longer look for novelty or excitement.

The Cyrenaics, by contrast, are vital, positive, and spirited. They want to take risks and affirm existence, saying yes rather than no to experience. To view the world the way the Epicureans do would negate all impulsive action and spontaneity. And we are not at all sure that intensity should be avoided simply because there could be painful consequences, any more than we are sure that tranquility is a blessing simply because it will be followed by more peace; intense joys may be worth the price.

The Cyrenaic philosophy is a young person's philosophy, stressing the pleasures of the body that are immediate, intense, and fleeting, and although this approach may not be prudent or wise in an Epicurean sense, nevertheless it can yield a better life than the careful, premeditated attitudes of maturity. To be reasonable in all of our decisions does not bring much joy, and the adultness of the Epicureans chills the blood; it can be a truth that kills.

It is uncertain, then, whether the Epicurean theory is an improvement or a deterioration in hedonistic ethics. Both the Cyrenaic and Epicurean theories have their merits, and we might like to combine the two to build a solid system. However, this may not be possible; their characteristics seem opposite to each other. We cannot, for example, have brief enjoyment of long duration, or an intense tranquility. Venturing may be incompatible with centering. We might vacillate between these alternatives, choosing to be Cyrenaic when young and Epicurean when old, or divide them between play and work, summer and winter, night and day, but it is hard to achieve harmony or to live a consistent life by embracing both. Besides, to attempt a pleasing mixture, extracting what we regard to be the merits of each, is really choosing an Epicurean balance.

Both theories have a self-centered, individualistic character, and this has troubled ethicists for some time. The Cyrenaics desire physical pleasure of short duration that is immediate and intense, but they want it for themselves. The Epicureans seek extended, tranquil, mental happiness in life as a whole, but they too want this for themselves. Neither adopted a universalistic ethic of altruism, or seemed concerned about harming others so long as the action promoted personal enjoyment. Epicurus spoke for the Cyrenaics too when he wrote, "No one loves another except for his own interests," and "Injustice is not in itself a bad thing but only in the fear, arising from anxiety on the part of the wrongdoer, that he will not escape punishment." That is, crime should be avoided because fear of being caught might disturb our sleep.

This pursuit of individual pleasure also lays hedonism open to a criticism called the hedonistic paradox."[4] This paradox, quite simply, is that pleasure or happiness is not an object that can be obtained directly but comes about as a side effect or unintended consequence of the pursuit of other goals. For example, people who strive for self-realization or to help others may find that they are happy in their dedication, but people who deliberately try to be happy usually discover that happiness eludes them. Happiness or pleasure seems to be a state that is attained indirectly and is destroyed when it becomes our goal; any conscious pursuit is self-defeating. Paradoxically, the search for happiness is an unhappy one, and hedonists are faced with the further paradox that by advocating happiness they are decreasing the likelihood of people's achieving it.

One figure, John Stuart Mill (discussed below), made this concession in his *Autobiography* (to the embarrassment of hedonism): "Those only are happy who have their minds fixed on some object other than their own happiness. . . . Ask yourself whether you are happy, and you cease to be so. . . . Treat not happiness, but some end external to it, as the purpose of your life . . . and if otherwise fortunately circumstanced you will inhale happiness with the air you breathe."[5] This observation appears to be true but it also gives the game away.

Other criticisms of hedonism center on the idea of "false happiness"; that is, happiness based on illusion. For example, a wife might be pleased to think that her husband loves her deeply when, in fact, he does not. A boss might believe that his employees are happy with him when they actually find him lacking. If people are living in a fool's paradise, their happiness may not be worth having.

In the same way, electrodes could be inserted into "pleasure centers" of the brain, which are then stimulated. The resulting pleasure that people feel would not be due to any experience in the usual sense but be simulated rather than genuine.

There is also the problem of "wrongful happiness." Wealthy people might enjoy having several houses, boats, and expensive vacations, but suppose they acquired their wealth through dishonest means—by cheating shareholders, for example. Is enjoyment worthwhile that comes from dishonesty and is undeserved? Similarly, the Germans have a word, *Schadenfreude*, which means pleasure at someone else's misery; obviously, such pleasures are not admirable.

Considerations of this kind make us wonder whether pleasure is good on any terms, and even whether it is dignified enough to be the goal of human existence.

D. UNIVERSALISTIC HEDONISM—UTILITARIANISM

The theory of hedonism did not undergo substantial changes during the Middle Ages or the Renaissance, and appears to have gone into a state of eclipse. Some development of the theory did occur in the seventeenth century at the hands of the English philosophers Thomas Hobbes (1588–1679) and John Locke (1632–1704), but significant work was not done until the nineteenth century, when Jeremy Bentham (1748–1832) and, subsequently, John Stuart Mill (1806–1873) gave hedonism a new lease on life.[6] Both men pursued their theories along universalistic rather than individualistic lines, developing a social hedonism which they termed *utilitarianism*.

The principle of utility, which forms the core of the utilitarian ethic, maintains that we should seek "the greatest amount of happiness for the greatest number of persons." In other words, we should not seek pleasure or happiness for ourselves but for humanity in general, and this happiness should be as great and extensive as possible. We can measure the rightness of our actions and the worth of our goals by whether more people have been made happy and to a greater extent. This is ethically better than making fewer people happy to a lesser degree. Success in living is thus gauged by the extent and degree to which we have made the lives of others happy or pleasurable.

The utilitarians obviously endorsed an altruistic and humanitarian doctrine, in contrast to the Cyrenaics and the Epicureans. The latter were concerned with whether enjoyment should be physical, mental, immediate, extended, and so forth, but it was always enjoyment for the individual that was at issue. The utilitarians, by contrast, were concerned with happiness or pleasure for society. They considered the agent performing the action as one among those affected by the action, so that the agent did not count for any more or any less than other people. Therefore, according to utilitarianism, it is not a matter of sacrificing oneself for the good of others or putting oneself before others, but of treating one's own happiness as having an equal claim beside that of everyone else.

Jeremy Bentham

The first hedonist to adopt a utilitarian position was Jeremy Bentham, an English philosopher and social theorist who was interested in political reform aimed at increasing the well-being of all social classes. Bentham was also impressed by science, which was emerging strongly in his day, and he thought he could employ science in the service of ethics.[7] He wanted to bring about an increase in the social good through the scientific application of social principles. To Bentham's mind, ethics had been much too vague and imprecise in the past, but the time was ripe to introduce scientific rigor and exactitude into ethical thinking.

Since Bentham was a utilitarian, he was interested in determining the amount of happiness that any action would yield, and he thought this could be quantified and precisely measured. If we are to bring the greatest amount of happiness to the greatest number of persons, we have to know the extent to which various actions provide happiness, and we need to establish which of two actions will produce greater happiness for more people.

With this as his intention, Bentham devised what he called the *hedonic calculus*, *felicific calculus*, or *calculus of pleasures*—a scheme for scientifically measuring the amount of pleasure and pain any action would yield. He thought he could reduce pleasure to certain "hedons"; that is, units of pleasure or pain capable of being added or subtracted. Furthermore, he wanted to isolate each of the factors involved in the receipt of pleasure and pain, and to rate actions according to the number of hedons provided by all of these factors.

Being aware of the history of hedonism, Bentham knew that the Cyrenaics had identified some important considerations such as intensity, immediacy, and physicality, and that the Epicureans had incorporated several good points in their definition of happiness: tranquility, duration, and mental satisfaction. These two earlier forms of hedonism should not be pitted against each other as mutually exclusive, Bentham maintained, but both schools of thought ought to be taken into account. An action should be given numerical values relative to the degree of pleasure or pain that was attained by either Cyrenaic or Epicurean means. Bentham isolated the factors involved in actions and reduced them to what he termed seven marks, which were largely a combination of Cyrenaic and Epicurean elements.

Intensity, the first mark, was stressed more strongly by the Cyrenaics. All else being equal, we would want our pleasures to be as strong as possible. *Duration*, the second factor, refers to the length of the pleasure, whether extended or brief. A pleasure of long duration is obviously preferable to one of short duration, and this consideration counted heavily with the Epicureans.

By their very nature, intensity and duration are usually opposed, for one cannot have a long, intense pleasure; nevertheless, both seem important considerations. Many activities have prolongation as their purpose rather than an acute pleasure. For example, the purpose of dining is not to have strong sensations but to savor the tastes and enjoy good company.

Certainty or *uncertainty* is another mark, the meaning of which is self-evident. An experience we are certain to enjoy would have a higher rating than one we might find enjoyable. In this case, Bentham is recognizing the Cyrenaic concern with pleasure that is sure to be enjoyed rather than that which is merely possible, likely, or dubious. The certainty or uncertainty of a pleasure could be a function of its nearness, and this leads to Bentham's fourth mark, *propinquity* or *remoteness*. This mark states that a pleasurable experience that can be enjoyed immediately is superior to that which one hopes to obtain at some future time. The greater the proximity, the better; because as we defer pleasures, hoping to enjoy them at some point in the future, we run the risk of never actually experiencing them at all. Closer pleasures are much more reliable, as the Cyrenaics pointed out.

A fifth factor, *fecundity*, refers to the tendency of a pleasure to be "followed by sensations of the *same* kind: That is, pleasures, if it be a pleasure: pains, if it be a pain." If either an enjoyable or a disagreeable experience leads to similar experiences rather than those of an opposite kind, then it can be rated high in fecundity. Bentham was here recognizing the merit of the Epicurean point, that one must be concerned with the future effects of our pleasures and pains rather than seizing or avoiding experience thoughtlessly. By including fecundity, Bentham was also counterbalancing the factor of intensity. For as intensity increases, fecundity tends to decrease; the two vary in inverse proportion, at least with regard to pleasure; the greater the intensity of a pleasure, the more likely it is to be followed by pain and the lower it is in fecundity. The mark of fecundity, as well as that of duration, therefore, qualify Bentham's endorsement of intensity.

Still another element in Bentham's list is *purity*, which he defined as the chance a pleasure or pain has "of *not* being followed by sensations of the *opposite* kind: that is, pains, if it be a pleasure: pleasures, if it be a pain." This too pays respect to the Epicurean concern with the future consequences of action and the overall pleasure content of our lives.

The final mark is *extent*, meaning the number of persons to whom the pleasure or pain extends. A pleasurable action that affects more people is better than one affecting fewer people, whereas painful action is undesirable and its extent should be minimized. As a utilitarian, Bentham was naturally concerned with bringing pleasure or happiness to the greatest number of people.

Bentham assumed that these seven marks were an exhaustive list of the factors involved in the attainment of pleasure. He also believed that he had culled the best of hedonistic thinking of the past since he had incorporated into his system the Cyrenaic factors of intensity, certainty, and propinquity, and the Epicurean considerations of duration, fecundity, and purity. In addition, he had added his own utilitarian factor of extent in order to ensure that the happiness of all was included as a factor.

Having isolated the relevant elements, Bentham employed them in his hedonic calculus. The seven marks would be applied to a given action, and the sum of hedons would be determined, perhaps according to a scale of +5 to -5. The same process would be carried out with regard to pains. Then the negatives would be subtracted from the positives to see whether the act was pleasurable overall. If the result proved to be positive, then the act was generally pleasurable and should be carried out, but if a negative result occurred, the act was shown to be largely painful and should not be performed.

Two points about the calculus should be made in passing. First, it is the individual who decides the number of hedons to award each factor, but the factors rated are an objective matter. Thus, there is a blend of subjectivity and objectivity in the scheme, and two people might well assign very different numbers to the same factor. Second, anyone using the calculus should give a truthful appraisal of the amount of hedons involved in each mark and not "fudge" the numbers in terms of a preferred result. This would be self-defeating, since an honest operation of the calculus would reveal which action will actually provide more pleasure to the person.

1. Bentham's scheme possesses a certain practicality and efficiency, a rough-and-ready usefulness. Also, the attempt to put ethics on a

scientific footing is commendable, although whether the hedonic calculus successfully accomplishes this aim is questionable. One criticism that can be leveled against the calculus concerns its utilitarian aspect. As a utilitarian Bentham should be very concerned with the number of people affected by a pleasurable action, yet the factor of extent is only one of seven marks in his system; that is, it counts only one-seventh in the calculation. If Bentham had made extent count more than any of the other factors, or perhaps more than their total value, then a utilitarian result would be more likely. But as the calculus stands, it is not guaranteed that the action that touches more people will come out to have the higher number of hedons and should be chosen. In his eagerness to construct a scientific ethic, Bentham seems to have betrayed a fundamental tenet of utilitarianism.

In Bentham's defense, it should be stated that he believed society as a whole would be made happy by each individual pursuing his or her own happiness. But this is willful blindness since there is frequent conflict between the happiness of the individual and that of society. A better approach would have been to place a good deal more weight on extent in the calculus, rather than assuming that the parts automatically enrich the whole. For example, someone whose company pollutes the environment and makes a fortune may live happily ever after, but that does not increase the happiness of everyone. Adam Smith's "invisible hand" cannot be counted on.[8]

2. A second major problem with Bentham's calculus of pleasures has to do with the specific numerical values that are assigned to each factor. There seems to be considerable imprecision in the number of hedons that should be awarded. If an experience promises to last an hour, should it be given a 3, 4, or 2 in duration? If an action brings pleasure to five people does that mean it is worth 1 or 3 in extension? With regard to a comparison of two actions, the problem is not so much deciding which action should be given a higher number of hedons but knowing how much higher. For example, a free fall from a plane is certainly a more intense experience than trout fishing, but is it twice or three times as intense? The overall difficulty comes in trying to obtain an exact measurement of something as amorphous as pleasure, and for the calculus to work, precision is required. With a change of only one or two numbers, the alternative action could be indicated as best in the final arithmetic.

It might seem that a narrower range of numbers would solve the problem, say 1 to 3, so that the variation would not be so great and the decision less arbitrary. But a scheme of this type would not do justice to the extreme differences that could exist between actions. If one action extended to ten thousand people, while another applied only to one person, the difference could only be indicated by awarding the first +1 and the second +3. That hardly indicates the greater superiority of the first action with respect to extent.

On the other hand, if we broaden the range to, say, 1 to 100 in order to show these differences, then we would be at a loss to decide the particular number that would be appropriate. For example, would watching a football game on a cold day in December rate 37 in impurity, 65, or perhaps 12? In other words, the wider the spread of the numbers, the more inexact the system becomes.

The general problem comes down to the fact that pleasure is not amenable to quantification. Bentham attempted to apply numerical terms to something that defies exactitude. With regard to states or feelings, there simply cannot be any moral arithmetic. As a consequence, Bentham's hedonic calculus breaks down and appears artificial, strained, and unreliable as an instrument for determining the greatest amount of happiness for the greatest number of persons.

3. We also wonder about the moral aspect of Bentham's theory. That is, by relying upon the maximization of pleasure as the criterion for conduct, we could endorse an immoral act that provides more pleasure over a moral act that yields less. This seems a serious flaw for a theory of ethics. That is, Bentham's utilitarianism tries to equate that which is most pleasurable with that which is most moral, but the two may not be equivalent. The morally right act does not always produce more pleasure, and as we all know, an action can be highly pleasurable and highly immoral. When we feel called upon to resist temptation, that tension is the reason for our struggle: we want to yield ourselves to a pleasurable experience but feel pangs of conscience because it is wrong.

Even an action that yields pleasure to a great many people is not necessarily moral as, for example, in the case of a majority that votes to exterminate a minority (one thinks of Native Americans, Jews in Nazi Germany). The pain of the victims might be less than the pleasure of the oppressors, but that does not justify mass murder. This means that the greatest happiness for the greatest number is not necessarily a criterion of morality.

With reference to our discussion of good and right, utilitarianism seems to offer a theory of the good which is often at variance with standards of right conduct. This disparity applies not only to Bentham's ethical position but to utilitarianism in general. An action that is highly pleasurable is not always morally right—even if the majority is pleased.

In contemporary society we commit this mistake when we use cost-benefit analyses to decide health care issues. A pharmaceutical company might, for example, decide to produce drugs for a widespread disease rather than for a rare but fatal one; that would be a sound business decision but not necessarily an ethical one. And on the basis of a cost-benefit analysis we could decide to practice non-voluntary euthanasia, that is, killing those whose illnesses are incurable and whose medical costs are high; we could then use the dollars we save to treat curable, widespread illnesses. We could even justify killing a healthy person if harvesting their organs could cure five others. When we engage in this type of utilitarian calculation, we ignore our moral obligation to preserve human life.

4. One additional problem with Bentham's theory should be pointed out. For one thing, he based his ethical hedonism on psychological hedonism, and this foundation is problematic, as we have already shown. "Nature has placed mankind under the governance of two sovereign masters," Bentham wrote, "pain and pleasure. It is for them alone to point out what we ought to do, as well as to determine what we shall do." Bentham thereby bases his belief that pleasure *ought* to be pursued on the fact that we *must* pursue it, and by doing so not only commits the naturalistic fallacy but makes it pointless to recommend pleasure; according to Bentham, we have no choice. If we have to pursue pleasure, then Bentham might approve of that fact but he cannot argue in favor of it; commending is not the same as recommending. In addition, even if people do pursue their own pleasure, that does not furnish any grounds for the utilitarian ideal of seeking the happiness of others.

John Stuart Mill

A final criticism of Bentham's hedonism is that he only takes into account the *amount* of pleasure that an action promises to yield and is unconcerned with the *kind* of pleasure involved. By implication, Bentham would compare activities such as hearing a classical concert and wallowing in mud only with regard to the quantity of pleasure produced by each; if the latter were more pleasurable, it would be the preferred activity. Bentham even went so far as to state that "quantity of pleasure being equal, pushpin [pick-up-sticks] is as good as poetry." But surely pleasures should be differentiated in terms of higher and lower kinds and not judged solely in terms of amount. Qualitative distinctions between pleasures seem at least as significant as quantitative ones, and might be more important altogether.

Because Bentham's utilitarianism consisted only of quantitative considerations, a reform was needed and this was introduced by his compatriot and successor John Stuart Mill. According to Mill, hedonism had to take into account the qualitative aspect of pleasure if it was to become dignified enough to be the goal of human life. In his book *Utilitarianism*, Mill wrote, "It is quite compatible with the principle of utility to recognize the fact, that some kinds of pleasure are more desirable and more valuable than others. It would be absurd that while, in estimating all other things, quality is considered as well as quantity, the estimation of pleasures should be supposed to depend on quantity alone."[9] Mill is here acknowledging the need for a modification and refinement of utilitarianism in terms of the quality factor.

Because of Bentham's failure to consider quality as well as quantity in his assessment of pleasures, and his treatment of animal pleasures as equal to those of human beings, his philosophy was referred to as "pig philosophy" (by Thomas Carlyle). The pleasures of a pig and a person were not considered any different in value if they were the same in degree. Bentham's concern was with more or less pleasure, not with better or worse, and this implies that he would approve the mode of life of a happy pig for human beings as well.

What Mill has in mind can be illustrated by the following example. When we see a herd of animals grazing, we might feel a sense of envy and think it would be marvelous to lead the life of a sheep or cow, with food readily available and nothing to do but crop the grass, roam about, sleep and stare, and reproduce the species. But even though an uncomplicated existence might be appealing for a moment, we really would not want to trade places. If we had the choice, we would elect to be human even if it involves more pain. We want a higher existence and are unimpressed by the fact that a sheep or a cow might have more pleasure.

But how are we to determine which of two pleasurable activities is qualitatively superior? What makes one pleasure higher and another lower?

Mill's answer is that the better pleasure is the one chosen by the majority of people. He wrote, "Of two pleasures, if there be one to which all or almost all who have experience of both give a decided preference, irrespective of any feeling of moral obligation to prefer it, that is the more desirable pleasure."[10]

The choices of experienced people, then, can be safely taken as the index of higher quality, since no knowledgeable person would ever elect a worse pleasure over a better one. As Mill noted: "No intelligent being would consent to be a fool; no instructed person would be an ignoramus, no person of feeling and conscience would be selfish and base, even though they should be persuaded that the fool, the dunce, or the rascal is better satisfied with his lot than they are with theirs." Mill went on to say, "It is better to be a human being dissatisfied than a pig satisfied; better to be a Socrates dissatisfied than a fool satisfied." The superior pleasures are also those that engage the higher faculties of human beings.

Certainly utilitarianism needed the addition of qualitative considerations as a corrective, since the principle of the greatest happiness for the greatest number can produce a vulgar philosophy. Also, Mill's criterion for establishing higher and lower pleasures appears persuasive. Upon analysis, though, certain flaws appear that throw Mill's utilitarianism, and perhaps the whole of hedonism, into question.

1. First, it is simply mistaken to believe that people who have experienced two pleasures will necessarily choose the higher one—however broadly we define "higher." The millions of people who watch soap operas on television are, by and large, acquainted with fine plays but prefer to watch these programs instead. And in choosing soap operas they do not claim to be enjoying higher pleasures; they simply want the lower ones. The same holds true with regard to mud-wrestling compared to visiting an art gallery, demolition derbies compared to a ballet performance. Blood sports attract far more people than cultural events but that does not prove them to be more elevated. Even within the same field, the higher type of pleasure is less popular than the lower type, and not because people have never been exposed to excellence. Better literature sells fewer copies, artistic films have a shorter run at the cinemas, and TV horror shows attract a wider audience than thoughtful dramas. In short, mass taste is not necessarily good taste, which means that, contrary to Mill's contention, the choice of the majority cannot be taken as indicative of higher-quality pleasures.

2. Second, Mill's concern with qualitative experience inadvertently led him to deny the primary importance of pleasure itself. When Mill stated that it is better to be a dissatisfied person than a satisfied pig, or a Socrates dissatisfied than a fool satisfied, he was saying that a certain quality of life is more valuable than enjoyment. A consistent hedonist would never approve of *dissatisfaction* (unless it led to greater pleasure in the long run) but Mill championed this over superficial pleasures. In this way, he was subordinating the hedonistic goal of pleasure to a better type of existence—that associated with the higher life of human beings.

The general point is that when Mill (or anyone else) attempts to refine hedonism by introducing qualitative distinctions, he places himself outside of hedonism altogether. That is to say, the qualitative standard used to differentiate between higher and lower pleasures becomes the basic ethic, displacing pleasure as the criterion for the good life. Without realizing it, Mill ultimately took as his ethic the qualitatively better life of the more fully evolved human being, but at this point hedonism has been left behind.

3. As a minor criticism of Mill, we should also mention that, as in the case of Bentham, he based his ethical views on descriptive information. He wrote, "The sole evidence it is possible to produce that anything is desirable, is that people do desire it. . . . No reason can be given why the general happiness is desirable except that each person, so far as he believes it to be attainable, desires his own happiness. This however being a fact, we have not only all the proof which the case admits of, but all which it is possible to require, that happiness is a good."[11]

In saying this, Mill clearly commits the naturalistic fallacy of deriving values from facts. His argument is that whatever is seen is visible, whatever is heard is audible, and whatever is desired is desirable. But what people desire may not be desirable, that is, worthy of being desired. What is valued may not be valuable; someone who is praised may not be praiseworthy. If an addict desires drugs, that does not make drugs desirable—even for the addict.

Our discussion of Mill's ethical theory, particularly the criticisms regarding qualitative factors, leads us to an evaluation of hedonism in general. To many moral philosophers, experiencing maximum pleasure does not seem sufficiently elevated or substantial to serve as the goal of human existence. We feel the need to raise ourselves from our animal roots but any refinement points beyond hedonism and suggests other theories of the good life. Pleasure or happiness may be a common and natural goal to seek but, upon reflection, we might want a life purpose that is higher.

Also, as was pointed out in the discussion of Bentham, there is no necessary connection between moral conduct and conduct that will secure maximum happiness, either for oneself or the majority. An extremely pleasurable action can also be highly immoral. It would be very odd, therefore, to endorse a theory of ethics that sanctioned all pleasurable actions regardless of their immorality.[12]

In an effort to counteract such criticisms, Mill argued that utilitarian principles in no way contradict morality but function as the basis for moral precepts. Murder, for example, can be judged wrong on utilitarian grounds because it runs counter to the greatest happiness for the greatest number; it militates against the social welfare and would therefore be immoral in general. This has been called *rule utilitarianism*, as distinguished from *act utilitarianism*, for instead of evaluating actions it evaluates the rules by which actions are judged. According to Mill, this forges a necessary link between the greatest happiness goal and moral principles.

An act-utilitarian might condemn a murder if that act failed to maximize happiness, but he could not offer any objections if the general happiness was increased by the action, as in assassinating a tyrant. A rule utilitarian, on the other hand, could disapprove of murder and similar crimes because they would be injurious to the happiness of society; such actions, therefore, could not be justified as rules of behavior.

In this way Mill believed he could escape the charge that utilitarianism would condone immoral actions that produced an increase in human happiness. According to rule-utilitarianism, that could never occur because the meaning of "immoral" is "deleterious to happiness when practiced as a rule," and "moral" refers to whatever is conducive to the happiness of the majority. Mill referred to justice, for example, as "a name for certain moral requirements which, regarded collectively, stand higher in the scale of social utility, and are therefore of more paramount obligation."

However, some ethicists disagree with this approach. They argue that actions should be judged right or wrong in themselves, independent of the pleasure they provide for the majority. Our endorsement of moral rules should not depend on the happiness they promote but on their intrinsic rightness. Even if the majority were to find pleasure in hanging the minority, we would not call it morally justified as a rule of conduct. Utilitarian ethics, therefore, may not provide us with a proper standard of behavior even in its rule utilitarian form.

As we have seen, hedonism contains some serious defects, whether formulated by the Cyrenaics, the Epicureans, or the utilitarians, and these defects serve as a counterbalance to the common-sense notion that happiness is the reason for living.

But the advantages and drawbacks of hedonism must now be judged by the reader. At this point, the individual must decide whether the weaknesses render the theory untenable or whether hedonism is still sufficiently strong to be chosen as the good in life. For there is a natural appeal to hedonism as expressed by Homer when he wrote "Dear to us ever is the banquet and the harp and changes of raiment and the warm bath and love and sleep." More philosophically, Joseph Butler (1692–1752) commented, "When we sit down in a cool hour we cannot justify any pursuit 'til we are convinced that it will be for our happiness, or at least not contrary to it."

REVIEW QUESTIONS

1. Differentiate between psychological and ethical hedonism, and between individualistic and universalistic hedonism.
2. Compare and contrast Cyrenaic and Epicurean hedonism. On what grounds do you judge one or the other as a stronger theory?
3. Discuss Jeremy Bentham's hedonic calculus, describing its operation and assessing its validity.
4. Explain the grounds on which John Stuart Mill asserts that one action can be qualitatively superior to another. Why would you agree or disagree with Mill?
5. Discuss the hedonistic paradox and the way in which it undermines the hedonistic theory. Does it apply equally well to utilitarianism?

5

SELF-REALIZATION

Self-realization is an ancient doctrine, first articulated by Greek philosophers several centuries before Christ, but it has re-emerged as a contemporary theory as to what would constitute a good life. Perhaps it is not surprising that the ancient Greeks, who were becoming more individualistic, should develop some of the same ideals as modern thinkers who treat the person as the locus of values.

It was Aristotle among the Greeks who developed the theory of self-realization most fully, although the virtue "know thyself" and the value of achieving excellence as a human being were part of the general culture. Another prominent name in the history of the movement is G. W. F. Hegel (1770–1831), a major German philosopher, but his theory is highly specialized and part of an elaborate system of thought. Other representatives include T. H. Green (1836–1882) and F. H. Bradley (1846–1924) in Great Britain,[1] and the American philosophers W. F. Hocking (1873–1966) and Josiah Royce (1855–1916).[2] Interestingly enough, some of the strongest advocates of self-realization in the twentieth century were psychologists rather than philosophers—humanistic psychologists such as Abraham Maslow (1908–1970), Carl Rogers (1902–1987), and Erich Fromm (1900–1987).[3]

A. DEVELOPING OUR POTENTIALITIES

As a theory of the good life, self-realization maintains that the fulfillment of our potentialities is the goal in living. We should strive to develop our capacities and actualize our talents: in other words, to develop our self to the utmost. The self to be realized is not the self of any given moment but our ideal self—the self that would exist if all our abilities and interests were fully developed. The self-realizationist is looking for the closest approach to our perfect self. Sometimes the self-realizationist will concentrate upon human nature and say that we should be as human as we can be; that is, to strive to become a complete human being. At other times, the emphasis is placed upon our individual personalities, on developing our own unique self. But whether our human nature is emphasized or our individual person, the self-realizationist takes ideal development as the goal.

As with all ideals, of course, the total realization of our self can never be achieved, for we can always imagine becoming more than we ever are. Nevertheless, it gives direction to our lives and a principle of selection for competing impulses.

We are never complete, never full-grown, for there is always more that we could do or know or be. Unlike a frog or a squirrel that develops to a maximum point at which it resembles every other frog or squirrel, human beings can always conceive of other states that they have not yet achieved. We are always short of our goal, forever lacking, so that a gap continually exists between what we are and what we want to be. The horizon line moves as we do. Perhaps a hedonist will one day be able to say, "At last I am happy," but the self-realizationists know that their ideal will never be realized. We throw the ball ahead of ourselves and chase after it in a recurrent, continual dance. Nevertheless, in that process, of challenging ourselves to reach increasingly more distant goals, we are constantly expanded. The ideal provides a shape, orientation, and narrative to our lives. By striving to realize our selves as fully as possible, we feel we are thriving and growing.

Becoming Fully Actualized

In order to develop our selves in the best way possible, it is necessary to decide which of our tendencies are dominant, for they are the ones that should take precedence, governing the realization of the rest. Some of our capacities, interests, and abilities are minor and should not be emphasized; other deserve cultivation.

It would be impossible to develop all our talents equally. There simply is not enough time, and if we tried, conflicts would inevitably occur. Furthermore, it is not desirable to achieve breadth at the expense of depth, or to award equal place to the major and minor parts of ourselves. Unless our principal interests are given priority, we will not realize our essential selves.

For these reason the self-realizationist wants us to develop under the guidance of our dominant abilities and interests. We should engage in those actions that will realize more of our selves, rather than those that realize less. Of course, we should develop as broadly as possible with the understanding that actualizing our essential self is more important than the variety, diversity, or range of our development. The American philosopher George Santayana (1863–1952), in discussing Goethe's *Faust*, explains this point as follows:

> It is characteristic of the absolute romantic spirit that when it has finished with something it must invent a new interest. It beats the bush for fresh game; it is always on the verge of being utterly bored. . . . [However] man is constituted by his limitations, by his station contrasted with all other stations, and his purposes chosen from amongst all other purposes. His understanding may render him universal; his life never can. . . . To be at all you must be something in particular.[4]

Our contemporary attitude stands opposed to Santayana's wisdom. We want to do everything and be everything, to expose ourselves to all possibilities. We resist making commitments to jobs or people or to determinate ways of being. We refuse to decide on the type of person we want to become, and imagine ourselves capable of any number of different lives. We want to leave all options open and not close any doors, thinking of ourselves as flexible, diversified, open-minded.

But if we try to be everything in general, we will be nothing in particular. If we regard every type of life as consistent with ourselves, then we are generalized beings rather than individuals with unique identities. We must decide what we are and what we are not; otherwise, we are a set of random numbers and have no selves at all. This is Santayana's point and the attitude of most advocates of the self-realization ethic. In order to become someone, we must focus upon our dominant interests and abilities; then self-realization can occur.[5]

Utilizing this type of approach, the self-realizationist can make qualitative distinctions between experiences that the hedonist is debarred from making. Higher kinds of activities to the self-realizationist are those that will develop the more essential parts of our being; the qualitatively inferior activities are those that will realize only a minor part. If we are looking for the maximum development of our personalities under the control of our dominant tendencies, then we can judge certain activities as higher and other activities as lower, some qualitatively superior and others inferior in terms of our overall goal. In that regard, self-realization has the advantage over hedonism. We might quibble with the definition of better and worse, but at least it is consistent with self-realization to make a distinction of this kind.

In relation to hedonism, self-realizationists are not saying they want to develop themselves in order to be happy. This ideal is not desirable as a means to happiness, but is *preferred* to happiness as the end of life. Like a mountain peak, it leads nowhere. Rather than pursuing a life aimed at happiness, self-realizationists want to actualize their potentialities as fully as possible. If, in the course of realizing themselves, they find happiness, that would certainly be welcome; but it would be an accidental consequence, not the final goal.

Very often the realization of oneself will conflict with the achievement of happiness, because the person will act to achieve personal growth but not pleasure. For example, the son of a millionaire could choose to strike out on his own rather than depend on the family fortune. He may know that the money he is due to inherit will give him an enjoyable life, but he may also feel that his chances of developing his talents and abilities would be compromised. The pleasures that the wealth provides would militate against his becoming a worthwhile person. Knowing the weaknesses of his own character and preferring a life of self-actualization to one of pleasurable experience, he could decide not to run the risk of remaining in "the land of the lotos-eaters."[6] *Becoming* might be thought more important than *having*. The person who chooses to be a second-rate violinist rather than a first-rate insurance executive might have a similar motive in mind, viz, not to amass money but to fulfill his or her essential self.

In the case of the potential heir, he is not afraid he will be unhappy but that he will be happy, and being happy, stop growing as a person. He dreads taking the line of least resistance rather than choosing the path of greatest advantage.

Therefore, just as in the case of hedonism, it would make no sense to ask people why they want to develop themselves, implying that it must be for the sake of some further end. Self-realization is itself an ultimate goal, standing on a par with hedonism and competing with it as a theory of a worthwhile life.

B. DEFINING THE SELF IN TIME AND SPACE

One of the first questions faced by the self-realizationist is deciding what the individual self is that is supposed to be realized. It is all well and good to say that we should realize ourselves, but what exactly is the self? This is a more difficult question than one might think, for in attempting to answer it we become involved in issues concerning the basic nature of selfhood and humanness. What are the particular factors that constitute the identity of an individual? How is a person to be defined as a unique human being, distinct from all others? And at the more general level, how is humanness to be defined? What specific characteristics can be formulated of humanity, and what differentiates us from other animals in the world? These issues of identifying selves and human beings are related, as well as being critically important to the self-realization theory.

In trying to uncover what constitutes selfhood, we are unconcerned with peripheral or transitory qualities that might identify a person externally; we want to discover whatever is constant and essential to the individual, that without which a person would no longer be the same.

The Self in Space

Initially, questions like this seem only the concern of fools or philosophers, but if we take the matter seriously we might, for example, identify ourselves with our bodies. We might respond that we know ourselves and other people through the material beings that we are, by our physical appearance.

But suppose that we have a friend named Joe, whom we describe as having brown hair and light skin, who dresses informally, and likes to drink red wine. But if Joe dyed his hair blonde, got a deep tan, began to dress up in stylish clothes, and switched to Perrier, he would still be Joe. We would say that his look and tastes had changed but we would not mean that he had actually become another person; he would remain Joe with a different image. If that is so, then physical appearance cannot be the constituent of selfhood. In other words, if Joe is still himself even though he looks different, then appearance is not what makes him Joe.

A more difficult case would be if Joe had a change-of-sex operation and subsequently renamed himself Joanna. We might be tempted to say that he was now another person, but it would be more accurate to say that he was the same person, but of a different gender and with a new name. *He* had now become *she*, but had not become somebody else. Even with a physical change of such a radical character, the same self would exist.

This might indicate that the essence of our selves does not consist of physical parts, even our sexual characteristics, much less hair or skin color. Perhaps our identity does not consist of our bodies at all. If a person becomes disfigured in a terrible accident, the person is not diminished; he or she remains that person although disfigured. Similarly, people who lose a limb and have a prosthesis attached are not any less themselves.

One objection to this might be that people will change when a bodily trauma occurs. The actor whose face is burned in a fire, the athlete who is crippled in war, the pianist whose fingers are gnarled by arthritis—they can all become different as a result. But if they are different it is not because of the physical change but because of their reaction to the change. They may become embittered, or introspective, or despondent; this would make us say they are different people. If they had not undergone any psychological alteration, then, regardless of the physical changes, they would remain the same individuals.

Judging by these considerations, then, the self appears to reside in what is internal rather than external, a matter of mind not body, the spiritual not the material part. The loss of sensitivity, the hardening of feelings, or a loss of memory could create a different self in a way that the loss of a limb could not. That is, a major mental change, as contrasted with a major physical change, could more easily be viewed as a change in identity.

However, certain difficulties also accrue to this interpretation of self. For example, if there could be such a thing as the isolation of a person's mind, suspended in a vat and connected by tubes and wires to a variety of life-support equipment, it would be difficult to say that the person himself was there. Just the presence of a disembodied mind does not seem sufficient to constitute a person.

In the same way, it has been difficult for people to accept the religious idea of the soul being the essential self. The self seems more than just the spiritual part, and the soul which is said to survive the body when we give up the ghost may be an important element of the self but is not synonymous with it. Even within Christian theology a debate has been carried on over whether resurrection should be interpreted as including the body as well as the soul. Many theologians and laypeople alike feel that an afterlife without the body would be seriously lacking.

If, then, mind alone is insufficient to constitute a self, and body is inessential to the self, how are we to define selfhood? We are left as perplexed as Oscar Wilde when he wrote,

> Soul and body, body and soul—how mysterious they were! There was animalism in the soul, and the body had its moments of spirituality. The senses could refine, and the intellect could degrade. Who could say where the fleshy impulse ceased, or the physical impulse began? How

shallow are the arbitrary definitions of ordinary psychologists! And yet how difficult to decide between the claims of the various schools! Was the soul a shadow seated in the house of sin? Or was the body really in the soul, as Giordano Bruno thought? The separation of spirit from matter was a mystery, and the union of spirit and matter was a mystery also.[7]

The Self in Time

A further problem has to do with the continuity of the self through time. Whatever defines a person should remain constant throughout his or her life. Whether we are referring to an aspect of mind or body that makes up an individual, that element must be the same from birth to death; otherwise the person is not the same. The problem comes in identifying the common denominator, the thread of continuity that makes a person the same self through time.

An analogy with an automobile may focus the problem. If we replace the engine of a car, then the upholstery, the electrical wiring, the tires, the drive train, and so on, until nothing of the original car remains, we could not call it the same car. More simply, if we had an axe and we changed the head, and then the handle, it would not be the same axe. Similarly, if someone changed in all respects from one time to another, we could not think of them as the same person. And it seems as though that is the case with human beings: nothing remains constant throughout a lifetime, either physically or mentally, that would entitle us to call a person by the same name.

Our bodies grow, mature, and decay, changing radically in size, shape, and character from birth to death. Our skin expands and grows slack; our hair thickens then becomes sparse and changes color; our muscles gain in strength then atrophy; our senses become more acute then degenerate in old age. Even our cells are replaced every seven years, the RNA in our nerve cells changes, and our organs, skeleton, glands, and systems also change in texture and composition.

Perpetual flux and mutability also characterize our mental makeup, for every element from personality to thoughts can alter. Our ideas are certainly different at six years of age and at sixty, our outlook can be transformed from optimism to profound pessimism; cynics, in fact, tend to be former idealists. Our memory can change from a steel trap to a sieve, our strength of will can grow feeble, our attitudes and disposition can be altered as a result of brutalizing experiences, and so forth.

It should be added that even though a person always remains the son or daughter of the same biological parents, this only serves as a means of identification in the way that a birth certificate does; it hardly defines a person. Furthermore, what would then differentiate a man from his brother, a woman from her sister, or, for that matter, identical twins, whose DNA is identical?[8]

What, then, constitutes the identity of the self through time? If we change in all respects, which seems to be the case, we would not be the same person but a series of different selves; beads on a chain rather than the chain itself. And, as a corollary, we would not be accountable for what our previous selves did, and no future selves would be bound by a promise. If there is a complete metamorphosis, the butterfly is not responsible for what it did as a caterpillar, the frog for its life as a tadpole . . .

As this brief description shows, the self-realizationist has a difficult time defining the nature of the self, as do all philosophers, and these difficulties stand as a stumbling block to endorsing self-realization, Obviously, if we are to pursue the development of our selves, we should know what the self is that we are striving to develop.[9]

Criticisms

The self-realizationist is recommending that we should find out "who we are" and concentrate on becoming the person we discover ourselves to be. The more we actualize our latent self, the better our existence will be. In elaborating and affirming this position Erich Fromm wrote,

> Existence and the unfolding of the specific powers of an organism are one and the same. All organisms have an inherent tendency to actualize their specific potentialities. The aim of man's life, therefore, is to be understood as the unfolding of his powers according to the laws of his nature. Man, however, does not exist "in general." While sharing the core of human qualities with all members of his species, he is always an individual, a unique entity, different from everybody else. He differs by his particular blending of character, temperament, talents, disposition, just as he differs at his fingertips. He can affirm his human potentialities only by realizing his individuality. The duty to be alive is the same as the duty to become oneself, to develop into the individual one potentially is.[10]

However, suppose one's individual potential lies in useless or harmful activities. A torturer might well be developing his personal abilities, in fact, calling into play his major tendencies. He may be extremely talented at inflicting pain and derive basic satisfaction from sadism, but his life could hardly be called commendable. Perhaps he has found his calling, his niche in the world, and is realizing the principal traits of his nature; nevertheless, torturing people cannot be judged worthwhile, even though a self is being realized in the process. In the same way, the drunkard may be satisfying his or her main interest in life and developing it to the utmost, but living in a continual alcoholic stupor seems a wasted existence. More significantly, we do not praise Jack the Ripper or Al Capone, Hitler or Pol Pot, even if each was expressing his true self. We would rather that they had suppressed their dominant tendencies (for brutality) and favored their minor tendencies (for benevolence). We would prefer that they had actualized less of what they were and became more of what they were not. Contrary to Fromm, their duty lies in not becoming themselves.

This means that the realization of one's self is not necessarily desirable; it very much depends upon the nature of the person. And if it is not always good to realize one's self, then the good cannot be defined as self-realization. If Attila the Hun or Genghis Khan were to claim that they were just expressing their nature, we would rather that they repressed it.

In addition, not all potentialities are worth developing, yet the theory of self-realization favors the maximum realization of our selves. That would include the worst as well as the best parts, so long as they constituted our dominant tendencies. Such a view is morally intolerable since cruelty, insensitivity, miserliness, and so forth would all have to claim to be developed if they were an essential part of the person.

The claim that awful actions never express a person's *real* self is dubious at best. It assumes that the basic part of any person cannot be bad, which is an unproven assumption; it might be patently false altogether. There may be some good in everyone, as the Quakers believe, but that is not to say that everyone is basically good inside.[11]

To become yourself, then, does not necessarily mean becoming something commendable, either in terms of one's own life or the welfare of other people. This reference to the well-being of others introduces a final criticism of the self-realization ethic: The theory offers no restraint whatsoever to an egotistical and selfish life. There is nothing in the self-realization position that encourages us to consider others as we pursue our own development. Sometimes it is suggested that we cannot realize our own selves without helping others to realize theirs, but this necessity is never made clear. It seems more likely that we need not pay much attention to the self-actualization of other people in order to expand personally. We may need others to develop ourselves socially, but we do not have to be concerned with their development in order to realize our own. To the self-realizationist, other people are only important for our personal nourishment.

This means that self-realization, as a theory of the good, can be at variance with what is right. It could justify cruelty rather than kindness, for example, so long as it led to personal development. And if self-realization, by its very nature, can approve immoral conduct, then it contains a serious defect.

This essential selfishness has often been noted, and stands as a major obstacle to the acceptance of self-realization as the ultimate goal in life. Any ethical theory that condones the pursuit of one's own advantage at the expense of other people is difficult to accept.

As we have seen, then, self-realization as applied to the individual can be criticized in several fundamental ways, and if we are to accept it as the purpose of our existence, these criticisms must be met. The realization of oneself appears to be a finer goal than pleasure, but it is by no means unequivocally good. Perhaps a combination of self-realization and another theory would be best in order to eliminate the weaknesses. For example, perhaps our purpose should be the realization of those aspects of ourselves that yield happiness. But then our maximum development might lie in one direction and personal happiness in another. And if we realized those tendencies that brought happiness to society, then utilitarianism would become our ethic, replacing the ideal of self-realization.

C. REALIZING OURSELVES AS HUMAN BEINGS

Another version of self-realization recommends that we develop not our individual selves but our humanness. We should become fully realized human beings, ideal representatives of humankind. Sometimes human life is contrasted with the existence of animals, and we are urged to differentiate ourselves from beasts. Sometimes, as in humanism, becoming perfect as a human being is considered a worthy aim, unattainable ultimately but providing a goal in living. At the outset, however, we face the same problem of definition. How are we to define humanness?

An extensive list could be compiled of the definitions of that have been proposed throughout intellectual history, and some philosophers assert that human nature is a myth altogether. Human beings have been variously called the social or political animals, the intelligent or rational animals *(Homo sapiens)*, the language user, the tool users *(Homo faber)*, the aesthetic being, the being that wants to know, the being that possesses self-consciousness, the religious creature, the creature that learns from his mistakes, the creature that laughs, plays, gets bored, or kills its own kind. Humans have been referred to as apes or angels (Disraeli), heaven's masterpiece (Quarles), nature's sole mistake (Gilbert), the creature that makes progress (Browning), a bundle of contradictions (Colton), the glory, jest, and riddle of the world (Pope), the only animal that is ashamed of himself—or needs to be (Twain), and the only animal that eats when he isn't hungry, drinks when he isn't thirsty, and makes love all year round.

However, if we are to differentiate humans from other creatures, all of these definitions are questionable. Humans are not the only social or political organisms; a variety of animals from ants and bees to deer and beaver live in organized groups. They have a hierarchical order, mutual cooperation, and a distinct division of labor. Intelligence and reasoning, including problem solving, are certainly not unique to human beings. Although we may be the most intelligent creatures, that does not make us unique in kind but only in degree; we stand at the top of an intelligence spectrum that includes the higher apes, tamarins, macaques, grey parrots, and even the octopus. Whales parallel people in startling ways. In a sense, computers too may be said to think, even though they do not possess consciousness.

The use of language and tools is also shared by animals; for example, by chimpanzees, which will use rocks to crack nuts and can learn an extensive vocabulary of sign language, including the use of abstract terms. They can converse in a sophisticated way with their trainers, as do dolphins, who have an elaborate communications system of their own. As for consciousness, this is not an exclusive possession of human beings, and self-consciousness, long thought to be a distinctively human characteristic, has recently been found in the higher apes: gorillas, chimpanzees, and orangutans.[12] They can look in a mirror and sign "me." These creatures also have an opposable thumb and forefinger; koala bears have this feature on both hands and feet. With regard to creating and appreciating art, chimpanzees and elephants can paint, and their work has won prizes in juried competitions.[13]

The same criticisms apply to other definitions of human beings, for it is not at all certain that human beings are the only creatures that become bored, kill their own kind, want to know (are inquisitive), eat when they are not hungry, perform homosexual acts, have imagination or a sense of humor, or love to play. We certainly cannot say "to err is human" or "man is mortal" since these are not distinctive to humans (and may not continue to be true). And to call a human being an "*animal bipes implume*" ("two-legged animal without feathers") seems beside the point. What then is human nature?

But passing over the difficulty of precise definition for the moment, self-realizationists do present a rough conception of humanness, which they believe adequately serves their purposes. They view people in terms of interests and needs: the desire for material goods, relationships, friendship, and love; and the wish to acquire knowledge, to pursue ideals, to experience beauty; and to fulfill the biological drives for food, sex, warmth, and shelter. These factors may not uniquely define people, differentiating them from chimpanzees and robots, but they are a definite part of being human, whatever else they may be part of, and our development should include them.

Is Human Nature Good?

However, if human beings are described in this way, further problems arise which parallel the problems with personal self-realization. For example, to strive for the development of our human nature can only be good if human nature is good, and this assumption is questionable. Judging by human history, the impulse to murder, steal, and rape, to maim, enslave, and exploit, seems very much a part of human beings. Sadomasochism, domination, and degradation of others are likewise characteristic of the human species, but these tendencies should be suppressed rather than cultivated. We seem able and willing to destroy as well as create, to be lazy as well as vital, to be harmful as well as helpful, but surely we would not want to become as destructive, lazy, or damaging as possible. The list of undesirable traits could be extended much further, but the point is that not everything human is commendable; a portion, at least, is shameful. And if that is so, we cannot take the unrestricted development of our human capacities as the ideal.

Self-realizationists may reply to this criticism that they would not want people to realize the unattractive parts of human beings but only the desirable aspects. They would say, in rebuttal, that the self to be realized is the good self, the pure gold within the coarse ore. But that brings us back to square one. Self-realization defines good as the development of our human capabilities; but if that is not always desirable, then the development of our capabilities cannot be the definition of the good. That is, self-realization cannot say that we should develop only the good tendencies in ourselves, since they have defined "good" as complete human realization. We would need some external criterion for differentiating between our benevolent and malevolent parts, and this takes us outside of self-realization for our ultimate standard of conduct. In judging some humanness as bad we are referring to a more basic standard of what is good than self-realization.

To bypass this criticism, self-realizationists have replied that they advocate the development of the *dominant* tendencies of human beings, and in the main, human nature is good. Therefore, there is no ethical tension within their system. However, self-realization has consistently championed the development of as much of our nature as possible, with our dominant tendencies given priority. Therefore, even if our main tendencies are considered to be positive, the minor tendencies should also be developed, and that would necessarily include some awful parts.

Furthermore, the assumption that human beings are good at heart is far from an established fact. A continual debate has raged for several hundred years over this very point. For example, Jean Jacques Rousseau (1712–1778) believed that, in a state of nature, people are basically good, but society and modern civilization corrupt their purity.[14] On the other hand, his predecessor Thomas Hobbes claimed that selfishness lies at the core of each human being, so that, prior to the establishment of governmental protection, each individual lived a life that was "solitary, poor, nasty, brutish, and short."[15]

The contemporary argument takes place between psychologists and anthropologists, and in newer subfields such as evolutionary psychology. Some social scientists are convinced there are no innate tendencies that constitute human nature, that each person, to use John Locke's phrase, is a *tabula rasa*, a "blank tablet." Others claim that people are basically loving, compassionate, and generous, and will remain so unless their development is distorted; for example, we may be hardwired for justice (as well as language acquisition). Still others maintain that our basic drives are toward self-preservation, acquisitiveness, and power over others. This is in keeping with the Freudian characterization of the id, which produces fundamental passions, and with the Christian notion of original sin that produces perversity and malice.

The issue is vast and far from decided, so that at this point in time we do not know that humanness necessarily means goodness. We cannot, therefore, advocate the realization of our essential humanness and feel assured that we are thereby endorsing what is worth endorsing. That which is human is not necessarily humane, and at least a portion of our potential may not be worth actualizing.

D. ARISTOTLE

The most renowned champion of the self-realization ethic is Aristotle, an ancient Greek philosopher whose ideas are very much alive today. His version of self-realization is sometimes regarded as hedonistic, but although he has been classified as a hedonist by some philosophers this may be misleading; he regarded pleasure as the accompaniment of activities aimed at self-realization.

Aristotle studied at Plato's Academy before founding his own school, called the Lyceum—an institute of philosophy which vied for prestige with the Academy. The name survives today in the French "*lyceé*," which is modeled on the Greek example, although teachers throughout the world are referred to as "academics." The main expression of Aristotle's ethics is contained in a book entitled the *Nicomachean Ethics,* which was named after Aristotle's son, Nicomachus. This work stands as one of perhaps four outstanding treatises in the history of ethics.[16]

At the beginning of the *Nicomachean Ethics* Aristotle famously states that "the good is that at which all things aim." Then, in a pedantic way, he defines what he means by the terms "aim" and "good."

By aim, Aristotle referred to the ultimate end of all activity, something not a means toward anything further but that for which everything else is done. To illustrate his meaning, he takes the case of bridle making, saying this activity is not an end in itself but a means toward the end of fine horsemanship. But horsemanship is not a final goal either; it, in turn, is a means toward victory in war (horses at the time being used primarily for military purposes). By these examples Aristotle was showing the distinction between means and ends, and saying that the aim he was referring to is the final aim, the aim that is never an instrument for reaching a more ultimate goal.[17]

Aristotle defined good as "*eudaimonia,*" which has been translated as "well-being," "vital well-being," or simply "happiness." "Vital well-being" is perhaps closest to the Greek, for it implies a dynamic state of personal satisfaction as well as health, attractiveness, material comforts, achievements, etc.; this seems to be what Aristotle had in mind. In any case, Aristotle took *eudaimonia* to be the *summum bonum*: the "highest good" that human beings can attain.

In order to achieve *eudaimonia*, we must first understand what it is to be human—which is the question we considered earlier. Aristotle believed that the ethical ideal must be integral to us, a part of our humanness. If we know what it is to be human, then we know the domain within which the good can be found.

Aristotle addressed the question in a distinctive way by asking what can be the *function* of a human being. A knife's function is to cut; a wing enables a bird to fly; a house provides shelter; an apple tree's function is to bear apples. Since everything has a function, what, then, is the human function? To Aristotle, the function of something is whatever is unique to it or that which it does uniquely well.

Initially, Aristotle examines the possibility that nourishment and growth may be man's function but he dismisses this conjecture by pointing out that this is the life of a vegetable, fit for plants but not for people.

Aristotle then considers the possibility that having feelings or emotions, being able to sense the exterior world, is distinctly human; perhaps the good for man may be found in this function. But he immediately rejects this suggestion by reminding us that animals also have sensations and feelings and live appetitive lives. There is nothing preeminently human in that.

But if plants are the organisms that feed and grow, and animals are the organisms that sense and feel, what function has man in the scheme of things? Aristotle's answer was that reason alone distinguishes human beings, and the good for man must in some way involve our reasoning faculty. Humans are the rational beings ("a thing that thinks," as Rene Descartes later phrased it), and man's purpose in living must be connected with the proper use of this central and primary ability.

The next question, of course, is "How should we exercise our rational function so as to attain the good?" The best life for human beings may involve the use of reason, but how, exactly, should our powers of reasoning be employed so as to achieve *eudaimonia*?

Aristotle replied in a somewhat circuitous way by saying that we should aim at achieving excellence for ourselves as rational beings. Excellent functioning, or *arête* in our area of supremacy will yield a good life. Just as the excellence of flutists consists in their skill at playing the flute and the excellence of sculptors lies in their ability to sculpt, human excellence must be judged by the degree to which we excel at being rational in conducting our lives. Since reason is central to man, *arête* in the functioning of reason will bring about the ultimate good for man; that is, *eudaimonia*.

More specifically, reason should he exercised in two ways: to engage in contemplation; and to make wise choices by controlling the extreme tendencies of our emotions. The former is more important, but the latter occupies a larger place in Aristotle's system, so we will examine that primarily.

The Golden Mean

For Aristotle, as for Plato, it is the unruliness of the passions that causes a great deal of trouble for individuals and for the human race in general. We have to control the sensuous and impulsive parts of ourselves, our emotive and animal feelings, through the exercise of reason. Our rationality should be our guide in striking the proper balance between the extremes that the passions promote.

Specifically, Aristotle maintained that we must strive to attain the mean between extremes by allowing reason to adjudicate between conflicting claims, choosing that area of moderation between excess and deficiency. What is needed is for reason to select, deliberately and objectively, mean states and activities. We must not allow the individual to be misled by emotion into extreme behavior for that way leads to an unharmonious life. "*Meden agan*," Aristotle declares: "Nothing in excess," and it is reason that will keep us moderate in all things.

The emotions can cause people to miss the mark by swaying them too far to the right or to the left, thereby bringing about an excess or a deficiency of the ideal condition. Excellence is destroyed by excess or deficiency but secured by observing the middle way; so in action we must aim at the mean under the guidance of reason. Aristotle elaborated upon this point by saying,

> For instance, it is possible to feel fear, confidence, desire, anger, pity, and generally to be affected pleasantly and painfully, either too much or too little, in either case wrongly; but to be thus affected at the right times, and on the right occasions, and towards the right persons, and with the right object, and in the right fashion, is the mean course and the best course—excess is wrong and deficiency also is blamed, but the mean amount is praised and is right.

We should strive to achieve what is called the "*aurea mediocritas*" or the "golden mean."[18]

Aristotle realized that these generalizations do not help us in a practical sense in the conduct of our lives, and since he wanted to give us a handbook of morality, he then specified particular states and actions that would be covered by his doctrine of the golden mean. With regard to feelings of fear and confidence, the mean is courage, the excess foolhardiness, and the deficiency cowardice. With respect to pleasures and pains, the mean is temperance, the excess profligacy (dissipation), and the deficiency,

Aristotle said, has not been given a name because it is hardly ever found (sic!). In money matters involving large sums, moderation is magnificence, while excess and deficiency are vulgarity and meanness, respectively. With regard to honor and disgrace, the mean is pride, the excess vanity, and the deficiency, humility. The virtue of wit is a mean between buffoonery and boorishness, and friendliness is the moderate path between obsequiousness and quarrelsomeness.

Aristotle did not say that we should try to strike the precise midpoint between extremes; rather, that we should find a middle range along the continuum from excess to deficiency. He also stated that certain virtues may not fall toward the center of the range. In other words, if 10 is an excess and 2 a deficiency, the mean may not be 6; it might be closer to 8 or 5.

In order to determine where correct behavior lies, Aristotle advised us to avoid the extreme that is more opposed to the mean; this usually works out to be the deficiency more often than the excess. For example, if we are looking to achieve courage, that would be closer to foolhardiness than to cowardice, so we would want to act more rashly than timidly. In the same way, being without a sense of humor is farthest away from wit, so in trying to achieve wittiness, we should move closer to the side of clownishness; and being a miser is much further from generosity than being a spendthrift, so we would avoid miserliness more.

Aristotle also instructed us to notice the errors to which we are ourselves most prone, and to resist those most vigorously. In other words, if our inclination is to be vain, we have to fight hardest against that tendency in order to strike the mean of pride. We must analyze ourselves to discover our weaknesses, and lean away from those particular vices. Last, Aristotle warned us to be on guard against what is pleasant and against pleasure. An action may be pleasurable but not right in terms of the mean between extremes; pleasure can, in fact, induce us to adopt non-virtuous actions. By saying this, Aristotle clearly differentiated his ethical theory from that of hedonism.

To forestall criticism, Aristotle also wrote,

> It is not all actions nor all passions that admit of moderation; there are some whose very names imply badness, as malevolence, shamelessness, envy, and, among acts, adultery, theft, murder. These and all other like things are blamed as being bad in themselves, and not merely in their excess or deficiency. It is impossible therefore to go right in them; they are always wrong: rightness and wrongness in such things [e.g., in

adultery] does not depend upon whether it is the right person and occasion and manner, but the mere doing of any one of them is wrong. It would be equally absurd to look for moderation or excess or deficiency in unjust cowardly or profligate conduct; for then there would be moderation in excess or deficiency, and excess in excess, and deficiency in deficiency. The fact is that just as there can be no excess or deficiency in temperance or courage because the mean or moderate amount is, in a sense, an extreme, so in these kinds of conduct also there can be no moderation or excess or deficiency, but the acts are wrong however they be done. For, to put it generally, there cannot be moderation in excess or deficiency, nor excess or deficiency in moderation.[19]

This would also imply that we cannot practice the doctrine of the mean too much, or that being moderate about moderation would be an extreme.

In summation, Aristotle argued that if we use our primary function of reasoning in an excellent way, we will choose the mean between extremes and thereby bring about our vital well-being. It is unlikely we will feel a sense of satisfaction if we behave in a foolhardy way or as buffoons or spendthrifts. It is equally unlikely we will attain a sense of well-being if we are cowardly, humorless, or miserly. But if we reach a condition in which we are courageous, witty, generous, and the like, we will have arrived at the ideal state of being. When we develop ourselves in this way under the control of our dominant trait of rationality, we can achieve the highest good of *eudaimonia*.

We said previously that, according to Aristotle, reason has two uses and the second is to engage in reflection. Reason is sometimes considered as an end in itself rather than an instrument for finding our way between excess and deficiency. It is the highest activity of which human beings are capable, the fullest development of a human being. Here we are not concerned with accomplishing any practical goal through our contemplation, but contemplation is considered worthwhile in and of itself. Aristotle referred to it sometimes as "*theoria*," pure intellect or theoretical understanding. At one point he called it consummated knowledge of the most exalted objects. In other words, if we reflect upon eternal, timeless truths, if we meditate upon basic questions, this will be good in itself.

This portion of Aristotle's theory, as well as his list of virtues, has been criticized as too elitist and smacking of privilege. Contemplation may be fine for people who have a great deal of money and leisure time but that hardly characterizes the mass of humankind. Nevertheless, in a larger sense, contemplation is not just a luxury of the rich; people in any walk of life can engage in it, just as they may practice meditation or yoga.

In any case, we are more concerned with the use of reason for achieving moderation in our behavior, and certainly this notion has great appeal. It is part of conventional wisdom that we should not be extremists, not be extravagant or miserly but spend our money in the right way; we ought not to be too silly or too serious but have a good sense of humor. We speak of people loving not wisely but too well, of being blinded by anger, over agitated, and losing balance and control. At the other extreme, we criticize those who seem incapable of loving others, people who are self-involved, like a snake swallowing its own tail. To charge someone with a lack of proportion has a certain commonsense appeal.

Aristotle is concerned with equilibrium and homeostasis, an overall harmony in our feelings and actions. If we go to extremes, our development will be distorted. To live in such a way that we achieve just the right amount, at the proper time and place, guided by our dominant element of reason—that is successful living.

Evaluation

1. In criticizing Aristotle, we should first notice his concept of function. He inquired into the human function because good is rooted in our nature, and he presupposed that, since everything has a function, that includes human beings. But this assumption is problematic. Artifacts such as knives and hammers, clothes and houses have been designed to serve a function, but that is not to say that natural objects such as plants, animals, or people also have a function. Natural objects have various characteristics and capabilities, different uses to which they can be put, but these may not be their reason for being.

    Aristotle embraced what is called *teleologism*,[20] the belief that everything has an end or purpose, a potentiality seeking actuality. But there may not be an end for which everything is intended or an inherent purpose that all things must fulfill. Plants give oxygen and cows give milk, but that is not to say these activities are their function. They are abilities or qualities that they possess. There may not be a reason for anything aside from the artifacts man creates specifically to serve some purpose. Besides, if objects have functions, it may not be a single function. The mouth, for example, can take in food, talk, smile, or kiss.

Human beings in particular may not have a function aside from a self-created one. Perhaps we do not have any intrinsic calling, no meaning that can be discovered through introspection and actualized. The entire approach of seeing objects, animals, or people in terms of function is highly controversial.

Although the thought that everything has a purpose can be reassuring because it grounds human beings in the universe, it could also have a negative effect. For example, suppose a woman aspires to a professional career but she is told that a woman's function is to be a wife and mother: "Unless you are a wife and mother, you are hardly a woman, because you have failed to fulfill your unique function." But this kind of reasoning seems pernicious. Although women have the capability of marrying and having children, that is not necessarily a woman's purpose. Women can choose, from a range of their abilities, which they wish to realize. They can freely decide, depending upon what they want to gain out of life. By choosing to remain single or not to have children, they are not necessarily thwarting any inherent function.

Another criticism of Aristotle in connection with this concept is that, when Aristotle tried to determine the human function, he meant by this our unique function as distinguished from that of animals, and he concluded that the human function is reason. But as was said earlier, humans do not necessarily differ from animals in their ability to reason; animals also reason, albeit at a lower level. Reason is not something unique to human beings; we simply do it better than animals. We also realize today that if human beings are unique, they could be unique in other respects besides reason—in religious awareness, for example, or aesthetic appreciation. Animals feel pain but perhaps people are distinctive in that we experience suffering.

In addition, why look for uniqueness at all in order to find out how human beings should live? It could be that a major part of being human is something shared with animals. In the present day we are rediscovering that pure animal energy is good, that work and play, bathing and sleeping, eating natural foods and drinking pure water are all positive. We would not want to do away with such things just because we share them with animals; they seem satisfying for people too. Aristotle seems to cut people off from their natural roots, but perhaps we should focus on activities we share with animals and not just on whatever differentiates us from them.

2. Apart from the problems surrounding the concept of function, a second criticism of Aristotle has to do with his championing of moderation. Reason achieves *aréte*, Aristotle believes, when it serves as a guide to the mean. But is the mean always best? Surely we would be justified in going to extremes in some cases, and perhaps temperance should not be our guiding principle if we want to lead a rich life overall. A painter, for example, might be justified in going to extremes in his or her passion for art, as van Gogh and Gaugin did. Christianity is based on complete dedication to God, an extreme of self-denial and an altruistic love for humankind. Should the artist, the saint, the political reformer, and the gifted scientist live temperately, or to the limits of their abilities? Don't we celebrate great people of the past for their single-minded dedication?

We also feel that we ought not to be moderate in our pursuits of justice, goodness, truth, or virtue itself. As was mentioned, Aristotle defended his principle of moderation by saying that such virtues are good in themselves and can be taken to extremes; moderation in them would be a vice. But this implies that moderation is not always best, which is inconsistent with Aristotle's position. And how do we know in advance which feelings and actions are virtuous in themselves and should not be done in moderation? Virtuous behavior, after all, is defined as that which is moderate.

In short, correct conduct is supposed to emerge from Aristotle's scheme, but we do not know beforehand which cases fall outside of his scheme. It would seem as though Aristotle had already established to his own satisfaction the states and actions that are right, and then took these pre-established virtues and fitted them into his general system. But neither he nor anyone else can determine ethical behavior by asking whether an action is a mean; an extreme can be virtuous. In short, Aristotle's system does not tell us how to conduct ourselves and thereby fails in its intention.[21]

3. This leads to a third problem in Aristotle's ethics, which numerous analyses have disclosed. Far from presenting us with an original theory of ethics, Aristotle merely took the conventional Greek virtues and found a structure of thought to contain them—a system that is itself the product of conventional wisdom. Aristotle stated that we should be temperate, courageous, truthful, gentle, modest, and so forth, enumerating a string of clichés and truisms that cannot be disputed but are also banal. And the system within which we find

these prosaic virtues, the system of choosing everything in moderation and nothing in excess, reflected an equally pedestrian mentality of Greek society. They are the values emphasized by conservatives and conformists, the middle class, middle-aged, and middlebrow, the people opposed to risk and afraid of being impetuous. Aristotle thus became a spokesman for a safe and commonplace morality that may be sensible but is not inspiring.

In view of the problems connected with Aristotle's version of self-realization, it may not be the path to successful living. But the readers must now make this determination for themselves in the light of the positive and negative features that have been described. As in the case of hedonism, the final judgment rests with the individual as to whether individual or human self-realization, or Aristotelianism in particular, constitutes the good life.

REVIEW QUESTIONS

1. Explain what the self-realizationist means by asserting that our dominant tendencies should take precedence in our development, and that if we try to be everything in general, we will be nothing in particular.
2. Describe the two tracks that self-realization can take: developing humanness or selfhood. Why is it difficult to define human nature and the self?
3. What is meant by the criticism that self-realization offers no restraints to an egotistical or selfish life? Why would you agree or disagree?
4. Explain Aristotle's doctrine of "the golden mean" with examples of how various virtues are derived within his system.
5. Present an exposition and critical analysis of Aristotle's concept of function. Why would you affirm or reject the notion that all objects have a function?

6

FOLLOWING NATURE

The term "natural" is one of the vaguer and more ambiguous words in our language, meaning by vagueness seeing dimly and by ambiguity seeing double. The word has caused particular trouble to students of ethics and to those who want to follow a "natural" way of life, because living naturally or being natural is hard to translate into concrete conduct. What does it actually mean to oppose an unnatural or artificial existence and to endorse living in a natural way? Our first task, then, in examining this theory is to differentiate the various senses of naturalism and the several ways of living that are intended. By a naturalistic ethic one can mean:

(a) being natural or living physically close to nature and satisfying our basic needs in simple, elemental ways—the type of naturalism of Henry David Thoreau (1817–1862), the nineteenth-century romantic poets such as William Wordsworth (1770–1850), and the "back to nature" movement of the 1960s;

(b) following the divine spirit within nature and being guided by its inherent character, laws, and manifestations—the view of American transcendentalism and ancient Roman Stoicism; and

(c) cooperating with the natural evolution of life as it has unfolded and progressed throughout biological history, doing nothing to counteract its dynamic movement toward greater integration and development.

We will examine each of these interpretations in turn as the principal forms of naturalism; other alleged types will be subsumed under these categories as subsets. The first two will be covered in this chapter; evolutionism in the following chapter, for it is sufficiently different from other forms of naturalism to warrant separate treatment.[1]

A. NATURE AS OUR MODEL

In the 1960s a movement principally concerned with the values surrounding a natural life spread across the country, fostered mainly by young people. The followers of this mode of living preferred the natural environment of the country over the artificiality of urban life, the tenderness of making love in place of the violence of making war; they sought the rhythm of the days and seasons as their measure of time, the simplicity and space and silence of the land to make them gentle, balanced, sensitive, and tranquil. They wanted to eat organic foods without pesticides or preservatives, to drink pure water and breathe unpolluted air, to maintain good health through balanced nutrition and physical activity with minimum reliance on machines. They also wanted to express themselves through folk crafts and popular music rather than being spectators of high art, and to wear comfortable working clothes instead of dressing up in the latest expensive fashions. Following Thoreau, they said that security consists not of what one has but of what one can do without. There was an emphasis on joy instead of status, feeling rather than intellect, communion in place of verbal communication, and direct experience rather than ideas contained in books. They also believed in magic and, perhaps, the insights obtained through hallucinogenic drugs rather than the methods of science and discursive reasoning. Culture, learning, sophistication, achievement, and urbanity were all considered suspect as artificial overlays on the natural life, while plainness, simplicity, openness, and rusticity were prized as elemental and good.

In the twenty-first century some of these ideas have been absorbed into our thinking. The concern about the environment, pollution, and conserving natural resources derive from this movement, as does the interest in being healthy and physically fit; eating natural foods, especially fruits and vegetables; and dressing down in natural materials. We are concerned with protecting the environment, including endangered species; and with the humane treatment of animals on factory farms, at the slaughterhouse, and as domesticated pets. In addition we worry about the morality of hunting, of caging animals in zoos, and of training them to do tricks in circuses: tigers do not jump through flaming hoops in the wild. There is also a large vegetarian movement, opposed to using animals for food, and vegans refuse animal products such as wool, milk, or eggs. Both groups lobby for a ban on animal experimentation—even to save human lives, much less for cosmetics. Many naturalists even oppose the use of animals for clothing, from fur coats and leather boots to snakeskin belts and rabbit-lined gloves; wearing an animal seems primitive, especially when synthetic fabrics are available.

Living Naturally

The roots of naturalism can be traced far back in intellectual history, perhaps to the Cynics in ancient Greece. But the recent "be natural" movement was triggered by specific ills of modern life, including air and water pollution; pesticides; genetically engineered animals; questionable food additives; carcinogens such as lead, asbestos, and mercury, and overcrowded, noisy, unsafe cities.

In the nineteenth century Thoreau, who was a transcendentalist, expressed the pastoral ideal of retreating to nature for the sake of achieving clarity and simplicity in living. As he wrote in *Walden,*

> I went to the woods because I wished to live deliberately, to front only the essential facts of life, and see if I could not learn what it had to teach, and not, when I came to die, discover that I had not lived. I did not wish to practice resignation, unless it was quite necessary. I wanted to live deep and suck out all the marrow of life, to live so sturdily and Spartan-like as to put to rout all that was not life, to cut a broad swath and shave close, to drive life into a corner, and reduce it to its lowest terms.[2]

"Most men," he said, "lead lives of quiet desperation and go to the grave with the song still in them."

Thoreau was retreating from a world that entices people to obtain more and more in the way of inessential goods, to live in debilitating comfort, and to spend an inordinate portion of their lifetime earning money to support a wasteful, superfluous, artificial existence. He believed that life in the towns diverts people from the satisfaction of their primary needs and encourages them to rounds of frivolity and superficiality. It separates them from the beauties of nature and the dignity of labor—especially labor that bears the stamp of their personality. Instead of being self-reliant, people grow weak and dependent, self-indulgent, and pusillanimous. Above all, towns render people oblivious to what is essential in life, whereas the demands of rural living make them aware of the basic terms of human existence.

The nineteenth-century Romantic poets also found in nature the truths and models that they sought, and evoked an ideal of receptivity to the lessons that nature could impart. In "The Tables Turned," for example, William Wordsworth urged readers, "let Nature be your teacher":

> Books! 'tis a dull and endless strife:
> Come, hear the woodland linnet,
> How sweet his music! on my life,
> There's more of wisdom in it. . .
>
> One impulse from a vernal wood
> May teach you more of a man,
> Of moral evil and of good,
> Than all the sages can. . .
>
> Enough of Science and of Art;
> Close up those barren leaves;
> Come forth, and bring with you a heart
> That watches and receives.

Nature, not books, contains the wisdom that will nourish us, and the truth it contains can only be absorbed through a "wise passiveness"; if we operate deliberately and make an earnest effort we will stand in our own way. Communion with nature was regarded as an experience that happens to the sensitized person rather than one forced by an act of will. It is almost as though we have to become one with nature in a pantheistic sense to absorb its message. "Are not the mountains, waves, and skies, a part/ Of me and of my soul, as I of them?" Byron asks in "Childe Harold."

We must also become like children or perhaps even infants, Wordsworth declares in "Intimations of Immortality," for they are nature's priests:

> . . . trailing clouds of glory do we come
>   From God who is our home:
> Heaven lies about us in our infancy!
> Shades of the prison-house begin to close
>   Upon the growing Boy,
> But He beholds the light, and whence it flows,

> He sees it in his joy;
> The Youth, who daily farther from the east
> Must travel, still is Nature's Priest,
>   And by the vision splendid
>   Is on his way attended;
> At length the Man perceives it die away,
> And fade into the light of common day.
>
> Thou, whose exterior semblance doth belie
>   Thy Soul's immensity;
> Thou best Philosopher . . .
>   Mighty Prophet! Seer blest!
>   On whom those truths do rest,
> Which we are toiling all our lives to find . . .
>
> Thou little Child, yet glorious in the might
> Of heaven-born freedom on thy being's height . . .

According to this perspective, the innocent and natural child is wiser than the adult and closest to God. The cultured person must learn from simpler souls, children, and animals; from the wilderness, the sea, the seasons, and the diurnal pattern of nature. "Except as ye turn and become as little children ye shall in no wise enter into the kingdom of heaven," the Gospel of Matthew tells us (Mt. 18:3), and Luke counsels us to "Consider the lilies of the field, how they grow; they toil not, neither do they spin" (Lk. 12:27). Lilies are the epitome of beauty and purity, a part of nature as we once were until we severed ourselves in the Fall. Now the prodigal must return to the arms of nature which is, as Wordsworth declared in "Tintern Abbey,"

> The anchor of my purest thoughts, the nurse,
> The guide, the guardian of my heart, and soul
> Of all my moral being.

Or as he wrote elsewhere in the same poem, in extolling his boyhood emotions,

> For nature then
> (The coarser pleasures of my boyish days,
> And their glad animal movements all gone by)
> To me was all in all . . . I cannot paint
> What then I was. The sounding cataract

Haunted me like a passion: the tall rock,
'The mountain, and the deep and gloomy wood,
Their colours and their forms, were then to me
An appetite; a feeling and a love,
That had no need of a remoter charm,
By thought supplied, nor any interest
Unborrowed from the eye . . .

Keats too celebrated nature, conceiving it as our fundamental solace, an inexhaustible balm against despondency through the beauty it offered. In his celebrated "Endymion" he wrote,

A thing of beauty is a joy for ever:
Its loveliness increases; it will never
Pass into nothingness; but still will keep
A bower quiet for us, and a sleep
Full of sweet dreams, and health, and quiet breathing.
Therefore, on every morrow, are we wreathing
A flowery band to bind us to the earth,
Spite of despondence, of the inhuman dearth
Of noble natures.
Some shape of beauty moves away the pall
From our dark spirits. Such the sun, the moon,
Trees old, and young, sprouting a shady boon
For simple sheep; and such are daffodils
With the green world they live in; and clear rills
That for themselves a cooling covert make
'Gainst the hot season . . .
. . .whether there be shine, or gloom o'ercast,
They always must be with us, or we die.[3]

A Philosophic Evaluation

Many poems extolling nature are lyrical and lovely, but can commitment to a natural life survive the harsh light of logic? If we are to be natural in these various ways, admiring and emulating nature, will that provide us with a good life? Is the natural the ideal, and is nature a model teacher?

1. Country living certainly has some advantages over city life, but it lacks a great deal as well. In practical terms, good theater and films are difficult to find in rural areas, as are museums, art galleries, and concert halls. If we enjoy modern dance or ballet, or seeing fine

architecture in buildings or cathedrals, we will probably be at a loss in a farm community, and if we want a variety of food or enjoy dining in fine restaurants, we are much more likely to satisfy our tastes in the city. Urban life also offer a wide range of entertainment, from clubs to sports events, and provides a more extensive selection of products and services including clothing, cars, furniture, appliances, and so forth, as well as CDs, books, and magazines. We also find people to talk with who are generally better educated and more sophisticated than country people. The main cultural achievements of civilization are concentrated in cities, as well as the latest technological advances which provide increased comfort and convenience in living. Dental and medical care are also superior in cities, which have more highly trained doctors and teaching hospitals, and social services are more extensively developed, as are systems of public transportation and communication. In addition, city newspapers, libraries, and broadcasting stations are generally better than their rural counterparts.

Furthermore, a country existence may be more peaceful and serene, but it also can be dull, boring, and lonely, deadening people rather than enlivening them. It can reduce us to an animal level where we only meet our basic needs but do not live the higher, more complex existence of a human being. The means for satisfying a variety of our interests are less readily available, and with limited access to educational, social, and cultural institutions our personal development can be stunted. As Aristotle said, to live the good life one must live in a great city.

We also wonder whether it is desirable to minimize our material goods or to eliminate the labor-saving devices that modern science has developed. Surely it would be more impoverishing than enriching to do without refrigerators, stoves, washing machines, cars, running water, indoor plumbing, central heating, or electric lights. Too much time would be spent on sheer survival, on providing the basic necessities for maintaining ourselves in a reasonably comfortable way. And not only would the burden fall on the woman (if she were the one keeping the home) but on the man as well if he tried to produce goods without machinery or to operate a farm without a tractor or a combine. At least some technological devices free us from exhausting, repetitive, routine labor, and some material objects such as musical instruments, attractive furnishings, works of art, and cooking utensils enhance our lives and give us the means for self-expression. Having a spacious, comfortable, well-appointed house can do more for our spirit than living in a shack, even if the latter is a more natural dwelling.

Country living, then, with a minimal use of technological equipment and material goods, is not necessarily better than living in the city in a tastefully decorated home with a variety of cultural offerings and conveniences at our disposal.

2. In addition, the "be natural" theory does not tell us how elemental or primitive we should be in order to lead a truly natural life. Should we, for example, do without the wheel, metal tools, written or spoken language, electric lights, heating, or plumbing? Should we go without clothing even in winter, as animals do, and never wear shoes? Should we bathe infrequently, pay little attention to sanitation or manners, and never consult doctors, undergo surgery, or use any medication other than herbs? Must we abandon the use of silverware, napkins, and plates, or even tables, chairs, and beds, in keeping with the practices of early man? Should we only gather fruits, nuts, and berries, rather than raise cattle or crops? If we eat meat, must it be raw? Is it enough to use a hand plow to work the land, or should we use a stick in order to farm the natural way? And when we travel should we simply forgo trains, airplanes, and cars, using horses instead, or do we have to walk to be truly natural? Are boats and bridges natural, or must we swim across rivers? Can we live in houses, or must we live in caves or trees? Just how far back must we go in our history in order to reach the natural state—to an eighteenth-century peasant, an ancient Egyptian, Neanderthal man, a primate, an amphibian, an amoeba, a particle of inanimate matter? The dictum "be natural" simply does not tell us which stage is the truly natural one.

We could begin with the first human being, *Homo erectus* (although that stage of human life does not seem ideal). But the moment we admit that certain changes in our natural state still constitute a natural life, then we do not know where to stop; we cannot then say how extensively human beings can change the environment and still be living naturally. We certainly cannot claim that whatever human beings do is natural by virtue of the fact that we are natural beings, because then every development in science, medicine, engineering, and so forth would be natural. Usually, we consider such fields non-natural.

Therefore, in addition to the criticism that urban living in all of its aspects has numerous advantages over a rural existence, we can also find fault with the ethic for failing to provide a criterion for a natural, as opposed to an unnatural, life.

3. A third criticism has to do with the emphasis placed on nature as a model for human conduct. We are told we should emulate nature, live as simply and forthrightly as animals, and draw our inspiration from the pace and pattern of the natural world. However, although nature does provide solace and beauty it also contains brutality; as Tennyson said, it is "red in tooth and claw." We would not want to imitate nature insofar as it includes animals preying on one another: big fish eating little fish for survival, without justice, kindness, or mercy. Aside from the constant violence of carnivores such as tigers, panthers, bears, wolves, and so forth, even plants crowd each other out seeking water, nutrients, and space to grow.

Furthermore, to copy nature's catastrophes would hardly be desirable. Hurricanes, earthquakes, forest fires, tidal waves, blizzards, droughts, avalanches, floods, volcanic eruptions, and so forth are genuine manifestations of nature, but we would not want to duplicate them. There are also a host of naturally occurring diseases such as malaria, cholera, tuberculosis, asthma, multiple sclerosis, diabetes, and polio. Civilization is in many ways a fortress in the wilderness, and we fight to keep out the more brutal aspects of nature. We want to build a garden in the jungle, not import the jungle into our garden. As John Stuart Mill pointed out, in many respects nature is the enemy.

In sober truth, nearly all the things which men are hanged or imprisoned for doing to one another, are nature's every day performances. Killing, the most criminal act recognized by human laws, Nature does once to every human being that lives; and in a large proportion of cases, after protracted tortures. . . . Nature impales men, breaks them as if on the wheel, casts them to be devoured by wild beasts, burns them to death, crushes them with stones like the first Christian martyr, starves them with hunger, freezes them with cold, poisons them by the quick or slow venom of her exhalations, and has hundreds of other hideous deaths in reserve. . . . All this, Nature does with the most supercilious disregard both of mercy and justice, emptying her shafts upon the best and noblest indifferently with the meanest and worst. . . . She mows down those on whose existence hangs the well-being of a whole people, perhaps the prospects of the human race for generations to come, with as little compunction as those whose death is a relief to themselves, or a blessing to those under their noxious influence. Such are Nature's dealings with life. . . . Next to taking life (equal to it according to a high authority) is taking the means by which we live; and Nature does this too on the largest scale and with the most callous indifference. A single hurricane destroys the hopes of a season; a flight of locusts, or an inundation, desolates a district; a trifling chemical change in an edible root, starves a million people. The waves of the sea, like banditti seize and appropriate the wealth of the rich and the little all of the poor with the same accompaniments of stripping, wounding, and killing as their human antitypes. Everything in short, which the worst men commit either against life, or property is perpetrated on a larger scale by natural agents.[4]

Nature, then, is by no means exemplary in all of its forms. Animals often bring pain to each other, in addition to suffering under the conditions of their environment: rain, cold, starvation, predators. When we say "Don't behave like an animal," we mean that the beasts are often beastly, the brutes can be brutal. Suffering and death are a definite part of nature, and we are all subject to natural catastrophes, but we would not want to call them good.

Civilization is at the opposite end of the spectrum, so that the closer we get to nature the further we are from civilized society. That may not be a good thing. Between cave dwellers and modern man we seem to have advanced in health, education, medicine, transportation, art, engineering, government, communication, science, and so forth. It would be regress, not progress, to ignore the improvements that have been made in human life and to revert to an elemental mode of existence. Lightning rods and levies, surgery and inoculations, serve a useful purpose. Irrigation can turn a desert into a farm, and pesticides can save the crop from insects.

Perhaps we have to accept the fact that we are unique within nature or, at this stage in our evolution, outside of nature altogether. We control our environment as no other creature can, and seem closer to computers than chimpanzees. In fact, we do not mind incorporating machines into our bodies to enhance our quality of life. We use contact lenses and hearing aids; have teeth implants and pacemakers; insert mechanical joints in our fingers, elbows, or knees; put plastic disks in our spinal column; and attach prosthetic devices such as artificial arms or legs. In a larger sense, clothing is a protective skin shielding us from the weather, and cars, trains, ships, and planes are our technological outer layer, giving us speed and mobility in three dimensions.

This brings us to the general criticism, which applies to every type of naturalism: that which is natural is not necessarily good. Some aspects of a nature are worth following but others are not, just as the unnatural contains both good and bad parts. Eating natural vegetables seems better than consuming prepared foods with large doses of chemical additives, preservatives, and pesticides, but we would not want to cure a ruptured appendix with herbal remedies; here we want the skills of a modern surgeon. We may have a romantic longing for a primitive life but we would want to bring antibiotics and novocaine. And not every organism in nature is benevolent. We do not value all the viruses and bacteria that are on the planet, because some cause awful illnesses and diseases. And would it really destroy the balance of nature if there were no rattlesnakes or black widow spiders, no crocodiles, piranhas, or moray eels? Nature would establish a new order through time; 98 percent of all species that have lived are now extinct but there is still balance.

In short, to call something "natural" is not always to commend it, and if something can be natural but not good, then good cannot be defined as the natural. When something is judged to be good, the judgment is made not because it is natural, but for some other reason. A natural event could be judged good because it enhances happiness, provides rich experience, realizes the individual, and so forth. But the event is not good simply because it is natural.

This criticism stands as a stumbling block to all forms of naturalism that attempt to equate the good with the natural. For our present purposes, it certainly constitutes a viable criticism of the "be natural" ethic. Rather than blindly following a natural life, it seems far more sensible to select, from among the natural and the unnatural, that which is worthwhile.[5]

B. AMERICAN TRANSCENDENTALISM

A second form of naturalism urges us to follow nature in the sense of harmonizing with its inner purpose and structure, its essential character and developing spirit. This is a more mystical form of naturalism that treats nature in a reverent, pantheistic way.

According to American transcendentalists such as Ralph Waldo Emerson and Henry David Thoreau, there is a universal force moving through nature to which we should ally ourselves, finding our reason for being in fulfilling its will. Rather than conceiving of a god behind natural phenomena, this type of naturalism sees nature as a transcendental force in itself, moving through all things and imbuing them with destiny. Nature here becomes God, not a personal being but an abstract spiritual power with an overall design. Unconsciously, without direction from a cosmic mind, nature tends toward certain ends and contains an internal, dynamic order. Without being directed, nature contains direction, and the natural world is shot throughout with discernible purpose. All events occur as a consequence of the operation of a grand scheme and everything happens in a beneficial way, for the scheme is supremely moral. If human beings live in tune with the system of nature, understanding its inherent tendencies and following its direction, they will achieve a satisfying existence, individually and collectively. If, on the other hand, they oppose the plan of nature, they will live in a state of disequilibrium, divided from both the natural order and their own nature.

The "be natural" movement seems to stress conformity to nature in a more external and romantic sense, whereas this theory looks to an active power within natural forms and claims that we should become one with nature in a more fundamental way. Here the purposive thrust of nature is emphasized in contrast to its external manifestations; physical appearances are only indicative of inner forces. Our duty is consequently seen in deeper perspective; it consists in following the disposition of nature, its vital, spiritual essence.

The American transcendental movement embraced a "Neoplatonism," which is usually identified with the founder Plotinus (205–270 CE). It preached that nature is the expression of "mind," and natural laws embody moral principles. A supreme but impersonal force was thought inherent in the natural world.

Ralph Waldo Emerson

As Ralph Waldo Emerson (1803–1882) rendered it, "at the center of nature lies the moral law, radiating to the circumference." In order to understand the inner workings of the universe, an intuitive perception is needed to take us beneath the surface. Systematic reasoning or scientific discoveries can only teach us facts, cram the filing cabinet, but a direct vision of reality is required. Those who discount empiricism and dismiss the outer world as "a dream and a shade" realize that nature is divine; and insofar as human beings are a part of nature, they too carry a spiritual spark inside them and transcendental worth. "Every natural fact is a symbol of some spiritual fact," Emerson wrote. "The whole of nature is a metaphor of the human mind." He further claimed that "Within man is the soul of the whole." Therefore, by looking either outward or inward, by understanding ourselves or nature, the fundamental reality is revealed to the aware and patient seeker.[6]

In addition to opening our minds to nature's spirit within and without, we also have a duty to correct injustices against humanity in civil society. Crimes against man are sins against nature because the two are one, and we can have confidence in our judgments because our conscience is rooted in the natural moral law. We are, therefore, obliged to adopt a humanistic stance, and for the nineteenth-century transcendentalists this took the form of an active protest against slavery and a call for women's rights, free public education, and prison reform. Most of the major figures of the movement defied the Fugitive Slave Law, and several were imprisoned for subversion. But whatever the particular issues of the age, the transcendentalists advocated a life of moral commitment, specifically to redress the offenses against civil rights. It was conceived as something of a holy mission to resist the desecration of the human spirit—a spirit that was the epitome of nature and the divine. Bronson Alcott, the father of the writer Louisa May Alcott, founded a school in Boston that promoted such principles.

Because of the insistence on a supernatural reality within the physical world of nature, transcendentalism is sometimes considered to be in opposition to naturalism. A case can be made for this position, particularly if naturalism is closely identified with materialism.[7] But insofar as the transcendental movement regarded nature as having an inner soul, it was a type of spiritualized naturalism. Belief in the reality of the unseen was faith in nature's divine essence. "Everything in Nature contains all the powers of Nature. Everything is made of one hidden stuff," Emerson declared. Spirit is immanent in nature, residing in every part, not an independent force behind it. There is a divine energy inherent in all living things.

It is difficult to judge whether transcendentalism is correct in its assessment of reality, particularly since it disqualified the rational and scientific approaches to truth. Is there a cosmic spirit permeating the natural world, and a mind or soul in each human being that reflects nature, a spiritual essence? Do only biological and physical laws operate in the universe? Perhaps the transcendentalists felt the force of conscience so strongly that they experienced it as an external obligation, and perhaps their entrancement with nature was so great that they imagined an animistic spirit within natural phenomena. This is the metaphysical question that has come down to us from the transcendentalists, and our acceptance of their ethical theory depends upon our answer to it. Today's manifestation of transcendentalism is the Unitarian Church, which originated through the writing and preaching of William Ellery Channing, Margaret Fuller, and Theodore Parker.

C. STOIC FATALISM

To examine naturalism in the form of Stoicism, we must go back to ancient Rome. Stoicism was a philosophy most closely identified with Seneca (c. 5 BCE – 65 CE), Epictetus (c. 55 – c. 135 CE), and Marcus Aurelius (121–180 CE), but its intellectual framework lay in the Greek thought of Zeno of Citium (c. 334–262 BCE) and Chrysippus (c. 280–207 BCE). The name derives from the painted *stoa* (or colonnade) where Zeno taught in Athens.

The philosophy was a blend of Greek rationality, Roman practicality, and an abiding theological belief in *logos,* which is an active, divine, and rational force informing every aspect of the universe. The external manifestations of nature were considered to be expressions of *logos,* and the spiritual force within directed all natural events in an orderly and purposive way. In Stoicism, as in transcendentalism, there was the idea of a divine power coursing through nature, but unlike transcendentalism, the power was considered to be rational and, therefore, comprehensible through the human intellect. And God and nature were so closely identified that the universe was sometimes spoken of as a living whole; the physical world was considered the body of God, its inherent *logos* God's very spirit.

Epictetus and Marcus Aurelius

According to the Stoics, nothing occurs in vain or by chance in this universe suffused with divine reason, and the good for human beings therefore lies in conforming to its benevolent purposes. We must live "in harmony with nature,"[8] acting "with good reason in the selection of what is natural,"[9] and "hold fast to the things that are by nature fit to be chosen; for indeed we are born for this."[10]

By definition, nothing that is natural can be evil in any ultimate sense, and it is childish of people to fear or criticize natural occurrences. It is equally foolish to seek our life purpose anywhere except in universal nature and the answering call of our human nature. "Do not look around thee to discover other men's ruling principles, but look straight to this, to what nature leads thee . . . following thy own nature and the common nature."[11]

As in much Eastern philosophy, the inner and the outer are one; internal and external are fundamentally the same, and both embody the workings of reason.[12]

When the rational governance of the universe is understood, a necessary pattern of events is revealed, for nothing happens fortuitously or by chance. A rigid predestination operates throughout the natural world, an infinite chain of causes and effects to which human beings too are linked in their physical life. The fatalistic universe always works for the good of the whole, but no material event is free from its ineluctable progress, including the events that constitute the outer experience of human beings. Whatever happens is wholly beyond our control despite the fact that some actions may appear to be the result of our decisions. All events occur as they must and we have no choice in the matter. As in the case of material objects, everything that befalls us is part of the necessary design, a thread in the tapestry of destiny.

However, human beings are not physical entities only, any more than the universe is purely material. We have an inner spirit that is capable of responding to the inevitable occurrences in our lives. Events may be predestined, but our attitude toward those events is not; here we possess free will and are our own masters. Our reaction to fate lies within our power.

Although we are free in our response to nature's inevitable decrees, if we are wise we will respond in a positive and rational way. We can rail against our fate, which is particularly tempting when tragedies occur, but that would be pointless and, in a sense, blasphemous. We can do nothing about the diseases or disasters that afflict us, neither to prevent nor to avoid them, and since destiny is ultimately good it ought not to be opposed in any case. Just as the Christian or Jew says that, despite the suffering we experience, we must have faith that God is good, the Stoic believes that everything happens for the best in a world governed by the divine *logos* of nature.

The only rational and moral response, then, is to condone actively whatever occurs. Not only should we accept our lot in life and remain poised and tranquil even in the face of catastrophe, but we should positively endorse whatever circumstances fate has ordained for us. Although our emotional reaction to disasters might be anxiety or frustration, curses or rebellion, we should exercise rational control over our feelings; we must behave with equanimity and maintain an attitude of calm approval. "Ask not that events should happen as you will," Epictetus advises us, "but let your will be that events should happen as they do, and you should have peace." Any other attitude is foolish and contrary to our duty to follow nature's will.

Intelligent people distinguish between that which is within our control, principally their mental attitude, and that which is not, namely, external events. We should realize that our well-being depends on knowing the difference between the two, accepting what we cannot change and managing that which is within our control. Nothing can be done about a drought or a plague, but we can cultivate the right attitude toward such disasters and achieve peace of mind. As Epictetus stated, we should "make the best of what is in our power, and take the rest as it occurs," separating "what is *ours,* and what is not ours, what is right, and what is wrong. I must die, and must I die groaning too? I must be fettered; must I be lamenting too? I must be exiled; and what hinders me, then, but that I may go smiling, and cheerful, and serene? 'Betray a secret.' I will not betray it, for this is in my own power. 'Then I will fetter you. What do you say, man?' Fetter me? You will fetter my leg, but not Zeus himself can get the better of my free will."[13]

Our essential self, then, possesses free will, which means we are capable of gaining power over our lives in a very basic sense. But in order to do this, we must agree to be ruled by rationality. Only reason can give us freedom because it enables us to recognize those circumstances we cannot change and to rise above them, not allowing any physical happening to affect the felt quality of our existence.

Conformity to nature, therefore, has a deeper meaning than it appeared to have at the outset. To the Stoic it signified following the rational part of our being that corresponds to the rational spirit within nature. It also meant using this rationality to realize that all operations of nature are beneficial to the universe at large and therefore should be approved. We cannot control our fate, but we can and should actively assent to it, and by this assent we will lead tranquil and satisfying lives. In our inner and inaccessible being we will remain unharmed by any catastrophe and pass through life in a serene manner, confident that the divine spirit moving through the natural order will inevitably bring about the ultimate good. In this way we will attain the ideal state of *apatheia*, the complete absence of feeling or emotional involvement.

The Stoic approach to successful living is extremely appealing at times of insecurity when people live in unsafe conditions and the political and social order is in ferment—which was the case during the later period of the Roman Empire. In such times, the tendency is to turn inward for our well-being rather than rely upon anything external, to concentrate on the satisfactions that are within our power to achieve and not external goods beyond our reach and uncertain. We are impressed by the fact that our health or safety cannot be guaranteed any more than we can count on wealth or fame; and if we pin our hopes on these things, we may well be disappointed. But we can take the proper attitude toward anything that occurs, and find contentment even in pain or poverty.

This polished sphere of Stoic philosophy can be attractive today when economic conditions are unstable in the world. People can feel that they have little power over their wealth or income, that larger economic forces determine their future. Working hard will not ensure employment any more than merit will ward off unemployment, and, in general, achievement will not guarantee security. There does not seem to be any universal justice, so the system will not always provide for those who do their part. People may feel their efforts are largely inconsequential in affecting their economic future; what happens to them is outside their control. In such circumstances, there is comfort in saying, "There's no sense worrying, it doesn't do any good; we might as well make the best of things."

D. AN EVALUATION

However, adherence to Stoic attitudes can be problematic; in fact, there are a number of criticisms which can be made:

1. By adopting the Stoic approach, whether in ancient Rome or contemporary America, we may be turning away from the world too much, denying ourselves its benefits in order to minimize its pains and losses. We might be inclined to take too few chances and therefore gain less than we could. In brief, our concern with avoiding discomfort can limit our satisfactions, making our lives more cramped, resigned, and withdrawn than they need be.

   This point has often been made against the Stoic mentality, which seems overly concerned with personal control and ensuring peace of mind to the detriment of fullness of living. In this, Stoicism echoes a recurrent theme in Eastern philosophy and religion (especially Buddhism); namely, that attachments to this world render us subject to pain at their loss. If we love or desire nothing, then we are invulnerable. But achieving satisfactions may be worth the risk of pain.

Furthermore, if we adopt the Stoic viewpoint, we may believe we have less control over our affairs than we actually do, resigning ourselves to our fate when we should be masters of it. We might make a virtue of necessity when an expenditure of effort could improve our circumstances. In short, by following Stoicism we tend to underestimate the degree of control we have over events, and, without confidence in our own power, surrender before we have tested our ability to change our lives.

A first criticism of Stoicism, then, is that it needlessly constricts our lives by advising us to forgo satisfactions and to accept various circumstances that we well might be able to alter. It seems far better to try to gain all we can out of life even though we run the risk of disappointment. Our efforts may be fruitless, but that is hardly a good reason not to strive for a richer life; being safe is no substitute for being fully alive. The Stoic saying, "*Abstine et sustine*" (abstain and endure) is a sad motto.

2. This leads to a second criticism, which has to do with the Stoic belief in fate ruling all external events. Obviously there is no point in trying to improve our situation if we have no control over it. However, few people today believe in fate or destiny; it has lost the widespread acceptance it had in the ancient world. Even contemporary Christianity holds a limited view of providence, which allows for free will and our consequent responsibility to God for the lives we choose.

Although pre-determinism has been discarded more than disproven, the grounds offered by the Stoics for its acceptance appear weak. The Stoic argument is that all past events are frozen in time and cannot be altered by any act of will; as the English poet John Dryden wrote, "Not heaven itself upon the past has power." Certain future events are also unalterable, such as the succession of night and day and our planet's death in about seven billion years. From such considerations the Stoic concludes that, since the past and part of the future are fixed and determined, we can assume that all temporal events occur according to destiny. The entire universe—past, present, and future—is one bloc, a predetermined whole.

Obviously, this is not sound reasoning. From the fact that past events are unchangeable, we cannot infer that another class of events, namely those in the future, are unchangeable. Equally illogical is the claim that, because some future occurrences are inevitable, the future is as fixed as the past. This is technically referred to as the *fallacy of composition*, for it claims that what is true of the part is true of the whole. It would be like saying that since straws are light, a load of straw will be light. Not only is the logic faulty, but we cannot claim there are necessities in nature—even with regard to such commonsense notions as that the sun will appear tomorrow or that man is mortal. The earth could cease its rotation at some point in time, and if we should control the aging process, then it would not be inevitable that people die. No future event is sure to occur; only the conclusion to a logical train of reasoning may be called certain.[14]

3. In addition to the weaknesses in the argument for pre-determinism, another objection against Stoicism pertains to the fact that a doctrine of predestination makes all effort pointless. This has become such a standard objection that it has acquired a name: the *lazy argument*. According to this criticism, there would be no point in doing anything at all if every event were destined to occur. We could simply stretch out on our beds, confident that to do so was fated. Furthermore, no one would be accountable for anything that occurred, since events must happen as they do. People would not be guilty of any wrongdoing; rather, they would be regarded as wholly innocent, an instrument in the hands of fate. Blame or praise would be inappropriate, as would be punishment or reward. Why try, after all, if nothing we do makes any difference,? In the Stoic system there is some question as to the extent to which our will has an effect on our actions. It would seem odd to believe that, when a person decides to throw a rock, and the rock then flies from his hand, the decision had nothing to do with the rock hurtling through the air. The Stoic is rather vague on this point, sometimes extending the power of will only as far as speech, as when Epictetus said he would not betray a secret; sometimes implying a greater degree of power over our actions. By and large, Stoicism separates volition and action in a radical way, and this creates certain puzzles which have plagued the movement from its inception.

Another way of presenting the objection is to say that if we do believe a connection exists between will and action, and if we do think people are largely responsible for their conduct, then we are rejecting the claim of Stoic fatalism. One way of criticizing an ethical theory is to show that its consequences violate certain basic beliefs and contradict our moral experience. Stoicism does this; therefore, the philosophic standpoint becomes questionable.

4. A final criticism has to do with the impoverishment of our emotional life that comes about when we only allow ourselves to respond to events in practical ways. For example, if we were concerned about someone we love who is undergoing surgery, the Stoic would advise us to control our emotions because they serve no useful purpose; it does not help the situation and it works against our peace of mind. But we are feeling anxious not because we think it will do any good, but as a result of our love for the person. Our concern is not meant to be a cause of anything but is an effect of our caring, and to refuse to feel this emotion would mean stifling our feelings.

If the Stoic recommendation were carried out, it would make genuine love impossible, for the emotions associated with love are not always "useful." A great deal of our emotional life, in fact, would be disallowed because it does not do any good; it would be "wasted emotion." But surely we want to have the full range of emotional experience, including those emotions that serve no practical purpose. And the very process of controlling our emotions to the extent advocated by the Stoic is destructive in itself. To allow ourselves to feel only certain emotions severely reduces our openness, sensitivity, spontaneity, and involvement. It transforms the richness of our feelings to a carefully regulated set of prudent responses. For a person to say, "I will feel a certain emotion if it is helpful; otherwise I will not feel it," is far too limiting. Blaise Pascal once remarked "There are two equally dangerous extremes, to shut reason out, and to let nothing else in." The Stoic obviously commits the latter mistake.

If matters are out of our control the wisest course would be to accept the situation, but psychologically the lack of power only increases our anxiety. Not only is it difficult to remain passive at such times but the self-control could actually be harmful, like a pressure cooker without a vent. We might not be able to help the situation, but expressing our frustration might be helpful in itself.

The controlled, deliberate, and rational approach to life is characteristic of the authoritarian personality. The authoritarian (as contrasted with the democratic) personality has such a rigid structure of responses that any genuine reactions are deeply buried beneath an extensive system of defenses. To be affected by genuine emotion means to risk a crack in the foundation of the personality, threatening it with collapse; therefore, a strong, implacable, enameled surface is presented to the world. But such strength is basically weakness, for it is grounded in an anxiety about exposing oneself; the person is most afraid of being unguarded, that is, of being himself and vulnerable. The real person lies cowering behind an elaborate network of fortifications.

Oddly enough, this self-protective attitude that is assumed to provide freedom from injury becomes the opposite of authentic freedom, for one locks oneself away from others and oneself, becoming separate and self-alienated. The castle is actually a prison, with little nourishment being delivered from outside the walls. The person feeds off himself: he cannot be injured very readily but also cannot communicate with others or be nourished by them. In forming an obsessive routine, or building psychological calluses that make him incapable of feeling, or becoming a member of a strict, hierarchical organization, the authoritarian personality loses his reality as a person. Petrified by fear, the individual becomes part of the castle rock itself, unassailable and less than human.

Perhaps freedom does not come about through independence but by being secure enough to risk depending on people outside ourselves. Then we are in command of our lives.

Is Nature the Ideal?

All four of these criticisms cast doubt on the Stoic doctrine as a theory of the good life. Following nature as Stoicism would have us do tends to constrict our conduct, to make moral effort futile, and generally to impoverish our emotional life. And as we have seen, the belief in destiny, which lies at the heart of Stoicism, can be questioned; that may not be the way the universe functions.

Even if it were, that does not mean nature should be emulated. For as we have seen in our discussion of the naturalistic fallacy, what is the case is not necessarily what ought to be the case. The "is" cannot be the basis for the "ought." In Stoicism, even if events are predetermined, that does not mean we should accept disasters cheerfully. Inevitability does not breed equanimity; in fact, we might want to rage against the dying of the light. And in the "be natural" ethic, the violence of nature is not something we want in human society, and the fact that it is the law of the jungle does not make it desirable.

Some features of nature are positive, while others are not. Rather than approving of nature as a whole, we must select only those aspects that are worthwhile to incorporate into our lives.

REVIEW QUESTIONS

1. Describe and criticize the "be natural" theory as an ideal of the good life.
2. Explain the philosophy of transcendentalism and show how it is a form of naturalism despite its spiritual dimension
3. Discuss the grounds on which Stoicism maintains that all external events are fated. Why would you agree or disagree?
4. Explain and evaluate the "lazy argument" as a criticism of the Stoic ethic.
5. Describe how all varieties of naturalistic ethics violate the naturalistic fallacy.

7

EVOLUTIONISM

This brings us to the evolutionary theory of Charles Darwin (1809–1882) and Herbert Spencer (1820–1903), as well as that of T. H. Huxley (1825–1895) whose last work, *Evolution and Ethics*, is especially relevant. Darwin's *On the Origin of Species*, published in 1859, is one of the books that changed the world.

A. THE MEANING OF EVOLUTION

As many people know, Darwin did biological research on the H.M.S. *Beagle*, mainly in the Galapagos Islands on tortoises and finches, which he combined with the demographic theory of Thomas Malthus (1766–1834). Malthus had written that the population increases at a geometric ratio (1, 2, 4, 8, . . .) and the available food at an arithmetic ratio (1, 2, 3, 4, . . .), so that continual competition exists among species as the population outstrips the food supply.

Using the evidence he gathered along with Malthus's projections, Darwin formulated the theory of natural selection. He postulated that those creatures possessing the characteristics called for by the environment were selected-for in the struggle for survival. Chance mutations among species and members of species determined which animals would live, breed, and transmit their characteristics to the next generation. Those creatures lacking the traits necessary to compete successfully simply perished, and their line became extinct. In the continual battle for life, animals fought for territory, sexual dominance, and food, and to the victors went the spoils of continued existence. The strongest species were able to dominate and to survive. "Survival of the fittest" was nature's mechanism for eliminating the inferior and preserving the superior organisms, just as farmers selectively breed their finest cattle, sheep, or horses.

The theory of evolution created a furor at the outset because it opposed several articles of faith. The Bible stated that "God made the beast of the earth after its kind, and the cattle after their kind, and every thing that creepeth upon the ground after its kind," and he did it in six days. That is, there were fixed species created at a distinct point in time, all of which are still in existence having been preserved from the flood by Noah. Following this special creation, the species remained immutable.

Darwinism opposed this tableau, claiming that progressively more sophisticated species developed over vast amounts of time. And like the rest of the animals, human beings are not unique but continuous with prior, natural forms. Life developed from a "primal soup" acted on by the sun's rays, so that increasingly complex organisms were produced: bacteria, plants, fungi, insects, reptiles, birds, and finally mammals.

This was contrary to the biblical account that put creation at several thousand years ago; Sir John Lightfoot opined that it occurred at exactly nine o'clock on October 23, 4004 BCE. Darwin, however, trading upon scientific evidence, asserted that life has existed for millions of years; the earth and universe as well. In fact, we now estimate the start of the universe with the explosion of the Big Bang at about 13.7 billion years ago, the sun as forming 9 billion years later, the earth as 4.5 billion years old, and the genus *Homo* as having existed for 1.5 to 2.4 million years. *Homo sapiens* (or homo but not very sapien) originated some 200,000 years ago.

Evolution and Religion

Prior to Darwin, one of the principal "proofs" for the existence of God was the *teleological* argument. In the last of his "five ways" in *Summa Theologica*, St. Thomas Aquinas argued in effect that the design of the world implies a designer, the plan a planner, the architectural scheme a divine architect. If nature is a work of art, then the landscape shows the brush strokes of God; there are "tongues in trees, books in the running brooks, sermons in stones" (Shakespeare).

William Paley (1743–1805) reinforced this argument from design with his famous watchmaker analogy, arguing that if we found a watch upon the ground in perfect working order, "with the gears properly positioned so as to interlock; the teeth, pointer, and balance all of the right shape and size to regulate the motion; the wheels made of brass to keep them from rusting; a spring of flexible steel; and glass over the face where a transparent material is required," we would be forced to conclude "that the watch must have had a maker . . . who formed it for the purpose which we find it actually to answer." By analogy, when we encounter the intricate mechanism of the world we must infer that it too had a maker; the parts could not have fallen together by chance in just the right combination to produce a perfectly functioning machine. "There cannot be a design without a designer," Paley wrote, "contrivance without a contriver; order without choice; arrangement without anything capable of arranging." That is, unless we assume "the presence of intelligence and mind," the world in its orderliness is inexplicable.[1]

The teleological argument points to various, remarkable facts as proof. For example, the earth has been perfectly positioned so as to sustain life. It rotates around the sun in an arc, which brings about the changing seasons, and at a distance that ensures a perfect temperature. If the earth were closer to the sun we would sizzle; farther away, we would freeze to death. In addition, an envelope of water surrounds the earth, and all organisms require water to live. Furthermore, human beings need to eat plants and animals, and edible plants and animals have been provided. Even the marvelous mechanism of the human body indicates a supreme designer who organized our complex systems and organs, our anatomy and physiology to operate in an ideal way. The intricacy of the human eye alone testifies to the genius of creation.

Evidence of design was also cited within the animal kingdom, where there is a perfect distribution of the qualities needed by various species: the hard shell of the turtle, the ability of the chameleon to camouflage itself, the giraffe's long neck enabling it to reach the leaves at the tops of trees, and so forth. Each creature has been given the exact attributes it needs to exist.

Darwin opposed this argument by offering an alternative explanation to account for the order in the world. He asserted that if turtles had not possessed hard shells, chameleons the ability to change color, or giraffes long necks, they would not have survived as a species. These were the characteristics needed in the struggle for life, so it is not remarkable that the species now living possess these characteristics. To regard it as uncanny would be like being surprised that all Olympic winners are good athletes; if they had not been good athletes, they would not be Olympic winners. Or it would be like being amazed that so many major cities are next to navigable rivers; if the rivers had not been navigable, settlements would not have become major cities.

In the same way, Darwin claimed, we can understand the ideal position of the earth relative to the sun, the edibleness of plants and animals, and the efficient functioning of the human body. All aspects of life had evolved in accordance with the principle of natural selection. Our hand was once a scaly fin and hairy paw; now it is used for brain surgery and piano concertos.

In essence, Darwin offered a natural explanation for the character of the world in place of a supernatural one.[2] For example, using the biblical story of creation, it is difficult to account for the extinction of dinosaurs, but it can be explained in terms of the Darwinian model. Paleontologists have found that a meteorite struck the earth about sixty-five million years ago, and the impact and sudden temperature change made life impossible for dinosaurs. When a species lacks the adaptations necessary for survival, then it ceases to exist. Hundreds of thousands of species have disappeared from the earth, from dinosaurs to the dodo bird, as a result of the mutation-selection mechanism; only fossils and imprints now remain.

In defense of the religious view, theologians sometimes used implausible arguments such as "God planted fossils on earth to test our faith," or "He made the world complete with dinosaur remains." However, critics have argued that this is not sound. It can always be argued that *for all we know* God planted fossils on earth as a test of faith, but that is unlikely. *For all we know* oysters may be doing differential equations, and hibernating bears are dreaming of the periodic table of the elements, but *as far as we know* they are not. In the same way, it seems more reasonable to regard fossils as preserved remains of organisms that once lived. Geologists debate whether fossils are bone or stone, but no one doubts that some are more than 6000 years old.

Theologians play a dangerous game if they call "God" whatever we do not know; for then the more we know, the less room there is for God. In this way, religion is edged out of the universe. This has, in fact, been a recurrent pattern. No one knew what caused lightning, plagues, earthquakes, or the Black Death, so these events were ascribed to the power of God, but that meant that the more science understood, the less was attributed to supernatural agency. Historically, as science has advanced, religion has retreated, partly because the divine was used as an explanation for the unknown. A "God of the gaps" is vulnerable.

Another major objection to the teleological argument took the form of the problem of evil. That is, there are elements in the design that cause people pain, and that does not seem consistent with a wholly loving, all-powerful, and all-knowing God. The environment in which we live does not resemble a perfectly functioning watch. As mentioned previously, nature includes disasters and catastrophes such as hurricanes, earthquakes, tsunamis, and volcanic eruptions, and diseases such as tuberculosis, polio, malaria, and typhus. There are dangerous creatures such as tigers, sharks, cobras, and scorpions; inhospitable regions of the earth such as deserts, jungles, Arctic wastes, and the oceans that cover the majority of the planet (while humans have not been given gill slits). The pain caused by carnivorous animals also requires justification, predator and prey, when the model of herbivores could have been used. There is the fact of death and the suffering of dying, and the deterioration of old age when people become caricatures of themselves. And why create humans with a need to sleep one third of every day, so if we live for sixty years we spend twenty years sleeping? More importantly, why let Beethoven go deaf and Monet go blind? Why are there handicapped children and genetic deformities in newborns? Such injustice and suffering is difficult to explain as part of an ideal plan.

On Darwin's view, these are all natural developments, but they would have to be laid at God's door if he designed everything. On the surface at least, the design seems flawed, wasteful, and even cruel. Perhaps there is a benevolent design beyond our understanding, but on the other hand, the unknown evil may be as pervasive as the unknown good; it could be even worse than we imagine.

Intelligent Design

The contemporary version of the teleological argument is called "intelligent design," which does not rely on the Bible but uses findings from modern science as proof.[3] For example, one version claims that natural selection cannot explain the "irreducible complexity" at the molecular level of many biological systems. As with Paley's watch-like world, the intricate mechanism requires a God. Another refers to the generation of "complex specific information," that is, the information contained in DNA, saying it is not remarkable that we have survived, but that we have arrived. Still other accounts hold that some intelligent force must drive the mathematical beauty and order in the universe; Keats could compose "Ode to a Nightingale" but only God could create a nightingale. According to one prominent approach, the chances of the universe developing as it did by accident are incredibly small.

Take the expansion rate—just one of the conditions that had to be right for life to develop. In *A Brief History of Time* Stephen Hawking wrote, "If the rate of the universe's expansion one second after the 'big bang' had been smaller by even one part in a hundred thousand million million, the universe would have collapsed into a hot fireball." Therefore, an intelligent being must have created the initial conditions.

Most biologists disagree, maintaining that Darwinian theory is sufficient to account for the complexity that exists, and that natural selection and mutations can provide the "information" needed. At a simple level, the mechanism of the eye was once a light-sensitive cell; the hand a pseudopod, protruding from protoplasm for locomotion and grasping. As for mathematical beauty, that need not be purposeful but a fortunate accident.

With regard to Hawking's point, that argument was addressed in the early twentieth century by the astronomer Sir Arthur Eddington (1882–1944). Eddington pointed out that if enough monkeys were typing on enough typewriters, they would eventually produce all the books in the British Museum. That is, chance can imitate order if the numbers are large. Therefore, if there were not one but millions of big bangs, it would not be unlikely that one would have the conditions necessary for life to exist. As Carl Sagan remarked, our universe was a winner at the cosmic slot machine, even though the odds were long.

In short, the scientific community at large treats evolution as an established principle; it explains the facts more comprehensively than any other option—a much better "just-so" story. Some philosophers even use evolution as an argument against the existence of God. For Darwinism could be interpreted as a naturalistic alternative to the religious worldview, treating the universe as physical rather than spiritual. Bertrand Russell was once asked what he would do, as an atheist, if he met God face to face. He answered, "I would say, 'Not enough evidence, Lord, not enough evidence.'"

In the philosophy of religion it is an open question where the burden of proof falls. Some philosophers maintain that we should believe in God until his existence is disproven. Others claim we should not believe until the reality is proven, that the absence of proof is proof of absence, or at least grounds for agnostic doubt.

Evolution continues to provoke controversy from the nineteenth century to the present. In 1860 Bishop Samuel Wilberforce had a debate with Thomas Huxley ("Darwin's Bulldog"), during which Wilberforce asked Huxley whether his monkey ancestry was from his mother's or his father's side. At the "Monkey Trial" in 1925 John Scopes was found guilty of teaching evolution in violation of state law, despite a brilliant defense by Clarence Darrow. Some theologians have suggested that if our ancestors were apes, God adopted us. More recently the states of Arkansas, Kansas, Kentucky, Louisiana, Ohio, Pennsylvania, and Tennessee have challenged the teaching of evolution in schools. Religious groups wanted intelligent design included as an alternative. However, the courts have not been sympathetic, ruling that such a doctrine is religion, not science; as such, it has no place in a science curriculum. And using the label "intelligent design" rather than creationism seems a subterfuge—an attempt to circumvent the separation of church and state.

It has been suggested as a compromise that God is behind evolution, using it as his instrument of creation. The billions of years of biological history, reckoned in the scale of human time, correspond to the days of creation described in Genesis, a day in the life of God being that much longer. But even this modest interpretation has met with considerable resistance because of a rule of thought called *Occam's Razor* or the *law of parsimony*. Named for its originator, William of Occam (1300–1349), this rule states that an explanation should not be compounded beyond what is required. In this case, since the theory of evolution alone can explain the orderliness and arrangement of the physical world, we need not have recourse to a further explanation in the form of a cosmic mind behind evolution.

Meanwhile, the biological data in support of evolution continues to mount and to be corroborated by anthropology, geology, paleontology, archaeology, and astronomy. Biologists now argue mainly about the exact process—whether there was "common descent" or "convergent evolution," "steady change" versus "punctuated equilibria." (Socio-biologists claim that a chicken is a device used by an egg to produce another egg.) Missing links are continually being found: for example, the discovery in 2005 of three specimens that help fill the gap between fish and land animals; and in 2006 the skull of a child was discovered, 3.3 million years old, that had both ape and human features.

Fairly recently, biologists have discovered that snakes, dolphins, and porpoises have limb buds in their early development, and whales have been found with atavistic hind limbs, some four feet long complete with feet and digits; this suggests their descent from terrestrial creatures. All mammals, including humans, have gill pouches in the embryonic stage, reflecting that they were once aquatic vertebrates, and human embryos have webbed feet and hands; they also develop tails. The last usually disappear *in utero* but some children are born with tails, some 1 to 5 inches long, and humans retain twice as many tail vertebrae as chimpanzees. In short, the embryo in its development goes through several of the stages of human evolution.

Because of the enormous weight of evidence behind it, evolution is no longer viewed as a "theory" but virtually a scientific law, similar to the laws of gravity and electromagnetism.

B. SOCIAL DARWINISM

Evolutionism did not remain within the realm of biology but was carried over to ethics as a theory of the ideal in human life. According to this application, the evolutionary development of the natural world provided a clear model for human behavior. The principle of conduct that should govern human relations was seen in the law of survival of the fittest. Anything that promotes the survival of life forms, especially human life, was declared good, and whatever impedes the development of life was declared bad. On this view, if we allow the law of nature to operate and the fittest alone to survive, then our conduct is moral, for the main thrust of evolution is thereby promoted. However, if we interfere with the course of evolution by helping the unfit to survive, then our conduct is ethically wrong. We must emulate in human life the operation of evolutionary laws so that continual progress could be achieved.

As previously described, some creatures survived because of their strength or agility, others by virtue of their speed and cunning. Some had defensive adaptations such as armor, quills, or wings; others had sharp teeth or horns or claws. Whatever the particular characteristics, each creature preyed upon others so that there was constant warfare in nature, a continual life-and-death struggle for the available food supply. Only those creatures that happened to possess the qualities demanded by their environment survived and produced offspring. The less favored creatures, which were too weak or inept or vulnerable, were inevitably destroyed.

In human life, therefore, we should not support the weaklings, the misfits, or the psychologically or physically handicapped, for they will only transmit a defective strain. They will produce a line of descendants who, raised in a tradition of defeat and carrying genetic weaknesses, will also be unsuccessful. The entire race would degenerate if we interfered in the process of natural selection by introducing a social safety net. Nature has shown us a pattern for human behavior. Just as animals in a natural state inexorably follow the law of survival of the fittest, so the human animal should conduct himself according to that governing principle. We must accept the hard code of the natural selection process whereby the weak perish and the strong survive, rather than artificially sustaining those members of the species that lack the ability to provide for themselves. If people succeed in life, that shows they have the requisite abilities and are fit to live. By the same token, if people fail, then they demonstrate by that failure their unfitness to survive.

Using this doctrine, the industrial entrepreneurs or "robber barons" of the late nineteenth century attempted to justify their business practices. They assumed that in a free market economy, their power and success showed their fitness to succeed. It demonstrated that they were brighter, stronger, and more capable than other people, and therefore deserved their wealth and position. By the same token, those who failed to succeed thereby showed their unfitness for success, and their position in the underclass was justified on evolutionary grounds. Poverty, in fact, was considered more of a shame than a pity, because it indicated that the person did not have what it takes.

The entrepreneurs argued that it was not unjust that certain people succeeded; their having used unscrupulous means did not imply they were not deserving of their position. The fact that they succeeded legitimized their success. They had thereby shown themselves to be the fittest individuals in an evolutionary sense; that is, the outstanding members of their species who could then transmit their qualities to their offspring. In this way the human race would be strengthened, refined, and uplifted.

Following the same reasoning, social welfare programs were sometimes condemned because they offered artificial help to the weaker members of the species, thereby enabling the unfit to survive. It was contrary to nature to have minimum-wage laws, social security programs, retirement benefits, health-care plans, and so forth; even unionization was considered wrong because it permitted the weak to band together against the strong. A sales tax may hurt the poor but it is fair to all, whereas the graduated income tax is unfair to the wealthy by requiring them to pay a higher percentage of their income; this is a disincentive to acquiring wealth.

All of these measures ran counter to natural evolution, for they allowed lazy, deficient people, the misfits, the sick, and the aged to be carried on the backs of the competent and the industrious. By allowing weakness to be perpetuated for generations, the entire species would deteriorate and the process of natural selection would be thwarted.

Recently we have experienced something of the same mentality under several presidents who championed a vigorous capitalism. Economists such as Milton Friedman argued that business has no social responsibility, that people should be self-reliant, pulling themselves up by their bootstraps; we should practice the work ethic rather than expecting handouts. In a democratic society a *laissez-faire* economic system should prevail, allowing the free market to operate with minimum government intervention. The climate of the times was opposed to entitlements, and even laws protecting consumers, the environment, or child labor. Individual responsibility was favored, as was the deregulation of the marketplace. The underlying assumption was that those who succeeded deserved their success and owed nothing to those who happened to fail in the free-market competition.

With the recent recession, this doctrine has come into question, if only for its capacity to ruin economies. Some attribute the economic downturn to deregulation, particularly of the financial markets, some to the non-enforcement of monopoly regulations, some to the unbridled greed of predatory mortgage lenders. The government has provided a bailout and a stimulus package to help those who are struggling and to subsidize banks, brokerage firms, and mortgage lenders, as well as the construction and manufacturing industry, especially carmakers. With widespread unemployment, dwindling retirement funds, and extensive home foreclosures, most people approve of the government's involvement to help its citizens, whether they are fit or unfit.

The Fittest and the Best

1. One point the nineteenth-century entrepreneurs and twentieth- and twenty-first-century capitalists neglected is that people do not necessarily succeed or fail because of their inherent qualities. A great deal depends on circumstances: the opportunities that are made available; introductions and connections; luck and timing; financial support; and so forth. For example, a person who inherits a railroad that transports an essential product such as wheat or oil is in a good position to make a great deal of money, and if that individual subsequently becomes a millionaire it will be due to this inheritance rather than superior intelligence, industry, or competence. Someone who is given a trust fund of several million dollars is not wealthy because of merit. In the same way, someone who owns a monopoly has an unfair advantage over others, which is why antitrust legislation was enacted. Financially successful persons, then, do not necessarily deserve their wealth by virtue of having superior abilities, and the poor are not necessarily poor as a result of biological deficiencies; many impoverished people are simply unfortunate victims of social forces. There does not seem to be any natural hierarchy in society which correlates directly to people's inherent qualities.

   Of course, some Marxists would say that even if there were such a natural hierarchy it would be unfair because people should not be rewarded for their inherent qualities—a high I.Q., musical talent, superior hand-eye coordination. Gifted people, they argue, rather than deserving a larger slice of the pie, have a greater responsibility to give to society because of their exceptional skills. Hence the Marxist dictum: "From each according to his abilities and to each according to his needs."

In any case, no correlation exists between success and personal qualities. Those at the top of the socioeconomic scale do not necessarily have superior abilities of the kind that can be genetically transmitted. The genes of the wealthy do not enrich the human race more than the genes of the poor. Economically successful people are not necessarily the outstanding biological specimens; in fact, they may only be the most fortunate.[4]

2. Another substantive criticism has to do with the implicit assumption that the fittest means the best. That is, it is not at all certain that the victors in the struggle for survival can be equated with the morally best of the human species. People who are deceitful and ruthless, self-centered, and manipulative, for example, may have the skills that fit them for success, but that is not a profile of a fine person. The fact that such a person succeeds does not mean that he or she merits that success in an ethical sense. The worst people may, in fact, "win" and the best may "lose"; but, morally speaking, that is no index of what they deserve. In other words, the fact that some people achieve worldly success where others fail does not show that the former are the fittest in the sense of being the best of the human race.

Obviously, we would not want humanity to consist of people who cannot survive, for that would lead to the extinction of our species, but neither would we want the race to be composed of cruel, callous, and selfish people who trample on others. We should not survive in a shameful way, and it is a real question whether a race of morally unfit people is worth preserving. Rather than either of these extremes, we would prefer individuals of good character who have sufficient survival ability to sustain themselves. In other words, we should value moral character above mere survival skills, while not denying the importance of succeeding in the struggle for existence.

Civilization has as one of its primary purposes fostering a high level of cultural development rather than just maintaining ourselves in being. Instead of the harsh principle of survival of the fittest that pertains in nature, civilization aims at a refinement of conduct, taste, and thought that transcends mere existence. We do not want to duplicate the brutal competition that characterizes carnivorous animals but rather build into our civilized world some moral improvements over nature such as care for the elderly and medical treatment for the sick and injured, and food and shelter for the destitute. In this way we will show compassion for the weak and not abandon them as unfit for survival. Instead of following nature in its awful aspects, we correct nature's brutality and live like human beings, closer to angels than beasts. A civilization should be judged not by its strength but by its compassion toward the less fortunate.

C. SPENCER'S EVOLUTIONARY ETHIC

Some of these criticisms were recognized by thinkers in the late nineteenth and early twentieth centuries, most notably Herbert Spencer. Spencer, in fact, published his "doctrine of development" two years before Darwin, and coined the phrase "survival of the fittest." He meant by this not that mutations were "random, mindless and blind" but that, in a moral sense, it was the best that survived. This sentiment enabled Andrew Carnegie to say "all is well since all grows better."

Like other evolutionists, Spencer was certainly concerned with the longevity of the human race and the maintenance of individual lives, for he wrote that "other things equal, conduct is right or wrong according as its special acts . . . do or do not further the general end of self-preservation."[5] Spencer clearly recognized that survival is a necessary condition without which all other values become impossible. He also agreed with the overall position of evolutionary ethics, "that the conduct to which we apply the name good is the relatively more evolved conduct; and that bad is the name we apply to conduct which is relatively less evolved."[6] But he placed special and unique emphasis on what he called breadth or fullness of life, which is the supreme value and the goal of evolution. The richer our lives, the better.

The Breadth of Life

The meaning of breadth or richness can be understood by examples Spencer draws from biology. The oyster, for instance, may live longer than the cuttlefish, but the oyster's life consists only of streaming water and absorbing nutrients, while the cuttlefish has more numerous and varied activities; in that respect, the cuttlefish experiences a higher mode of existence. The earthworm too, living in a secure and protected environment in the soil, might have a longer life than an insect exposed above ground. But the insect, Spencer wrote, "during its existence as larvae and pupae may experience a greater quantity of the changes which constitute life."

With regard to human beings, he makes the same point: Civilized people may have shorter life spans than "savages," but they have a greater aggregate of thoughts, feelings, and actions, in short, richer lives. Actually, Spencer believed that greater breadth of life tends to increase the length of life also, for he wrote that "each further evolution of conduct widens the aggregate of actions while conducing to elongation of it." In other words, more evolved does mean broader and richer, but along with this comes greater *longevity*. Length of life seems to follow richness of life in an automatic way, so that, with the improvements of civilization, modern people live longer than pre-technological people.

In Spencer's comprehensive view, breadth of life did not just mean whatever is more complex and varied but a moral existence also, which takes into account the harmonious development of the race. He saw evolution as tending toward a fullness of life that includes concern for the welfare of others. According to Spencer, the line of evolution does not lead to a selfish individualism but to *cooperation* and community, which are essential to the survival and satisfaction of human beings, individually and as a species.

Although conflict now occurs between the individual and the group over their separate interests, Spencer believed that, in the long run, the two will be recognized as harmonious. At some advanced stage of evolution, when we understand the interrelatedness of society and the individual, this conflict will disappear and humanity will live in peace. Altruism will completely replace egoism as the human race evolves to the moral stage of development. "Conduct gains ethical sanction," Spencer wrote, "in proportion as the activities becoming less and less militant and more and more industrial, are such as do not necessitate mutual injury or hindrance, but consist with, and are furthered by, cooperation and mutual aid."

In taking this position, Spencer was actually following the lead of Darwin, who wrote, "The term, general good, may be defined as the rearing of the greatest number of individuals in full vigour and health, with all their faculties perfect, under the conditions to which they are subjected."[7] Spencer then went on to say that rearing and preserving healthy, vigorous individuals could only be brought about by mutual justice and consideration among people. Since human beings possess a capacity for sympathy and are able to retain past experiences, social justice is thereby able to flourish.

Spencer elaborated and developed this idea of social justice and cooperation as part of evolutionary development by arguing that mutual helpfulness, rather than competition, tends to promote breadth of life for the group and, consequently, for the individual. For when a community cooperates, each individual benefits from the goodness of the whole and the species is advanced by the efforts of each member "to further the complete living of others." Murder, for example, is punished because it works against the good of the species; at the same time, refraining from murder does not involve any self-sacrifice because everyone profits from a nonthreatening environment. Benevolent conduct therefore furthers evolution; selfishness runs counter to the evolutionary flow and is in no way sanctioned by the law of survival of the fittest.

Spencer further argued that those activities conducive to survival and richness of living also bring *pleasure*, and those that are destructive bring discomfort and suffering. Thus, by seeking pleasure, human beings, as well as other species, act in ways that promote their continued existence. For example, eating brings pleasure through the experience of its flavor, and consuming food, of course, is necessary for survival. Rest provides the pleasure of refreshment from fatigue, and shelter offers the pleasures of warmth and comfort; both rest and shelter are vital to human existence. Spencer also mentions the pleasures that accompany being married, rearing children, and accumulating property, all of which are necessary to the survival of the species. Pleasure and survival are, therefore, perfectly adjusted to each other, which is a fortunate occurrence. As Spencer wrote, "those races of beings only can have survived in which, on the average, agreeable or desired feelings went along with activities conducive to the maintenance of life, while disagreeable and habitually avoided feelings went along with activities directly or indirectly destructive of life." If hunger, fatigue, and cold had been pleasurable, the human race would never have continued.

By combining these elements, Spencer constructed an ethic that is basically evolutionist but with hedonistic aspects. Pleasure is the index that our conduct is in conformity with evolutionary development, and evolved conduct is always "immediately pleasurable" and "conducive to future happiness." Spencer did not favor the pursuit of pleasure *per se* but advocated actions conducive to higher evolutionary development, which fortunately are accompanied by pleasure. In any case, Spencer declared, we never pursue pleasure but only objects that further evolution. If we are hungry, we want food, not the pleasure of eating; if we are cold, we seek heat, not the pleasure of warmth.

There is an interesting parallel between Spencer's refinement of the evolutionist ethic in terms of breadth of life and John Stuart Mill's addition of qualitative considerations to the theory of hedonism. Mill declared that of two pleasures, equal in amount, one could be judged higher because of its quality (for example, poetry over pushpin), while Spencer maintained that of two lives, perhaps equal in length, one can be judged superior to the other by its fullness (for example, the life of a civilized person over a Neanderthal). In their separate ways, each thinker tried to raise the level of their ethical theory and to render it dignified enough to serve as an ideal for human life. Both chose quality over quantity as the more important element in the good life.

D. A CRITICAL ASSESSMENT

Spencer can be commended for including a qualitative factor in his evolutionist ethic as well as a pleasure component, for pleasure in life is surely important. He also seems praiseworthy for integrating cooperation and community into the survival-of-the-fittest doctrine. He regarded both as more helpful to the survival of the individual and the species than ruthless competition. For these reasons, and because it offered a scientifically based ethic, Spencer's theory was highly celebrated in the late nineteenth century as a humane evolutionism. Today, however, Spencer is rarely read, for his theory is seriously flawed. From an evolutionary standpoint, since Darwin survived, that makes him the fittest . . .

1. For one thing, Spencer assumed that evolution will necessarily progress through all future biology by continually producing increased complexity and integration of functions, that an inexorable process of change from "incoherent homogeneity" to "coherent heterogeneity" will occur. His optimism echoed that of Darwin, who concluded *On the Origin of Species* by saying "we may look with some confidence to a secure future of great length. And as natural selection works solely by and for the good of each being, all corporeal and mental endowments will tend to progress toward perfection."

   However, since the nineteenth century when these confident words were penned, we have experienced two world wars that killed over five hundred thousand people; numerous smaller wars, revolutions, and genocides that killed hundreds of thousands; and we possess biological, chemical, and nuclear weapons capable of extinguishing life on earth altogether. Furthermore, we have caused global warming and polluted our air, land, and water to the point where the ecological balance of nature may be irreparably damaged. AIDS, cholera, and malaria are rampant in developing countries, and natural disasters such as earthquakes, tsunamis, and hurricanes are more frequent and destructive. Thousands of people in developing countries die of starvation every day, and the gap between the "haves" and the "have-nots" only increases. In the wake of such events, we can no longer believe that evolutionary progress is inevitable or that natural selection works toward perfection. In addition, the theory of evolution is not compatible with the principle of entropy, the second law of thermodynamics in physics, which holds that matter and energy are continually being transmuted into unusable forms; this degradation tends toward a state of inert uniformity for the entire universe. This presents a countermovement to evolutionary progress. Furthermore, astronomers have detected in galaxies the presence of "black holes," which could swallow stars and planets whole.

In short, evolution will not necessarily produce greater complexity and integration, breadth of life, harmony, and pleasure, and this presents an uncomfortable dilemma for Spencer's evolutionary ethics. For if it is claimed that we should follow evolution wherever it leads, we may well find ourselves endorsing a less coherent and diversified world, or one in which selfishness, violence, and ugliness are the principal elements. If, on the other hand, we are meant to affirm the values of complexity, integration, fullness, richness, cooperation, pleasure, and so forth, then we may not be able to endorse evolution as our model.

Spencer seemed to adopt the latter position. In other words, he appeared to claim that breadth of life is best, whether or not it is nature's direction, which means he would have to base that value on some grounds besides evolutionism. In a sense, Spencer and Mill fell into the same trap—perhaps a fortunate trap, in which quality was seen to be most valuable. In trying to refine their respective theories, they placed themselves outside of their theories altogether. That could mean that each system has a "fatal flaw," which cannot be eliminated without abandoning the ethic altogether.

2. Besides this major defect, Spencer's evolutionism has been criticized with regard to its emphasis on the importance of cooperation and mutual helpfulness. Neither one necessarily characterizes evolution. According to other interpretations, nature is "the tyrannically inconsiderate and relentless enforcement of the claims of

power" (Nietzsche) or "ruthless self-assertion," a "thrusting aside, or treading down" of all competitors, a "gladiatorial" existence (T. H. Huxley). Some creatures, such as bees or beavers, may live in cooperative communities, but tigers and cobras lead lives of independence and competitiveness; it is an open question as to which is more representative of the natural evolutionary process.

3. Spencer's belief that pleasurable activities are conducive to evolutionary advancement may also be challenged. Sometimes pleasure can accompany activities that do not have survival value or produce an enrichment of life. For example, the sexually active person is more likely to contract a social disease; the drunkard is prone to cirrhosis of the liver; and the pleasure of sleep can produce laziness. Gluttons can enjoy eating to the point where they are unhealthy and their movements restricted by obesity; in psychological terms, they are attacking themselves with a knife and fork.[8]

Naturalism Broadly Considered

This last criticism brings us back full circle to the first, for it indicates that evolutionary developments are not always good; therefore, conformity to the evolutionary process cannot be the criterion of good and bad. Every type of evolutionary theory of ethics runs afoul of this problem and is rendered highly dubious as a consequence. Not only Spencer but all advocates of evolutionism judge certain aspects of the evolutionary process beneficial and others harmful, and in doing so they must refer to some external standard of judgment.

Basically, evolutionary theory attempts to deduce a value system from a description of the natural world. The advocate of evolutionary ethics is arguing that because "survival of the fittest" is the operative principle in nature, therefore it ought to be the prevailing ethic in human society. But as we have seen, we cannot logically derive an "ought" from an "is"; because something *is* the case does not mean it *ought* to be the case.

Of all the theories of ethics, naturalism commits the naturalistic fallacy most blatantly, for it asserts that conduct is right if it conforms to some natural fact, whether that fact is the character of nature, destiny, or the evolutionary process. But we cannot logically derive a value from a fact. Just because nature exhibits characteristic *X*, that does not mean that therefore *X* is good. Conduct may be judged as right or wrong, praiseworthy or blameworthy, but not on the basis of whether it is actually done. Rather, we judge conduct, in the human or natural world, according to ethical standards; otherwise, the tail is wagging the dog.

In the case of evolutionary ethics, serious questions can be raised about the brutality of allowing the unfortunate members of society to die rather than being compassionate and supportive toward them. But in any case, it is illogical to argue that the facts of nature furnish the grounds for values. We must look beyond nature if we are to find a sound basis for our ethical judgments.

Naturalism nevertheless holds considerable attraction because it places human conduct within the context of a larger world, linking it to the surrounding environment in which we live. Rather than viewing action as essentially individual, performed in unique isolation, naturalism offers a comprehensive view of the natural world that includes human actions. Our lives become integral to the organic whole of nature, not a foreign body outside its skin. We are placed in relation to the natural world that envelops us; we belong as integral to the scheme of things. For this reason naturalism holds a very elemental appeal for us, whether nature is regarded as a basic model in its varied aspects of animals, seasons, growth, children, or beauty; a manifestation of the divine, in rational or irrational form; or a blind inexorable process of evolutionary advancement.

One of the most insistent problems in ethics today is to demonstrate how such a linkage between human beings and nature or the larger cosmos can be justified. We would like to view our actions not just against a backdrop of history but as intrinsic to the natural order. The problem comes in showing the logic of that relation; we need good reason for believing that our wish is answered by reality.

REVIEW QUESTIONS

1. Explain why Darwin's theory of evolution undermined the teleological argument for the existence of God and the recent version of intelligent design. Are evolutionism and theism compatible?
2. Present an assessment of the "survival of the fittest" doctrine as a theory of ethics. How can it be defended or criticized?
3. What does Herbert Spencer mean by "breadth of life" and by "cooperation"? Why would you agree or disagree that they are conducive to evolutionary survival and development?
4. In your view, does nature tend toward evolution or devolution, progress or entropy? Defend your position.
5. In what way can naturalism itself be criticized in all of its manifestations? Can ethics be linked to metaphysics and grounded in the natural world?

8

THE ETHIC OF DUTY

A. JUDGING THE WORTH OF CONDUCT

Thus far we have examined three ethical theories concerning the good life: hedonism, self-realization, and naturalism. One criticism common to them all is that a disparity can exist between their concepts of the good and conduct that is right. With regard to hedonism, we found that stealing can produce happiness for the thief; or if he is a Robin Hood, the greatest happiness for the greatest number. Nevertheless, that does not legitimize taking other people's property; it only romanticizes it. In the case of self-realization, we concluded that a tyrant may be realizing himself or even expressing a desire for power that is basic to human nature, but the tyranny is not thereby justified. And in naturalism, even if rampant selfishness were found in nature, that would not make it right in human society.

In the duty ethic of Immanuel Kant which we will examine in this chapter, and in the religious ethic that follows, the good and the right are combined in such a way that doing what is right becomes the definition of what is good. That is, a good life is conceived of as one in which people perform acts that are right. In this way, the disparity between the two is eliminated and the gap is bridged.

The Right and the Good

Right refers to actions that are ethically correct, usually in terms of specific rules of conduct. Philosophers might, for example, defend the rightness of honoring commitments, being honest, or respecting human life, and argue against treating people as objects. Or they might condemn acts of murder, theft, and adultery, and endorse principles such as paying one's debts, being just and generous, or acting in accordance with our responsibilities to one another.

Religion, too, has its set of right principles and moral laws, from the Code of Hammurabi in Mesopotamia (1800 BCE) and the Eightfold Path of Buddhism (c. 520 BCE) to the Ten Commandments and the Sermon on the Mount. Usually the "thou shalt nots" dominate the list, greatly outnumbering the "thou shalts," which is unfortunate since prohibitions can create a taste for that which they ban. From a psychological standpoint, positive reinforcement does far more to change conduct than forbidding behavior.

Those who follow an ethic of right claim that actions are right according to their inherent worth. For that reason we must accept them as obligations in our lives. An act is not right by virtue of its outcome, that is, by the fact that it promotes some good end, but because of some innate, moral quality; once we recognize this quality, we realize that our duty consists in carrying out the actions—regardless of whether good or bad is brought about. The emphasis is on the obligatory character of certain actions, apart from their results. Our duty is to act in moral ways, not necessarily to achieve prescribed ends, and we must act according to the qualities intrinsic to the act itself. If we do so, our existence will be justified.

Doing what is right has the advantage of focusing on conduct, not on the preceding motive or the subsequent result, and it uses as its standard the moral nature of the act. If an action is correct in itself, then the intention and the consequences are beside the point. Helping others, for example, might be regarded as ethically correct and, if it is, then no external considerations could make it wrong. The fact that the help later proved to be harmful, so that the people were worse off than before, would make no difference in the moral equation. Likewise, if people help others in order to help themselves, that fact is morally irrelevant. A correct action remains correct even if it turns out badly and even if the right thing is done for the wrong reasons.

Those who endorse the right usually accept an *objectivist* theory of ethics, whereby certain acts are considered intrinsically right apart from societal norms. Paying one's debts, for example, might be considered objectively correct even if one's culture views it otherwise because, by and large, we should keep our promises. Furthermore, most advocates of the right treat rightness as universal. That is, if certain acts are right in themselves, then they should be practiced everywhere and always. If paying one's debts is right in the United States in the twenty-first century, then it is equally right elsewhere in the world at any period in history. In short, that which is intrinsically right is an obligation for everyone; something cannot be right for one person without being right for all.

Some moral philosophers, however, endorse the *good* over the right, meaning that an act should be judged not by its nature but by its result, its effect or outcome. Whether there were beneficial or harmful consequences is the critical consideration in the moral reckoning.

According to this school of thought, what someone actually accomplishes is the relevant factor, not why or how a person acted. If, for example, some political program such as Affirmative Action were motivated by a sincere desire to remedy racism but, in fact, produced a backlash against blacks, we could not praise the program. Or if an act begins in benevolence but ends in violence, then the act is wrong and no amount of explanation as to the purity of the act can make it right.

In law, for example, when one person accidentally kills another in vehicular homicide or by knocking a flowerpot off a ledge, the person is tried for third-degree murder or manslaughter (the nomenclature varies between states). If the court finds that one person did cause the death of another, then the charge is substantiated. Because there was no "malice aforethought" or *mens rea*, an evil mind, the sentence is usually commuted and the defendant goes free, but the important point is that the court finds a wrong has been done. The consequences of the act make it reprehensible in the eyes of the law even though the person is excused.

This is precisely what is claimed by those who judge actions according to their results. Good people can do a great deal of harm, so moral worth should be determined by consequences alone. For this reason the Bible states "by their fruits ye shall know them," and Mao Tze-Tung declared "It does not matter whether the cat is black or white as long as it catches mice."

The term "good" is also used in reference to objects, as when we speak about a good watch, a good tree, a good dinner. These are obviously descriptive, not evaluative, uses of the term "good"; we mean that the object functions efficiently or is excellent in its qualities. As G. K. Chesterton said, "If a man were to shoot his mother at a range of five hundred yards, I should call him a good shot but not a good man."

Objects are value-neutral; they have no ethical quality in themselves. Our moral judgments with regard to objects have to do with the use to which they are put. An axe can be used to chop down trees to make furniture, baseball bats, or violins; or it can be wielded by an executioner to chop off people's heads. A buoy can save lives by marking a safe channel; or it can cause the loss of life if a boat should collide with it and capsize. Nuclear energy can be used to light and heat homes or as a terrible weapon in war. The examples are endless, but the point is that *things* are neither good nor bad, and people make a mistake when they make such judgments. Alcohol, drugs, and even guns cannot be categorically condemned as evil; it all depends on how they are used.

B. DEONTOLOGY AND TELEOLOGY

Deontology and teleology are the respective names for these positions. The *deontologist* or *formalist* maintains that doing what is right is most important, perhaps all-important; "deon," in fact, means duty. The *teleologist* judges an action in terms of whether it produces a beneficial result, good rather than bad.

The difference between the two approaches to ethics can be illustrated in our criminal justice system. That is, the reasoning behind the incarceration of a criminal can be either deontological or teleological in nature. On deontological grounds, the criminal is given a particular sentence according to the severity of the crime; the aim is fair retribution for wrongdoing. Perjury and fraud, for example, should be lightly punished, while armed robbery and kidnapping deserve stiffer sentences; murderers might be executed as a matter of justice. If people are imprisoned for thirty years for a trivial offense, common sense says they have been unfairly treated, but if a serial killer receives a sentence of six weeks, that also violates our sense of justice. When the punishment fits the crime, in the sense of being proportional to it, then we believe that justice has been served. We use language such as, "A debt to society has been paid," "The criminal received his just deserts," or "The person got what he had coming." On this model, justice means an equivalence between crime and punishment: the person got what he deserved.

In a cosmic sense, it is as though the equilibrium of the universe has been restored, the scales of justice had been balanced. This, incidentally, is the foundation of the Old Testament idea of an eye for an eye and a tooth for a tooth, which was thought just in the sight of God. By this the ancient Hebrews did not mean retaliating with the same offense so that robbers would be robbed or rapists raped, but responding in kind; that is, in proportion to the nature of the wrong or to a degree commensurate with its seriousness. It is a balanced, measure-for-measure morality, rather than the belief that we should get even with evildoers. In its pure form it represents fairness; in its corrupt form it may mask a desire for revenge.

In punishment theory, this approach is called *retributive*, for it takes fair retribution as the hallmark of justice. There is no thought of the effect that the punishment might produce upon the person or society but only the rightness of the punishment in relation to the offense. It is backward-looking not forward-looking, because punishment is meted out solely in response to the crime. Because John did X therefore he should receive Y, not in order to reform him but to give him what justice demands: people should get what they merit.

In contrast, a *utilitarian* theory of justice is based on teleology.[1] A criminal is punished in order to bring about certain results, both for him and for society. Under this model, the punishment is meant to reform and rehabilitate the offender so that he or she will not repeat the offense. The severity of the punishment does not depend on the nature of the crime but on what is needed to change the person's future behavior.[2]

The punishment is also aimed at deterring others from committing similar crimes by showing what will happen to them if they do. An example is made of the offender which, it is assumed, will have the effect of discouraging people from committing unlawful acts. In addition to reform, rehabilitation, and deterrence, criminals are imprisoned so that society will be protected from them; they are released or paroled only when they are considered safe. Until then, they are disabled and rendered harmless. In pronouncing the original sentence, the judge considers the time needed to bring about reform and rehabilitation, as well as the degree of harshness necessary to deter potential criminals and safeguard society.

The punishment is thus apportioned not to the crime but to the desired effect; the crime only serves as an index of the need for punishment and of the sentence required to reclaim the person as a productive member of society. Since it is forward-looking rather than backward-looking, it has a teleological character; the main concern is the ramifications of the action taken.

If, then, a bank robber is sentenced to ten years in prison because that is considered appropriate to the crime of grand larceny, a retributive theory of justice is being used that is formalistic in nature. If, however, the ten-year sentence is handed down because that is thought to be the time needed to reform and rehabilitate the criminal, to protect society, and to deter potential criminals, then a utilitarian theory is operative, with teleologism as its ethical foundation.

One point is worth noting here. Although the utilitarian theory appears to be more liberal, enlightened, and humane, and retributivism could disguise a primitive wish for revenge, the utilitarian approach has a serious weakness. Namely, it could be used to punish people who have not committed any crime. For if a psychological profile shows that someone is likely to commit a crime, or if society needs an example as a deterrent, then a person could be sent to prison even if he or she is innocent of any criminal offense. The retributivist theory may be too close to vengeance to make us comfortable, but at least it ties punishment to crime; punitive measures are taken because someone is guilty of unlawful conduct. In utilitarianism, punishment need not be connected to any crime, thus making it potentially dangerous.

Another example that will illustrate the difference is the abortion controversy, which has divided the nation and caused considerable anguish.

From our perspective, the pro-life faction believes in certain basic principles that should not be overridden: the value of human life, the wrongness of taking innocent life, and the special obligation we have to protect the helpless. The pro-life advocates can also maintain that it would be sinful to reject life, which is a precious gift from God, for we are not the arbiters of life and death but the servants of God's will.

They further assert that, even if life must sometimes be taken, it is only in cases where the person is guilty of some terrible offense. Capital punishment might be justifiable for murderers, especially serial killers; or in the case of aggravated murders in which the victims were also brutalized. Or killing might be necessary in a defensive war when the other side is threatening our homes, families, or nation. However, taking the life of a fetus or unborn child is unjustified because the fetus is entirely innocent. Here, killing is murder. There is no provocation or threat, so having an abortion is wrong.

The pro-choice advocates, on the other hand, stress the good that would be produced by allowing women to have an abortion. Family planning could take place, the world population problem could be alleviated, and the children who were born would be wanted. Men and women could decide when to have a baby, and the baby would be welcomed, with adequate financial and psychological preparation.

Furthermore, women would not be forced to bear children that were the result of rape or incest, nor would they undergo the trauma of raising a child who might resemble the father. They would not have to give birth to genetically defective children whose quality of life could be minimal, or be subject to the pain, expense, and daily problems that such a child brings.

In short, pro-life advocates emphasize that preserving life is the right thing to do, whereas pro-choice advocates maintain that abortion can promote good for the woman, the family, and society. Viewed from this standpoint, the abortion controversy concerns whether deontologism or teleologism should have priority.

Ideally, what is right and what is good should coincide, so that the good can be achieved by doing what is right. But sometimes a disparity exists between the two, and then a choice must be made that shows our basic ethical attitude.

Acts and Rules

Quite often a distinction is made between two kinds of deontologism. *Act-deontology* claims that, in particular situations, we will know which action is appropriate to that time and place. However, no rules of conduct can be formulated to decide how we should behave in general. Each situation is unique, so that actions that are right in one case are not transferrable to another. Judgments of obligation are particular, rather than generalizable in character. One cannot say, for example, "Human life should always be preserved," but only "In these circumstances, at this time, in regard to these people, I ought to preserve life."

Some act-deontologists, adopting a more moderate position, maintain that general principles can be constructed afterwards from particular judgments, but most believe that, because each situation is so different, no general rules can be formulated. In any event, judgments about particular situations occur first, and they always take precedence over any principles. No rules can ever be invoked as the ultimate and decisive criterion of right action.[3]

Rule-deontologism maintains that general principles always take precedence over particular judgments and they inform us as to which actions are appropriate. We must reason from the general to the particular, deducing our obligations in various cases from the broad rules of conduct that govern them. Situations are not individual and unique; they can be grouped according to type. Common denominators always exist that enable us to classify situations under the same category and therefore to judge them by the same rules. No two situations are identical, but they can be alike in essential respects so that a moral judgment can be made that covers both situations.[4]

To the rule-deontologist, moral principles are the best way to determine the mode of conduct we should follow. If an action can be seen as an instance of some general moral rule, then that act should be done, and adherence to such rules makes our behavior right.

The act- and rule-deontologists differ markedly regarding the question of whether the action or the rule should be referred to in determining our obligations, but they agree in maintaining that the recognition of certain moral qualities should govern our conduct, rather than the desire to promote a good end.

The ethic of duty as espoused by Immanuel Kant is generally considered to be the quintessence of deontologism, so we will examine it at some length as a proposal for the good life. It will quickly become apparent that Kant strongly advocated a rule- rather than an act-deontologism, and that he opposed all teleological ethics.

The Intention behind Action

Before examining Kant's theory, one other moral element should be mentioned: the intention of the agent performing the action. According to the intentionalist view, conduct should be evaluated in terms of the motive, or purpose of the moral agent. The results of action, it is argued, often fall outside the power of the person and cannot be foreseen; every act spreads ripples and ends in mystery, having unintended consequences. But the agent is in control of his or her own intentions, and that is what should be judged. If a person has commendable intentions in performing an act, then the act is praiseworthy regardless of whether it happens to turn out badly. In the same way, if someone has evil intentions, then the act is blameworthy, even if by some chance the results prove beneficial. If we intend to lie but tell the truth by accident, we have still done something wrong; the fact that we told the truth is beside the point. What matters is that people have a good will, that their heart is in the right place.

For example, if someone asks to borrow our car and subsequently has a terrible accident, we may feel partly responsible: "If only I hadn't lent him my car. . . ." But the intentionalist would say that we are praiseworthy, not blameworthy. Although the person would not have had the accident unless we loaned him our car, we cannot blame ourselves for what we could not foresee; on the contrary, we should be praised for being generous and responding to someone's need; the tragedy that resulted was beyond our control.

Obviously, in some cases ignorance about the results of action is avoidable, and in those cases, where we could have known that something awful might happen and should have known, we could be blamed.[5] But where our ignorance of the outcome is unavoidable, then only the intention behind our action matters in assessing its worth.

If we invite someone to visit us and they are struck by lightning on the way, our ignorance is unavoidable; it was not possible for us to predict that lightning would strike. However, it is not a viable excuse for a doctor to claim immunity in a malpractice suit because he or she did not know the latest treatment for a disease. The doctor could and should have kept up with the current literature, and his or her ignorance is avoidable. Likewise, a person who says "I did not know the gun was loaded" could have checked and is therefore responsible.

The intentionalist mainly stresses that if our heart is in the right place, if we meant well, if we intended to do the right thing, that is what makes the difference.

The concept of intention does not mean the yearning or vague hope that something will happen but the earnest striving to accomplish some purpose. When people say that the way to hell is paved with good intentions, it is the empty wish they have in mind; we would not want to praise people because they hoped something would occur. An honest and active attempt must be made; otherwise the person's intentions cannot be called genuine. An intention should be something that moves us to act. But when people try to the best of their ability, and earnestly desire to effect some worthwhile end, then, the intentionalist claims, what they did was right regardless of how it turns out.

C. THE KANTIAN ETHIC

Immanuel Kant is considered among the world's most eminent philosophers, although his fame derives more from his *Critique of Pure Reason*, which deals with epistemology and metaphysics, than from his work in ethics. Nevertheless, Kant did present a celebrated theory of ethics in his *Foundations of the Metaphysics of Morals* and the *Critique of Practical Reason*; his ideas about duty are worth considering.

"Nothing in the world . . . can possibly be conceived which could be called good without qualification except a good will,"[6] Kant wrote at the beginning of the *Foundations of the Metaphysics of Morals*, and with that opening statement we know him to be an intentionalist.

He is saying that the basis for evaluating conduct is not the consequences that follow from it but the will that lies behind it, that "good" does not stand for any end of action but can only be applied to the will of the agent performing the action. A person of good will, someone with high intentions and a noble nature, is praiseworthy regardless of whether his or her actions achieve some worthwhile result. Circumstances, chance, historical accidents, and so forth may prevent the accomplishment of that which a person wills, but such blockages are morally irrelevant. The significant factor is whether the motive of the moral agent is commendable. If so, then praise is appropriate; if not, then no praise may be given regardless of whether the action ultimately proves to be beneficial.

> A good will is good not because of what it performs or effects, not by its aptness for the attainment of some proposed end, but simply by virtue of the volition, that is, it is good in itself. . . . Even if it should happen that, owing to a special disfavor of fortune, or the niggardly provision of a stepmotherly nature, this will should wholly lack power to accomplish its purpose, if with its greatest efforts it should yet achieve nothing, and there should remain only the good will . . . then, like a jewel, it would shine by its own light, as a thing which has its whole value in itself.[7]

For the will to be good, however, Kant stipulated that it must not operate from inclination but out of the recognition of a moral obligation. For example, if we were moved to help a blind person out of a sudden rush of pity, that would not constitute a moral action, but if we offered our help because of a realization that we have a moral duty to help the handicapped, then the action would take on a moral character. Kant distrusted the emotions, regarding them as too fickle and unreliable to determine correct behavior. The emotions could induce acts of sympathy and generosity, but they could also impel us to cruelty and destructiveness. Just because we feel certain emotions, that is no justification to act upon them. On the other hand, if we recognize certain acts as morally binding upon us, we have a more trustworthy basis for action. It is not that our sense of obligation informs us as to which emotions are trustworthy, but that obligation rather than emotion should be used as the criterion of moral conduct.[8]

The next question addressed by Kant is how one is to know where one's obligation or duty lies. We might accept the notion that obligations rather than feelings are the foundation of morality, but how is one to determine which actions are obligatory? Kant answered this question by saying that if our act can be subsumed under some general principle of conduct, then we know that we are in the realm of moral obligations. If we can say that a contemplated action is an instance of some general rule of behavior, we can feel confident in proceeding with it. For example, suppose we are contemplating the rightness of stealing food rather than earning it by working. Maybe we are aggrieved about the unequal distribution of wealth and feel that blue-collar workers get too small a slice of the pie. In order to test the morality of the action, we must ask ourselves whether such action could be advocated universally as common practice. Could we in good conscience recommend that everyone steal food instead of working for it? Obviously not, for if no one worked, including farmers, there would not be any food to steal. The action does not fall under a general principle and is therefore wrong.

Kant sometimes described this standard of morality as respecting the moral law. By this he meant operating with deference to objective rules of rightness in contrast to behavior that springs from emotions or is based on the consequences of action; in other words, operating according to an objective, deontological ethic. "Duty is the necessity of an action executed from respect for law . . . ," Kant wrote.

> Now as an act from duty wholly excludes the influence of inclination and therewith every object of the will, nothing remains which can determine the will objectively except the law, and nothing subjectively except pure respect for this practical law. This subjective element is the maxim that I ought to follow such a law even if it thwarts all my inclinations.[9]

The Categorical and Practical Imperatives

However, the definitive formulation of Kant's views on duty and the core of his moral system are expressed in what he called the *categorical imperative*. Various descriptions of this are given by Kant, but broadly speaking, the categorical imperative can be stated as follows: We should act in such a way that the principle for our actions could become a universal law. That is, in order for an action to qualify as moral we should be able to say that all people at all times and all places should do likewise; that is, follow the same principle of conduct. Kant expressed the point as follows:

> But what kind of law can that be, the conception of which must determine the will without reference to the expected result? Under this condition alone the will can be called absolutely good without qualification. Since I have robbed the will of all impulses which could come to it from obedience to any law, nothing remains to serve as a principle of the will except universal conformity of its actions to law as such. That is, I should never act in such a way that I could not also will that my maxim should be a universal law.[10]

Kant elaborated his categorical imperative by saying that if we cannot declare that everyone ought to do what we have done, then we know our conduct is wrong. When we make an exception for ourselves, declaring that the action is generally incorrect but we can do it anyway, that is a certain indication that our action is immoral. A genuine rule of conduct has no exceptions, so that if the rule covering our action can be applied to everyone, then we know the action is right.

Kant gives various examples of the operation of the categorical imperative that help in grasping its meaning. Suppose we are considering borrowing some money, but in order to obtain the loan we must promise to repay it—which we do not intend to do. Should we, Kant asks, make an insincere promise to repay the loan in order to obtain the money? To decide this question in a moral way we must apply the categorical imperative. Could we will that everyone should act according to the same principle, that whoever wants to borrow money is justified in making a false promise to return it? Obviously not, Kant said, for if everyone did this no one would ever lend money, which means that the conduct cannot be universalized and cannot be right. Once we apply the test of the categorical imperative, we see that if everyone practiced this mode of conduct then the conduct would become impossible to practice; consequently, it must be immoral.

Another example is that of truth-telling. We may be tempted in various circumstances to tell a lie, perhaps to extricate ourselves from an awkward situation or to spare someone's feelings, but the acid test of the rightness of our behavior is whether it can be universalized. Can we will that everyone should lie? Apart from questions about the undesirability of a world operating that way, Kant maintained that lying would be impossible to universalize because if everyone said the opposite of what he or she believed to be the case, no one would ever be deceived. Universal lying, then, would be self-defeating, which means that lying is wrong.

It is important to realize that Kant did not say that a maxim could be considered wrong if the results of universalizing it would be bad; rather, Kant's point is that the wrongness could be determined by the inconsistency, impossibility, or self-contradiction involved if the maxim were universalized. To take still another example, to have a rule that a contract can be broken whenever a person finds it inconvenient would violate the nature of contracts, and this contradiction makes it impossible for such a rule to be universally practiced. It would be, Kant says, as though a contract with four clauses specifying the mutual obligations of the parties involved were to have a fifth clause stating that either party could break the contract whenever he or she wishes. Such a contract would negate itself and cease to be a contract at all. In the same way, any principle that contradicts itself when universalized is thereby revealed as being outside the realm of reason and morality.

Kant formulated the categorical imperative in another way that seems quite different from the concept of universalizability, although Kant regarded it as essentially the same. It is sometimes differentiated as the *practical imperative*. "Treat humanity," Kant states, "whether in thine own person or in that of any other, always as an end and never as a means only." He is here emphasizing respect for persons or, more specifically, rational beings, and affirming that people should not be used merely as instruments or objects. Notice that Kant says "as a means only," thereby acknowledging the fact that people must regard each other as means to some extent, whether as employers, shopkeepers, mothers, or doctors. But human relationships ought to be more than that. We should, Kant believes, have regard for people as worthy of respect in and of themselves and, insofar as possible, treat them as the ends of action not merely as a means for achieving our aims.

This version of the categorical imperative provides a second reason for condemning lying and suicide. In both cases we are treating someone only as a means. With regard to lying to another person about our intentions to repay a loan, we are using them in order to obtain money. This is the reason we feel humiliated when we discover that someone has lied to us: we have been regarded as an obstacle rather than a person. In the case of suicide, we are treating ourselves as a means of avoiding difficulties and ignoring the respect that should be accorded to all human beings, including ourselves. Kant's analysis may seem odd, but when suicide is condemned, whether by the church or some other authority, the argument is usually that the taking of human life is wrong, and that means one's own life as well as the lives of others.

Treating humanity as an end is an important element in Kant's ethics, but his theory hinges mainly on the concept of universalizability; this is the main formulation of the categorical imperative. If we cannot claim that the rule authorizing an action is universal, then the action cannot be called moral.[11]

In order to clarify and develop his point still further, Kant differentiated between a hypothetical type of imperative and a categorical one, saying that hypothetical imperatives always contain conditions under which it should be followed, whereas categorical imperatives are obligatory regardless of circumstances. For example, if we own a store and want customers to return, then we should be honest in our business dealings. This would be a hypothetical imperative because it is provisional; if one wants X, then one is obliged to do Y. A categorical imperative, on the other hand, would not be of an "if/then" type but would state that a certain principle is right and therefore should be done. Being honest would be categorically right, and not just right if we want others to trust us in the future.

According to Kant, the type of proposition that can be judged as truly moral is the categorical one in which there are no stipulations, provisions, or conditions made on our obligations. This led Kant to affirm the categorical imperative as the master rule of ethical conduct. In saying this, Kant is asserting that genuine moral principles have no exceptions. The categorical imperative is, therefore, the ultimate criterion for moral behavior.

In summary, Kant advocates an approach to ethics in which we perform actions that can be placed under a universal rule. An act is not right because it leads to good results or because it flows from moral inclinations. A good will alone is praiseworthy and the will is good when it acts out of pure respect for moral law. We must treat people mainly as ends rather than means and, above all, be sure that our conduct falls under principles that can be advocated for all human beings, categorically and without exception. Kant was thus an intentionalist and a deontologist while rejecting teleologism as a criterion of morality.

In Kant's system everything is subordinate to ethics, including religion, which is reduced to "the acknowledgment that our duties are God's commandments." Even human freedom is deduced from our sense of obligation: if we have a sense that we should, then we know that we can. For this reason also the soul is declared immortal, because it ought to fulfill itself, which cannot be accomplished in one lifetime. There ought to be endless progress, and that implies life beyond the grave.

Are There Universal Values?

But is deontologism the right way to evaluate conduct, and can we accept Kant's categorical imperative as the fundamental touchstone of morality?

1. When we begin analyzing the Kantian position, one of the problems that strikes us is the difficulty in finding any principle that is universal. For example, it might be right to keep our word, but some promises should never have been made and should not be kept. Furthermore, we have no obligation to stay with someone who abuses us, even though we promised "'til death do us part." In such cases, loyalty would be wrong; we do not have a duty to finish what we started, to stay the course. Or we may believe in the

value of human life, even its sanctity, nevertheless we can justify killing in self-defense or to protect those we love. Not long after Moses fetched the Ten Commandments down from Mt. Sinai, he was engaged in a bloody war, yet the Fifth Commandment says, "Thou shalt not kill." The rule, therefore, can be broken. Many people feel that the death penalty is a just response to crimes such as espionage, murder, and terrorism, and mercy killing can be considered a humane act even though, in general, we should preserve human life.

In light of the numerous exceptions that spring to mind, it seems impossible to defend any principle as being right all the time. We are told that agreements should be kept, but we are surely not obliged to return a package entrusted to us when we realize that it contains crack cocaine or a terrorist's bomb. We may believe that stealing is wrong, but if we are starving because of an unjust social system, then stealing food might be condoned; for a spy, the theft of enemy secrets is a patriotic duty. Or we may have been raised to think that violence is evil, but in a political situation in which the worst people hold the best people in a state of subjection, and all peaceful means have been exhausted, then an argument could be made for revolution. We might also accept truthfulness as a value, but would not want to be honest if a woman has a weak heart and the truth would kill her. Here we would have a moral duty to lie, and to do so as convincingly as possible.

There seem to be a problem, then, in finding any principle that can be applied without exception, including the seven classic virtues of prudence, fortitude, temperance, justice, faith, hope, and charity. As we have seen, Kant considered only universal rules as truly right, but we cannot find any rules that can be applied universally. Each principle covers a certain number of cases, perhaps a majority; but none can be said to cover all cases. Even though we do not feel right about stealing, lying, and breaking promises, there can be extenuating circumstances in which we are morally obliged to steal, lie, or break promises. By insisting that only those principles without exceptions are moral, Kant created an empty system without any genuine principles; none can satisfy the criterion

2. Setting aside that problem, another objection to Kant's ethic is that two universalized principles can contradict each other. Suppose, for instance, we maintain as part of our absolute principles that human life should be preserved, and also that one should always tell the

truth. Then one day a man with a smoking gun in his hand and a wild look in his eye asks us which way his wife went. In these circumstances we can either tell the truth and contribute indirectly to a murder, or protect a life by telling a lie. We are forced to choose between the two principles because we cannot both preserve life and tell the truth. Many moral principles will oppose each other in this way, and under Kant's system we are faced with a dilemma that cannot be resolved.

It might be argued that, in this case, we can decide which of the two principles takes precedence, and set up a hierarchy of values with the strongest on the top. Preserving life seems more important than telling the truth, so it should be given priority.

But then only the topmost principle would be considered right within the Kantian scheme of things, and all others would have to give way if they conflicted with it; that is, they could not always be carried out, and, therefore, would not qualify as moral principles. A moral theory with only one principle seems rather odd. Furthermore, how is this foremost principle to be determined? The preservation of life does seem to be the overriding consideration, but situations could arise in which other values would take precedence. A doctor, for example, is bound by the Hippocratic Oath to both preserve life and alleviate suffering, and that can pose a conflict. For instance, in the case of a burn victim who is in extreme pain and not expected to live, a doctor might decide against "exotic" or "heroic" measures to prolong the person's life, for that would mean prolonging his suffering. Killing might be more compassionate and courageous than keeping the patient alive or letting him die a painful death. The quality of a person's life can be more significant than its quantity, which means that preserving life is not always supremely important.[12]

The same problem—finding a rule that cannot be overridden—plagues us whenever we try to establish a scale leading to the highest moral principle. To arrive at one superlative principle which transcends the rest is difficult, if not impossible, to do. Therefore, under Kant's system, we cannot resolve a situation in which universalized principles clash.

3. In addition, some principles might be moral even though they are impossible to universalize. For example, self-sacrifice does seem commendable at various times but it cannot be practiced by all people at all times. For if everyone were self-sacrificing, there would be

no one left to accept the sacrifice. On Kantian grounds, therefore, we would have to reject self-sacrifice as a virtue. Nevertheless, it might be worthwhile to practice self-sacrifice sometimes. For example, suppose someone were starving to death and we were merely hungry; we should sacrifice our interests to that of the starving person and give him our meal. The point here is that if an action can be moral in certain circumstances, then an action need not be universal in order to be moral.

Conversely, some principles can be universalized even though they are not moral. For example, the rule that we should exploit the weaknesses of other people for our own advantage does not contradict itself when it is universalized; nevertheless, it is not moral. In other words, it is possible for people to operate by taking advantage of each other's weaknesses, but that does not make for an ideal society. The fact that exploitation is capable of being universalized does not legitimize it.

Kant recognized this problem and tried to protect himself by citing the *criterion of reversibility*, which differentiates between universal principles that are moral and those that are immoral. This standard is similar to the golden rule of Christianity: that we should do unto others as we would have them do unto us. Judaism (and Confucianism) believes that we should not do unto others as we would not have them do unto us; avoiding harm is more important than doing good. However, the sentiment is the same: An action is moral only if we would want it done to us. Using this criterion, Kant tells us that some conduct is immoral even though it can be universalized without logical contradiction. We can declare a universal principle to be moral only if we would want the same done to us; that is, if positions were reversed, we would agree to it.

But there is something rather odd about the standard of universalizability having exceptions. In other words, it seems inconsistent to claim that a universal principle holds true unless it violates the reversibility criterion, that there is an exception to the rule that genuine moral principles do not have exceptions. Passing over that criticism, reversibility itself seems problematic. It appears that Kant means by reversibility that we should do unto others as we would have them do to us; otherwise we run the risk of being treated badly in turn. If this is Kant's meaning, he is appealing to consequences in determining the morality of conduct, which is contrary to his deontology. Or to put the point differently, Kant appears to be saying that if we want to be treated well, then we should treat others the same way, which is a hypothetical rather than a categorical imperative; that violates his ethical stance. In order to be consistent, Kant would have to base the criterion of reversibility not on consequences but on some abstract ethical considerations. However, Kant seems to appeal to consequences, saying, for example, that we should desist from actions for which we would not want to be paid back in "our own coin." This contradicts his deontological position.

4. Kant's emphasis on intention also raises certain problems. One criticism is that intentionalism does not evaluate the moral nature of actions but only the character of the person performing the actions. The "good will" that Kant prizes is that of the agent, since actions do not possess a will, good or bad. And although people may be praised for what they intend to do, that is not the same as saying that they did what is right. The intention of the agent is separate from the act and cannot be used to impart a moral quality to it. And it would be odd to have a theory of moral evaluation that has no bearing on action but only judges the actor.

Furthermore, critics have pointed out that intentions are extremely difficult to determine. One can see what people do, but their inner motives are always hidden. Even when they report on what moved them to act, they tend to paint their motives in a favorable light. Intentions are intangible and elusive, a function of the person's mind, and what a person has in mind can be difficult to know.

As numerous critics have pointed out, Kant's general mistake has to do with the universality of right action as expressed in the categorical imperative. He fails to distinguish between qualifying a rule and making exceptions to it. That is, it seems legitimate to claim that we should not make an exception for ourselves in affirming a moral rule, but Kant assumes this means that no qualifications can be built into such a rule. Granted that it would be wrong to argue, for example, that "no one may break a promise except me"; nevertheless, that is not the same as qualifying promise-keeping by saying that "no one may break a promise unless a person's life would be endangered by keeping it." In the latter case, the qualified rule might be universalized without exceptions, which would satisfy the criterion of the categorical imperative. By failing to make this distinction, moral rules become stricter and narrower than they need be.

It should be added that Kant fails to make a proper distinction between the categorical and practical imperatives. He claimed that the criteria of universalizability and treating people as ends are versions of a single principle. They are actually different, for actions that are not universalizable could be performed for the sake of treating people as ends. For example, a man might steal food for the purpose of alleviating his family's hunger, but that might not be capable of being universalized. Kant has, in fact, several "versions" of the categorical imperative (H. J. Paton in his book *The Categorical Imperative* identified as many as five), and at least some of these are separate principles rather than formulations of a single doctrine.[13]

Because of the rigidity and strictness of the universality criterion, some neo-Kantians endorse the idea of *prima facie* obligations. Most notably, the philosopher W. D. Ross speaks of *prima facie* duties as those generally binding upon us unless other duties assume greater importance and displace them.[14] According to Ross, we have a subjective awareness of our objective duties, but these are in no sense absolute. Rather, one duty takes precedence over another and vice versa, depending upon the circumstances.

Although Ross's proposal seems an improvement, his theory fails to provide a reliable method of identifying which actions are *prima facie* obligations. To Kant, our duty is recognizable by its universal character, but Ross gives us no such standard. In addition, Ross does not adequately explain how we know when one *prima facie* obligation overrides another. Therefore, there is no basis for resolving conflicts.

The notion *of prima facie* obligations, although closer to common sense, still fails to solve many of the problems that plague Kantian ethics. How can objective moral principles be identified, and how are we to rank them in importance?

Oddly enough, one weakness in Kant may consist in ignoring the virtues of teleologism; in his concern to avoid the vices of this theory he throws out the baby with the bathwater. To judge actions solely in terms of their nature, without regard to their results, can make us blind to human suffering.

John Wesley stated, "I would not tell a willful lie to save the souls of the whole world," and Immanuel Kant said that if a sentence of death were just it should be carried out today even if the world were known to be ending tomorrow. Kant also wrote "If a woman cannot preserve her life any longer except by surrendering her person to the will of another, she is bound to give up her life rather than dishonor humanity." This type of formalistic thinking maintains principles at the expense of people. It might be worth telling a lie if that would save the world, and maybe we should not approve of the execution of a guilty man if there were no world to benefit by the example. What's more, perhaps a woman is not required to choose death before dishonor. John Stuart Mill declared that utilitarians value "only the dry and hard consideration of the consequences of actions," but Kant seems rigid and uncompromising in his commitment to duty; a "cold-hearted moral machine." To care for a rational system more than human beings can lead to blood and iron.

Now we generally assume that whatever is right ought to be done. It would be odd to say, "I know this act is right, but why did you do it?" Or stated differently, commending would seem to imply recommending; if we approve of certain conduct, then it seems appropriate to suggest it to others. However, right and ought are separable. As we have seen, keeping promises is right but there are circumstances in which we ought to break a promise, have second thoughts. In short, we are faced with the paradox that sometimes we should do what is wrong and ought not to do what is right. We then must undertake to prove or justify why the exception should be made. Kant assumes that right should prevail (*bonum fadendum*), but sometimes we ought not to perform an act even though it is principled, because of the consequences. Perhaps a child molester deserves to be tortured, but even if it is right we do not feel we should do that. And although our cause was just, we wonder whether we should have dropped atomic bombs on Hiroshima and Nagasaki.

One additional point should be made in this connection. If we should violate our principles of preserving life and go to war against an aggressor nation, we are not implying that killing is right, but only that in some cases it may be permissible. Killing is still wrong and preserving life is still right, but we are temporarily suspending that principle for the sake of larger considerations. Therefore, people who say that killing is sometimes right are being imprecise; killing remains wrong, but it may be allowable in certain circumstances.

Exceptions reinforce principles. That is, if we discover some cases contrary to what we believe to be right, then our belief is supported by the fact that there are only some contrary instances, in general, the belief holds true. Thus, the fact that the principles of being honest, preserving life, maintaining trust, and so forth all have exceptions in no way invalidates them, but rather verifies their general soundness.[15]

In conclusion, we find that Kant's ethical theory, although seriously flawed, is nonetheless intriguing and persuasive, perhaps because of its ethical purity. In some fundamental way, it seems appropriate to say that an intrinsically right action should always be done, and whatever can be proven to be a universal requirement is thereby shown to be correct.

As we have seen, a major weakness in the teleological theory is that the ends can justify the means. That is, if the results are what count, we need not be squeamish about the morality of our acts. Whatever is done, no matter how vile, is purified by the good that is achieved. This seems to invite pragmatic, unprincipled thinking. In Kant, the means justify the end, and that seems equally myopic. In following principles, we cannot ignore the consequences of actions, especially if those consequences entail human suffering.

Whenever too great a disparity exists between means and ends, then the moral integrity of an action is jeopardized. To wage war for the sake of preserving peace, to kill murderers as a deterrent to murder, to preserve justice by unjustly convicting someone who is a threat to justice—all of these paradoxes create a moral tension. And this tension occurs when we operate teleologically, looking toward some greater good and accepting awful means to that end.

Kant's emphasis on doing what is right because it is the right thing to do seems more in accord with our moral understanding. Nevertheless, if we are to accept a deontological system of Kant's type, the various criticisms must be met. Kant would be the last one to advise us to accept ethical ideas on the basis of emotional inclination. He would want any system of thought to satisfy canons of rationality—including his own deontological scheme.

REVIEW QUESTIONS

1. Explain the difference between right and good. When would the two coincide and when could there be a conflict?

2. Explain how the retributive theory of justice is deontological (formalistic) in character, whereas the utilitarian theory of justice is teleological in nature.
3. Why is it that people can be called good or bad, but objects cannot be evaluated that way? Are there exceptions, as in the case of guns, drugs, or nuclear power?
4. Explain the difference between act-deontology and rule-deontology. Which would you judge as superior? Why?
5. Explain the criticism that, in the Kantian system, two universalized principles can conflict, and that an act can be right but not universalizable.

9

THE TEACHINGS OF RELIGION

Ethical theories that are based on religion are also deontological in character, in that they approve of actions because they are right, rather than because of their consequences. However, instead of actions being right in themselves, their rightness derives from the commands of God. Certain rules should be followed, such as the Christian injunction to love thine enemy, because it is God's will.

According to most religious ethics, we should commit ourselves to a particular type of existence as pleasing in the sight of God. Scripture has revealed that we have a special relation to the being that created and sustains us, and to our fellow human beings on earth. A good life is one in which we believe in the dominion of God and accept his word as binding. We should regard ourselves as the agents of God's purpose, here to fulfill his design for human life which is part of the overall plan of the universe.

In the Kantian ethic, our duty consists in carrying out a certain type of behavior because we recognize it to be intrinsically and objectively right. In religious ethics we are called upon to perform actions because God has commanded us to do so. We must recognize obedience to God as our primary duty, which should be honored above all other considerations. For this reason the religious ethic is called "divine command theory."

There is comfort and reassurance in being part of a religion and a shared worldview. The mass worship with its familiar ritual, chanting, and liturgy reinforces the faith, uniting people and bonding them together in common beliefs. The sameness of the service offers continuity and order, and disbelief means exclusion from the community, a betrayal of a time-honored tradition. Belonging is critical to our personal well-being, linking us to others and to a cosmic purpose.

In Western religion, the Bible is considered the source of knowledge as to what God requires of human beings, and this sacred work, together with the theological interpretations in hermeneutics, provides our religious ethic. However, there is room for debate within denominations, for although many Jews and Christians regard scripture as infallible, that does not mean we interpret it infallibly; after all, to err is human. Whether God's word was transmitted by automatic writing or by inspired saints and prophets, mistakes are bound to occur. What's more, much of the Bible was communicated orally and over several generations, which further complicates the problem of authenticity. At best, we have only an approximation of the original message, and that means no religious sect can be certain it possesses the truth.[1]

A. JUDAISM—THE OLD TESTAMENT

The first section of the Bible, which is called the Old Testament, consists of a series of books produced by Hebrew writers over a period of four hundred years. In contrast to the view of Socrates and the Greeks in general, wrongdoing is due not to ignorance but to disobeying God's laws. To the Greeks, knowledge of the good is essential to doing the good; whereas to the Hebrews, it is right to submit ourselves to the will of God (Yahweh).

Beginning with Genesis and running throughout the Old Testament, the primary emphasis is on the wrongness of defying the Lord. In the story of the Fall, for example, in which Adam and Eve were banished from the Garden of Eden, the sin they committed lay in disobeying the explicit word of God. They had been told not to eat the forbidden fruit but they succumbed to the temptations of the devil (hidden in the snake) and were punished accordingly. "Ye shall not eat . . . of the fruit of the tree which is in the midst of the garden," God had said, warning that disobedience would be upon pain of death. But "when the woman saw that the tree was good for food, and that it was pleasant to the eyes, and a tree to be desired to make one wise, she took of the fruit thereof, and did eat, and gave also unto her husband with her; and he did eat" (Gen. 3:3–6).

Various interpretations have been offered as to what the fruit symbolizes: knowledge of good and evil, the acquisition of private property, an oblique representation of sensuality, and so forth. And it matters whether one thinks Eve was tempted by the snake or by the apple; the snake, for example, could be that serpent Reason or a phallic symbol.

But the wrongdoing of Adam and Eve consisted in their rebelling against God's wishes and his authority. As a consequence, they lost paradise for themselves and their descendants ("Adam's fall felled us all"), so that now human beings must live in a world of disasters and disease, suffering and death. We question whether anything the fruit might symbolize should be forbidden to man, including knowledge of good and evil, and whether one should dangle forbidden fruit. We also question whether subsequent generations should be punished for the original sin of their forebears, but this would have been blasphemous to the ancient Hebrew mind. In their view, God's commands cannot be questioned. It would be sheer arrogance, presumption, and pride (hubris) for finite creatures to doubt the perfect God, for human beings of limited power and intelligence to do anything but obey the will of Yahweh.

Other Biblical incidents reinforce this lesson. The Flood occurred because people were living sinfully in violation of God's laws (Gen. 6:5–7:10), and Sodom and Gomorrah were destroyed when people departed from God's ways (Gen. 19:16–28). When the Hebrew people worshiped Baals, the nature symbols of fertility, they were rebuked by the prophets Hosea, Elisha, and Elijah for disobeying God's commandment to Moses that "you shall worship no other God, for the Lord is a jealous God" (Ex. 34:14); for the same reason, Moses condemned the worship of the golden calf. And when Uzza tried to steady the Ark of the Covenant on the ox-cart on which it was being carried, he was struck dead because God had ordained that only the priests could touch the Ark (1 Chron. 13:10). Similarly, in a war with the Amalekites, Saul violated God's instruction to destroy all men, women, children, and animals. He spared the king, Agag, along with various animals for sacrificial offerings; but he was denounced by the prophet Samuel, who said that "to obey is better than sacrifice, and to hearken than the fat of rams" (1 Sam. 1:23). The conduct of some of these men seems justified to us, others appear unjustified, but the common failing is that they disobeyed God's will and for that reason they were thought to have acted wrongly and to deserve punishment.

In this same connection a great deal is made within Judaism of the covenant relation with God, which it is sacrilegious to break. In the Jewish tradition a special relationship has been established between the Hebrew peoples and their God. They took a solemn vow to obey the holy laws and, in return, were given the privileged status of God's chosen people. The covenant was considered inviolable, and unrighteousness was viewed as violating the compact with Yahweh.

Although the tenor of the Old Testament is to define rightness in terms of formal obedience, the Hebrews did advance from this conception, particularly through what is termed the *prophetic tradition*. There is a common tendency among early faiths to emphasize a strict adherence to rules and the ritual of worship above more substantive religious requirements. The ancient Hebrews were no exception, but they did begin to see a certain justice in God's demands and to follow his will not just as obedient children but as morally responsible adults.

In parts of the Old Testament, God is viewed as a being who commanded adherence to moral principles rather than a stern, judgmental, and wrathful father, perpetually jealous of his authority. His commands are no longer arbitrary and he does not exact vengeance so readily for transgressions. Mercy and forgiveness appear, paternal love becomes more prominent, and the actions he commands are seen to have a moral base. Sin still consists in disobedience, but God's laws can be followed out of respect for their moral character and not just through blind obedience and the fear of punishment. This advance is seen best, perhaps, in the later interpretation of the Ten Commandments as ethical principles of a high order.

The Ten Commandments, or Decalogue, are a summary of the most important rules of behavior laid down by God; they are accepted as bedrock by Jews, Christians, and Muslims alike. There are actually three versions in Hebrew scripture, Exodus 20:2–17, Exodus 34:12–26, and Deuteronomy 5:6–21, and different denominations have different lists. Exodus 20 is most often quoted and it has sixteen commandments, although Christians and Jews insist on ten. The King James translation is as follows.

1. I am the Lord thy God, which has brought thee out of the land of Egypt, out of the house of bondage.
2. Thou shalt have no other gods before me.
3. Thou shalt not make unto thee any graven images, or any likeness of any thing that is in heaven above, or that is in the earth beneath, or that is in the water under the earth.
4. Thou shalt not bow down thyself to them, nor serve them: for I the Lord thy God am a jealous God, visiting the iniquity of the fathers upon the children unto the third and fourth generation of them that hate me;
5. And shewing mercy unto thousands of them that love me, and keep my commandments.

6. Thou shalt not take the name of the Lord thy God in vain; for the Lord will not hold him guiltless that taketh his name in vain.
7. Remember the Sabbath day, to keep it holy.
8. Six days shalt thou labour, and do all thy work.
9. But the seventh is the Sabbath of the Lord thy God: in it thou shalt not do any work, thou, nor thy son, nor thy daughter, thy manservant nor thy maidservant, nor thy cattle, nor thy stranger that is within thy gates.
10. For in six days the Lord made heaven and earth, the sea, and all that in them is, and rested the seventh day: wherefore the Lord blessed the Sabbath day and hallowed it.
11. Honour thy father and thy mother: that thy days may be long upon the land which the Lord thy God giveth thee.
12. Thou shalt not kill.
13. Thou shalt not commit adultery.
14. Thou shalt not steal.
15. Thou shalt not bear false witness against thy neighbor.
16. Thou shalt not covet thy neighbour's house, thou shalt not covet thy neighbour's wife, nor his manservant, nor his maidservant, nor his ox, nor his ass, nor anything that is thy neighbour's.

To be sure, God requires that we follow these commandments in a legalistic way, but they are in no sense a mere expression of his will. Sin still lies in disobedience to divine commands, and goodness in fulfilling one's duty to our heavenly Father, nevertheless these commandments constitute some of our highest moral thinking. The "golden rule" has been especially influential: Do to no one what you yourself dislike.

B. CHRISTIANITY—THE NEW TESTAMENT

In contrast to this conception of religious obligations, the New Testament stresses not loyalty to God so much as love of him. The Christian emphasis is always placed on the spirit rather than on the letter of the law; the cultivation of our hearts more than our wills; proper attitudes, intentions, and beliefs instead of correctness, deference, and ritualistic observance. Hope should replace fear, according to Christianity, the hope of salvation through divine grace; and rather than cowering from God's wrath we should trust him to be merciful, compassionate, and forgiving toward the repentant soul.[2] Brotherhood and kindness are regarded as important virtues, particularly toward the poor and lowly, and in place of a special-people idea the Christian considers all human beings as having equal worth. Being impelled by love toward all humankind is more significant than performing particular acts, although social morality is important as the emulation of God's concern for humanity. To love our neighbor as ourselves and to forgive our enemy, rather than just loving our friends and retaliating against foes, reflects God's own treatment of human beings; it constitutes the worship of God through the spirit of love, forgiveness, and mercy. In Judaism we should return good for good, and justice for evil, but Christianity favored a loving response to all.

This transformed ethic is preached, of course, by Jesus, who is accepted as the Christ or Son of God. He is considered by Christians to be divine, the promised Messiah, sent to redeem the human race from sin: both original sin that was inherited from Adam and Eve, and the subsequent sin that humanity acquired itself.

Christians divide over the question of which way is best to serve Christ: through faith, whereby we believe in his divinity and accept certain dogmas such as the Trinity, the resurrection, and the day of judgment, or through works, which means living as closely as possible to the morally perfect life of Christ, following in his footsteps. Both ways are often thought to bring salvation, for there are many mansions in heaven (John 14:2), but the debate is ongoing as to which path is best. Saints of both persuasions have been canonized in the Catholic Church.

Concepts of Love and Justice

The ethical approach of Christianity concerns us most, and the principles of the Christian life are perhaps best expressed in the gospel according to Matthew. Here Jesus presents the main tenets of Christian ethics, which center around the concept of love.

The various forms of love that are identified and distinguished in our Western tradition stem mainly from Greek concepts and include sexual love ("lust"), *philia* ("brotherly love"), *eros* ("possessive love"), and *agape* or the Latin *caritas* ("selfless love"). It is the agape type of love that is endorsed by the Christian moralist, who contrasts it most sharply with eros, which is characterized by a desire to possess the person (or object) beloved.

In erotic love we want the person to belong to us, to assert our right of ownership—oftentimes in romantic relationships, exclusive ownership. It is essentially a self-centered form of love, because we are concerned with satisfying our own desire for the person rather than wanting to satisfy the other person's need for us. In some way we wish to be personally enriched by assimilating their traits or by appropriating the person altogether. By making another our own, incorporating them within ourselves, we experience an expansion of our being, even though it may mean the other's diminution. We do not exist for the other person; rather, he or she exists for us, and we maintain the relationship just so long as we continue to benefit from it. Sacrificing our own good for the sake of the other person is anathema to erotic love, for we do not desire what is best for another but only what is best for us.

In agape love, by contrast, our feelings for someone else are so strong and genuine that we desire his or her good even above our own. Our love impels us to dedicate ourselves to the other person's welfare, and that may even entail withdrawing from the relationship rather than continuing with it. That is, if we accept an agape ideal and feel that authentic love for others means acting selflessly instead of selfishly toward them, we will only remain in a relationship as long as we believe that the other person is benefited by having us there. If that point is passed, and the relationship is not good for the person we love, then regardless of whether it is good for us, we will sever the connection. The depth of our love for the other person makes us unwilling to be possessive if that is detrimental to them.

We should also not be jealous or resentful of the happiness he or she finds with another person, since our primary concern is the other's well-being. If, in these circumstances, we refuse to let go of the person we love, or feel bitterness about his or her happiness, this would indicate that we placed our own feelings above the other person's and that the relationship was essentially selfish throughout. In brief, "real" love consists of dedication to the other person more than to ourselves, and this implies a willingness to allow the person we love to find happiness with someone else if that happens to be greater than the happiness we could provide.

A love relationship, then, is not regarded as a business transaction in which each party seeks the utmost advantage, or even equal benefit, but a commitment to the other person's welfare above our own. In the words of the philosopher Martin Buber (1878–1965), we regard the other as "thou rather than it,"[3] and involve ourselves in a personal way, which means care, tenderness, and a self-denying generosity. And the agape love we give does not have to be earned by the other person, because it is not based on merit or deserts; in the same way, it will not be withdrawn if the person we love disappoints us. It is not what the person does, but what he or she is, that matters. People are lovable because of their nature, not their accomplishments; and we forgive them their sins while maintaining love for the person.

The Christian moralist who affirms agapeistic rather than erotic love wants this mode of relatedness to be applied not just to romantic attachments but to our attitude and conduct toward all humankind. Charity, as St. Thomas Aquinas said, is "the mother and root of all the virtues" (*"caritas est mater omnium virtutum, et radix"*), and to be charitable means loving humanity, our brothers, without reservation, as God the Father intended and Christ exemplified.[4] We may not be able to feel the same affection for all people or judge them of equal worth, but we can carry an identical love for them in our hearts. Agape love should typify all personal relations and replace envy, malice, spite, greed, lust, hate, and selfishness as our dominant attitude. Fellowship and brotherhood should supplant individualism and pride, especially in relation to the poor, the lowly, and the downtrodden. All souls are equally precious, and the destitute and homeless in particular should elicit our compassion.

For the Christian, the supreme prototype of agapeistic love is, of course, God's love for humankind, which compelled him to sacrifice his only Son. That love was not awarded because of any merit, that is, because people deserved it, but because pure love is of an unqualified character, an unreserved giving that is unconditional. God loves humanity for its own sake, and human beings should love God in the same way: not for the good he can provide by granting our prayers or guaranteeing us heaven, but solely because he is God. And our caring attitude toward our fellow human beings should be prompted by a sense of our common relationship to God in agape love: "This is my commandment, that you love one another as I have loved you" (Jn. 1:12), and, "Let no man seek his own but each his neighbor's good" (1 Cor. 10:24).[5]

In Christian ethics this leads to a paradox that is not a contradiction: as we give, so do we receive; as we lose ourselves we gain ourselves. When we subordinate our egos in agape love, deferring to our maker and our fellow human beings, we become infinitely richer. Rather than being absorbed by another, our dedication becomes a source of personal fulfillment. Instead of being anxious and dissatisfied, isolated in our selfishness, we arrive at a state of grace, reconciled with God and our inner soul.

The agape ideal also leads to a special conception of *justice*, which distinguishes Old and New Testament thinking. Unlike the Hebrews, who believed in giving a person his just deserts, the Christian wants to give a person what he needs. Starting with the metaphysical belief in the law of *talion*, according to which people can expect to have done to them whatever they do to others, the ancient Hebrews conceived of justice as balancing the scales, giving a person exactly what is deserved (as described under the theory of retribution). This meant "getting even"; that is, evening the scales of justice or punishing a person according to the severity of the crime. The doctrine of "an eye for an eye and a tooth for a tooth" pertained, and this was considered fair.

In contrast, Christian ethics tries to cater to a person's needs regardless of what the conduct might merit. Instead of rewarding or punishing people in proportion to what they deserve, the New Testament stresses our obligation to help people improve; their sins are used as a gauge of their need for love and care. No thought is given to paying for the crimes or being paid back for them, but only for meeting the fundamental need that motivated the crime. As discussed under the utilitarian theory of punishment, we do not want to make people pay, but to make them better, not pointing a finger but extending a hand; and that means focusing on how people can be supported rather than on what they have done.[6]

Divine justice, as the New Testament theory is called, thus concentrates on needs rather than deserts, redemption of the person rather than compensation for the crime. For example, a child caught stealing cookies from the cookie jar may deserve a "time out," a form of ostracism; or loss of a privilege, such as watching television; or even a spanking. But the child might need more affection, for which eating was a substitute; or be physically hungry; or want attention, preferring the negative attention of punishment to outright neglect. In this situation, the Christian approach would be to give the child love, nourishment, attention, or whatever is required rather than meting out the punishment that the wrongdoing merits. In the same way, murderers might be said to deserve capital punishment, but they might need a prison sentence during which time they can be reformed and rehabilitated. The Old Testament approach would be to punish the killer severely enough so the debt to society would be paid; whereas the New Testament approach favors forgiveness and salvation. Obviously, the case of the child and the murderer are at two extremes, but the principle of justice is the same, and to the Christian that means responding to human needs. Sometimes people need love most when they deserve it least.

The Christian view of violence is a natural consequence of the divine concept of justice and, more ultimately, the agapeistic ideal. In the New Testament Christ tells us not to return evil for evil but good for evil, fighting fire with water rather than with fire, responding not in a reciprocal or retributive way but with the kindness and caring that the other person lacks. Christ preached a gospel of understanding and forgiveness, peace and compassion, rather than a response of violence. God has ordained that harming others is wrong; therefore, it should not be done even when we are harmed.[7] "Forgive them for they know not what they do" is Christ's cry when he is being crucified. The people who killed him are ignorant of God's word, and if he copied their cruelty he would be guilty of betraying his principles.[8] In Matthew 5:44 Christ declares, "Love your enemies and pray for those who persecute you."

Christians hope that, by the example of their courage and fidelity to God's commands, as well as through preaching the Gospel, others will realize the virtue of a Christian way of life. By precept and example, the Christian hopes to lead people away from a self-centered existence in which personal pride provokes us to retaliatory measures. They preach an other-centered life where devotion and service to humanity become our primary focus.

The "Sermon on the Mount" (Mt. 4:25), including the beginning section called the "Beatitudes," encapsulates the Christian position most succinctly. The following are some critical excerpts:

Blessed are the poor in spirit, for theirs is the kingdom of heaven.

Blessed are the gentle, for they shall inherit the earth.

Blessed are the merciful, for they shall receive mercy.

Blessed are the peacemakers, for they shall be called sons of God.

You have heard that it was said, "You shall not commit adultery."
But I say to you that anyone who looks at a woman with lust for her has already committed adultery with her in his heart.

You have heard that it was said, "An eye for an eye, and a tooth for a tooth."
But I say to you, do not resist an evil person; but whoever strikes you on your right cheek, turn the other to him also.
If anyone wants to sue you and take your shirt, let him have your coat also. Whoever forces you to go one mile, go with him two.
Give to him who asks of you, and do not turn away from him who wants to borrow from you.

You have heard that it was said, "You shall love your neighbor and hate your enemy."

> But I say to you, love your enemies and pray for those who persecute you, so that you may be sons of your Father who is in heaven: for He causes His sun to rise on the evil and the good, and sends rain on the righteous and the unrighteous.
>
> For if you love those who love you, what rewards do you have? Do not even the tax collectors do the same? If you greet only your brothers, what more are you doing than others? Do not even the Gentiles do the same?
>
> Therefore you are to be perfect, as your heavenly Father is perfect.

A great deal more could be added about Christian ethics, especially as it has been developed by such Catholic theologians as St. Augustine, St. Anselm (1033[4]–1109), and St. Thomas Aquinas, and the Reformation leaders Martin Luther (1483–1546) and John Calvin (1509–1564). Modern Protestant theologians, such as Reinhold Niebuhr (1892–1971), Karl Barth (1886–1968), Emil Brunner (1889–1966), Dietrich Bonhoeffer (1906–1945), and Paul Tillich (1886–1965) have also contributed to the interpretation of scripture. The "golden rule" may be the most significant principle, which in Christian ethics is rendered: Love your neighbor as yourself.

Situation Ethics

Before leaving Christianity, however, mention should be made of a modern Christian movement that has attracted some attention as well as notoriety. This is "situation ethics" or "contextual ethics," which has come to be associated with Rudolf Bultmann (1884–1976), John A. T. Robinson (1919–1983), and Joseph Fletcher (1934–1984).

These theologians maintain that the Biblical conception of God is archaic, no longer applicable to the modern experience. Their main emphasis is on the primacy of love as the guiding principle for society. They are more concerned with the ethics than the metaphysics of Christian thought, and even if institutional religion entirely disappeared they would still want to salvage the ethic of love. These theologians want God redefined in a more adequate way so that we abandon the concept of a lawgiver, a righteous God who gives us codes engraved on stone tablets and specific dictums for the governance of our lives. Whether the laws are embodied in the Old Testament and concern stealing, or New Testament principles concerning divine justice and nonresistance to evil, they do not furnish us with a basic ethic. We can no longer affirm the notion of a God as an old man with a white beard sitting on a throne dictating laws *ex cathedra*, but must embrace a more nuanced, subtle, and ambiguous ethic.

To these theologians, ethics is situational; that is, the context determines whether or not a particular principle or value should be applied. Contrary to Kant, situation ethics does not necessarily condemn suicide or lying since the circumstances may mandate them, and fidelity, honor, loyalty, even life itself may have to be forfeited for the sake of some practical moral good. No ethical principle is universally right to practice, but each gains sanction within some specific context that makes it lawful. We must "tailor our ethical cloth to fit the back of each occasion."

The only norm of conduct that the situationist accepts is not a law at all but the spirit of agape love, which seeks only our neighbor's good. Instead of being governed by specific rules, the Christian ideal of love should be taken as the sole criterion for action. To the situationist, it does not matter which principle or value is chosen—provided that our choice is motivated by altruism. In some contexts, force will be appropriate, in others, pacifism will be indicated; both can be correct if some good is achieved for the people affected by the actions. In this way, the Christian can justify supporting the First and Second World Wars as well as the gentleness of St. Francis of Assisi (1182?–1226) preaching a sermon to birds. Sometimes honesty will be called for, at other times deceit; in some situations, humility is best, in others assertiveness—all according to the requirements of love. There are no absolutes for the situationist, only an attitude of concern for humanity that can legitimize the acceptance of any action according to love's demands.

The situationist goes so far as to say that, contrary to traditional Christian teaching, any action may be justified by its results; that is, by the good that is achieved. Joseph Fletcher has stated unequivocally that the end does justify the means and that nothing else can. We should operate according to "agapeistic expediency," adopting any means that love requires to bring about the well-being of humanity. As St. Paul said, it is not lawfulness that makes an act worthwhile, but whether it is constructive and edifying. If, in certain contexts, divorce, abortion, euthanasia, and even assassination and war would accomplish some beneficial end, then agape love would dictate their employment.[9]

To the situationist, then, the advantageousness of actions is what counts, and love impels us to perform these acts regardless of religious laws. As Fletcher wrote, Christian ethics is not "living according to a code but a continuous effort to relate love to a world of relativities . . . its constant task is to work out the strategy and tactics of love, for Christ's sake."[10]

Situation ethics can easily be related to orthodox Christian theory mainly through the common denominator of agape love. It does, however, diverge radically from traditional teachings by relying wholly upon the ends of action as moral criteria. In reacting against legalism and centering on the primacy of love it follows the main thrust of the New Testament.

1. Although the person of faith may believe that God is the source of ethics, that may not be logically true.[11] As mentioned in chapter 1, an act does not become right because God wills it; rather, God would will an act because it is right. Ethical value is not derived from God's approval; God approves of that which is valuable. Ethics, therefore, is independent of God rather than being based on his authority. He cannot make that which is wrong right by willing it, or that which is right wrong by prohibiting it. If cruelty is immoral, it cannot be made moral by God changing his mind, and if it is argued that God would not do such a thing, that only proves the point.

   Another way of putting it is that God does not approve of actions whimsically, but for good reason; meaning that he recognizes the inherent value of certain conduct and for that reason tells us to behave accordingly. And for our part, we can appreciate the worth of his commands and see them not as the expression of an arbitrary will but as ethically sound judgments; for that reason they deserve to be followed. The existence of God is, therefore, irrelevant to the rightness of actions, for they would remain right even if there were no God.

2. A further problem concerns the intentionalist aspect of Christianity. Sinning in thought is considered the same as sinning in deed; coveting thy neighbor's wife is as bad as committing adultery. But how is it possible not to think certain things? Our actions lie within our power, but can we tell ourselves not to have certain thoughts? For in telling ourselves not to think these thoughts, we are thinking of them. The situation is very like a game that can be played with children. We can tell them there is a treasure hidden in the garden but that they will only find it if they do not think of a white rabbit. If, after searching for it they return empty-handed, we can say "I'll bet you thought of a white rabbit." The children cannot deny it, because they had to remember the thing they were supposed to forget; they had to keep in mind what they had to put out of their mind.

   The point is that one cannot tell oneself not to have certain ideas, feelings, memories, etc., and if people cannot help what they think, then it makes no sense to blame them for their thoughts.

3. Christian ethics has also encountered opposition with regard to its impracticality. The principle of agape love and divine justice are certainly admirable ideals, but the person who operates a business on this basis is doomed to fail. A banker, for example, cannot follow the maxim "Give to him who asks of you, and do not turn away from him"; he would soon declare bankruptcy. And in international relations, Christians who act for the well-being of their nation's enemies would soon endanger their native country; they could help the progress of evil in the world by default; that is, by not opposing it. A brutal, totalitarian dictator, for instance, would like nothing better than nonresistance. To bring about positive change in the human condition, universal love seems ineffectual. If everyone adopted the agape ideal, then the Christian approach would work, but in a world where only some operate selflessly and the rest selfishly, altruistic people become casualties and victims. Little good is achieved, and a great deal of suffering can result.

   Christian theologians recognize the practical difficulties involved in applying agape love, and they make various concessions to the business economy and *realpolitik*. These compromises are more or less successful, but they stray very far from the pure ethics of Christianity. The American Protestant theologian Reinhold Niebuhr, for example, concluded that we must abandon the law of love and engage in evil actions if we are to improve the world politically.[12] Individuals may behave in just and loving ways toward one another, but "all human groups tend to be more predatory than the individuals which compose them . they take for themselves whatever their power can command." Therefore, we cannot expect to make widespread moral progress through withdrawal or pacifism, but only through employing the evil tactics of racial, economic, and national groups. We must get our hands dirty, and "if we repent, Christ will forgive and receive us." Niebuhr may be correct in his assessment, but his theory does point up the impracticality of using Christian ethics in real social contexts.

4. Still another problem with the agape concept has to do with the conflict that can occur between the spirit of love and the ethical laws listed in the Old and New Testaments. It appears right to choose Christian love over the letter of the law, and to adopt the

viewpoint of situation ethics that love is all important, but can moral rules always be violated in the name of love? It seems odd to be able to set aside principles regarding killing and stealing, lying and adultery, if love requires it.

Should we disregard all rules, the Ten Commandments and the Sermon on the Mount? Perhaps the role of agape love is being overemphasized if it can override any moral principle. Furthermore, in operating this way we are left without firm moral guidelines, with too great a burden placed on our consciences to decide which actions best express the spirit of love. Surely a loving attitude toward humanity would naturally lead to certain rules of conduct as the expression of that love, which is what we have in Christian ethics. Perhaps we should not apply fixed rules to our behavior, but moral rules do emerge from sympathetic experience.

Principles cannot simply be sacrificed to an attitude of love. Both elements must be considered, and this creates a tension within Christian ethics as to which should take priority in various circumstances. Old Testament legalism sins to the right and situation ethics sins to the left, which leaves us with a dilemma regarding the relation between love and principles.

It might also be pointed out that we should not always do unto others as we would have them do unto us, for as Oscar Wilde said, "They may not have the same tastes." If someone is suicidal, the golden rule would give them a license to kill, and a masochist could hurt others as he would like to be hurt.

In summation, Christian ethics is admirable and high-minded, but also fraught with flaws. These problems make us hesitate before adopting it as our basic reason for living. However, humility dictates that we be careful before dismissing any moral system that has been maintained for several thousand years.

C. ISLAM

Most of the theories studied in ethics derive from Western sources, and little attention is paid to the systems of the East. This seems a mistake, especially in an age of global conflict between the two cultures. In Eastern nations ethics has always been intertwined with religion, so we will examine two of the major religions for their philosophic and ethical content: Islam and Buddhism.

Islam is the most recent of the world religions, revealed to the prophet Muhammad "the Praised" in the seventh century, according to Muslim tradition. Muhammad was born in the city of Mecca in c.570, the posthumous son of a man named Abdullah; his mother died when he was about six, and he was raised by his grandfather, then his uncle. Some speculate that this background made Mohammed especially sympathetic to widows and orphans. We know that he joined caravans traveling through portions of Arabia, and encountered Jews and Christians, which broadened his religious ideas.

Muhammed managed a caravan for a wealthy widow named Khadijah fifteen years his senior, whom he subsequently married. The couple had five children, but unfortunately two sons died early in life, and only one daughter, Fatima, outlived her parents. After his wife's death, Muhammed began to see visions and hear voices in the desert around Mecca, especially one persistent voice saying "You are the chosen one, proclaim the name of the Lord." Finally, on a night known as *el Qadr*, the Night of Power and Excellence, a vision of Gabriel appeared to him. The Archangel either commanded him to "Recite thou," that is, preach the word of God or wrote certain words in fiery letters on a cloth revealing God's nature. But it was not until the second revelation, and through the faith of Khadijah, that Muhammed became convinced he was a prophet of God or Allah (a contraction of al-ilah, "the good"). Following this, he began preaching to his friends in Mecca, converting Abu Bakr, Ali, and finally Omar. There was considerable resistance and a period of exile; he was even stoned out of the city of Taif. Muhammed's flight from Mecca to Medina occurred in 622 AD or 1 AH (Anno Hegarae) in the Islamic calendar. Nevertheless, the faith spread throughout the Arab world, both by persuasion and by the sword; Islam, in fact, means "absolute submission to the will of Allah."

Muhammad is regarded as the "last and most perfect messenger to humanity," "unequaled among human beings," with lesser prophets preceding him from Adam to Abraham, Moses, and Jesus: Moses revealed the Ten Commandments; Jesus the Golden Rule. Although Jesus is revered as a true prophet and is believed to have cured the sick, raised the dead, and been born of a virgin, he is not regarded as divine. In the words of the Qur'an, the principal Islamic scripture in 114 *suras* (chapters), "They say the God of mercy has gotten to himself a son. Now have ye uttered a grievous thing . It is not meet for God to have children" (3:78, 19:93).

The cardinal principle stated in the Qur'an is an uncompromising monotheism, that "God is one God . There is no God but He—the Living, the Eternal" (2:158,255). Allah has ninety-nine most beautiful names that identify his attributes, which include being almighty, the sovereign of heaven and earth, the ruler of life and death, the being who holds dominion over man and nature. He is the sustainer of all the Worlds, an eternal refuge, omniscient, just and merciful but terrible in his wrath (13:16; 29:61,63; 31:25; 39:38; and 43:9). He does not beget nor is He begotten, and there is none equal to him (112:1–4).

At the end of time Allah will reveal himself fully and pronounce doom or blessings on everyone who has ever lived. In that day of reckoning, "[w]hen the sun shall be folded up, and the stars shall fall, and when the mountains shall be set in motion . . . and the seas shall boil . . . then shall every soul know what it hath done (81). . . . Every man's actions have we hung round his neck, and on the last day shall be laid before him a wide-open Book" (17:13). The afterlife is depicted in vivid, physical terms: heaven as a place of deep, cool rivers of crystal waters, succulent fruits, fertile fields, and beautiful mansions with attending virgins; Hell a place of molten metal, bubbling, sulfurous liquids, and all-consuming fire. To conservative Muslims, these descriptions are literally true; more liberal Muslims treat them as symbolic, since coolness and intense heat would resonate with a desert people.

The Five Pillars of Faith

This view of reality naturally led to various moral obligations, first the five articles of faith that Muslims are required to accept. The belief in: (1) the oneness of God; (2) the reality of angels; (3) the revealed books; (4) the prophets; and (5) the Day of Judgment. Also required is adherence to Shari'ah, the Islamic law, which prescribes the complete way in which life should be lived.

In terms of obligations, there are the Pillars of Islam, which all pious Muslims must practice: First, the recitation of the *shahadah*, the profession of faith, "There is no God but Allah, and Muhammad is the prophet of Allah." As one commentator remarks, "it is easy to learn and impossible to forget." This is Islam's creed, which must be uttered at least once during one's lifetime, carefully and thoughtfully, although most Muslims repeat it several times each day.

The second pillar is prayer, and the faithful are enjoined to "be constant" in their worship. During prayers the Muslim is to put his worldly life in perspective, to reflect on his dependence on Allah, and surrender himself as a creature to his creator. Five times a day believers must pray: upon rising, at high noon, in mid-afternoon (at the yellowing of the sun), after sunset, and when night finally comes. Friday is a holy day, and noon prayers are held in mosques with the service conducted by an imam, an officiating priest or leader, but the Muslim is required to pray "anywhere upon God's earth or under his heaven." As part of the ritual, the faithful bow, place their hands on their knees, prostrate themselves, and repeat "Allahu Akbar" (God is great). Facing toward the sacred city of Mecca, he utters prayers of praise and gratitude and asks for the strength to live righteously and to love God above all else.

> O Lord, grant me the love of Thee. Grant that I may love those that love Thee. Grant that I may do the deeds that win Thy love. Make Thy love to be dearer to me than self, family or wealth . . . I ask Thee for an innocent heart, which shall not incline to wickedness . . . for forgiveness of those faults, which Thou knowest . . . for verily Thou art the forgiver of offenses and the bestower of blessings on Thy servant.

Third is *zakat*, charity or almsgiving, which provides the blessing of purification. Those with much have an obligation to give to those with little; specifically, 2 1/2 percent of both income and wealth. And these alms should be distributed to slaves who are buying their freedom, to debtors unable to pay their debts, and to strangers and travelers in need.

The fourth pillar of Islam is the observance of *Ramadan*, a sacred month of fasting to commemorate significant events in the life of Muhammed. Muslims must fast from sunrise to sunset; they cannot eat, drink, or enjoy sensuous pleasures until night. One can tell that darkness has come when a white thread cannot be distinguished from a black one.

The final pillar is the *hajj*, or pilgrimage to Mecca, which must be undertaken once in a lifetime, health and wealth permitting. Since Mecca is the site of Allah's revelations to Muhammad, it is a sacred place and the journey is meant to deepen one's devotion to God. The worshiper must circle a small cubicle building called the *Kaba* seven times, touch the holy black stone it contains, and taste the blessed water from the *Zemzem* well.[13]

Such are the religious/ethical duties of the Muslim.

An Ethical Evaluation

1. The recent hostility of the United States toward the Islamic world arose, of course, from 9/11/01, when Muslims flew planes into the World Trade Center and the Pentagon, killing three thousand

people. The Taliban, Hamas, and al-Qa'ida further targeted civilians in suicide bombings and other acts of terror, including the beheading of hostages with swords. Terrorism has occurred not only in Iraq and Afghanistan but in Western Europe, Israel, India, Pakistan, and other nations. This violates the international rules of war that prohibit violence against non-combatants. There is widespread debate as to how much of this can be laid at the door of Islam.

Defenders of the faith point out that whoever kills without just cause carries the burden of killing all of humanity; and whoever saves a life, it is as if the whole of humanity has been rescued (5:32). But is killing the infidel a just cause, and does that include civilians as well as soldiers?

In this context, the principle of *jihad* is relevant—a religious duty imposed on all Muslims. In the Qur'an it appears as both Holy War and great effort. According to the mildest meaning, jihad signifies purification of the heart, fighting the devil, and supporting what is right with tongue and hand. According to a harsher meaning, it obligates Muslims to impose Islam on all non-Islamic peoples. The *dar ul-Harb* are the countries to be conquered; the *Ahl al-Islam* is the House of Islam. Insofar as Muslims follow the meaning of Holy War against unbelievers, jihad can be criticized in word and deed. This applies to the Sunni branch of Islam, with its orthodox theology, and the Shi'ite branch, which trusts exemplary leaders to reveal the truth of the Qur'an.[14]

2. The moral code of Islam, governing every aspect of daily life, has also been criticized for its severity. For example, although abortion is sometimes allowed (before the spirit enters the fetus at 120 days), homosexuality is strictly prohibited. Homosexuality is considered "unnatural," and penalties range from flogging to execution. Even discussing the issue can lead to excommunication. Temporary contraception is sometimes permitted but not vasectomy or hysterectomy; coitus interruptus is best.[15]

In many parts of the Muslim world, females cannot attend school, participate in government, hold jobs, drive cars, or appear in public without a male relative. Women are habitually covered in a *chador*, which shrouds them from head to foot, allowing only their faces to show, sometimes just their eyes. Imams claim this dress is necessary for the sake of modesty, but women elsewhere in the world regard it as oppressive, especially in an age of gender equality. In the name of Islam, clitoral circumcision is also performed in

Egypt, Yemen, Bahrain, Pakistan, the United Aram Emirates, and elsewhere; in some places it has become "a law by custom." Reports have also surfaced of "pride killings," in which a woman who has been raped is murdered by relatives because she brought shame on the family. At least some of these practices can be attributed to Islamic teaching and cannot be dismissed as deviations.

3. Along with the control of personal liberty, freedom of speech, press, and religion are often curtailed. No defection from Islam is allowed, nor dissent from traditional beliefs. Even irreverent cartoons can cause rioting, and a *fatwa*, or death sentence, has been issued against writers who are considered sacrilegious. A notable example is the prominent novelist Salman Rushdie, who was forced into hiding because of death threats.

In our moral thinking today we support tolerance and diversity and an open and respectful dialogue; we defend a person's right to express contrary opinions. A theocracy that regulates thought can suppress the development of individuality and freedom, which are important values in democracies.

That said, many Muslims are moderate in their beliefs, and Islam contains numerous virtues, especially the desire for self-improvement shown in prayer and charity toward the poor. Tithing is taken quite seriously, and generosity is a fundamental virtue within the Muslim community. Furthermore, Allah is seen not only as just, almighty, and righteous, but as merciful, kind, and forgiving. He is

> The Holy, the Peaceful, the Faithful, the Guardian over His servants, the Shelterer over the orphan, the Guide of the erring, the Deliverer from every affliction, the Friend of the bereaved, the Consoler of the afflicted; in His hand is good, and He is the generous Lord, the Gracious, the Hearer, the Near-at-Hand, the Compassionate, the Merciful, the Very-forgiving, whose love for man is more tender than that of a mother-bird for her young.

D. BUDDHISM

The Buddhist religion, which began in northeast India and spread to Sri Lanka, Thailand, Cambodia, Burma, Laos, China, Mongolia, and Japan, has an estimated 150 to 300 million followers. The extensive metaphysical structure of beliefs, with ethical ideals flowing from it, has also appealed to Americans, so that numerous Buddhist societies, meditation centers, and even monasteries have been established across the United States.

The religion proper was founded by Siddhartha Gautama, the Buddha or Enlightened One, who was born in 563 BCE, the son of a wealthy chieftain in Kapilavastu in northern India. "I wore garments of silk and my attendants held a white umbrella over me," he wrote. Although Gautama was surrounded by luxury and married a neighboring princess "full of dignity and exceeding grace," he felt compelled to renounce his material comforts. According to Buddhist legend, this was prompted by seeing an old man, a diseased man, and a corpse, which made him understand that "I also am subject to decay and am not free from the power of old age, sickness, and death . . . when I reflected thus, all the joy of life which there is in life died within me." In short, he was overwhelmed by the awareness of human decay, suffering, and death, which impelled him on a pilgrimage across India seeking enlightenment.

The main reason for Gautama's homelessness, searching, and meditation was the cycle of rebirths. According to the Hindu religion prevalent at the time, our souls undergo a series of reincarnations, inhabiting new bodies at the moment of death. The level of the caste, or fixed social class into which we are reborn, is determined by the quality of our previous lives, and this process is called the Law of Karma. In the Hindu system, those who have had the best thoughts, words, and deeds "enter a pleasant womb," that of a Brahmin priest or a Kshatriya nobleman; those with poor past lives become shopkeepers or craftsmen called Vaisyas or laborers called Sudras; while those whose conduct was despicable, that is, have bad *karma*, will even "enter the womb of a dog, or the womb of a swine, or the womb of an outcast."

This continuing existence of life after life, in different castes and forms, was not viewed by the Hindus as something positive; rather, they felt themselves chained to the wheel of rebirth (*samsara*) and sought ways to escape from it. They wanted deliverance from the round of change, from endless weariness and illusion, the perpetual becoming that never resolved itself into permanent being. If they could be reborn as a Brahmin then they would be in a position to merge with the universe at death, to lose their separateness and identity and become one with the All. They would enter *Nirvana*, a condition of ecstasy in which they were aware of finally being absorbed into *Brahma*, the world soul. The spark would then join the universal fire, the drop dissolve into the ocean of Being.

The Hindus long for this state but envision a future of almost endless reincarnations, until they attain the Brahmin caste and can achieve liberation from this earth of tears. In his six years of study and reflection, Gautama sought a better answer to human salvation, and refused numerous solutions that were urged on him. He rejected the way of knowledge, because it was too speculative and remote to be of practical help; the way of devotion, because he rejected the idea of gods and thought prayer was useless; and the way of asceticism and self-mortification, which only weakened his body rather than disciplining his mind. Gautama believed there had to be a Middle Way.

Meditating under a *bo* (fig) tree one day, he finally received the revelation he sought, and he began to teach his message throughout India, acquiring a group of close disciples (the *sangha*) and a growing mass of followers who regarded him as the *Buddha* or Enlightened One.

The Buddha left no written body of thought, but his teachings were recited and chanted by his disciples and transmitted orally. Several centuries later a written canon was created called the *Tripitaka*, or three baskets, because it consisted of three collections of writings: the *Vinaya Pitaka* or monastic rules; the *Sutta Pitaka* or discourses; and the *Adhehamma Pitaka* or supplement to the doctrines. The Buddha's first sermon was given at the Deer Park in Benares, and the teachings hold the same importance to Buddhists as Christ's Sermon on the Mount does to Christians. Here the Buddha declared his basic principles of a worthwhile life and for spiritual salvation, presented in the form of the four truths and eight instructions for correct behavior.

The Four Noble Truths and the Eightfold Path

The Noble Truth of Suffering is first: "Birth is suffering, decay is suffering, illness is suffering, death is suffering . . . clinging to existence is suffering." In other words, sorrow or *dukkha*, pervades all of life—hunger and disease, the breakdown of the body as it ages, and the pain that accompanies death. Even if one is not tormented by these inherent evils, the times will bring upheavals, turmoil, and destruction.

Second is the Noble Truth of the Cause of Suffering: "Thirst that leads to rebirth . . . thirst for pleasure, thirst for existence, thirst for prosperity." That is, the sorrow we experience springs from our desires or cravings. We yearn for material comfort, goods, and property, the satisfaction of our physical appetites and for intellectual, aesthetic, and spiritual satisfactions.

Each one of these proves disappointing, so we exist in a state of frustration, not having what we want and not wanting what we have. Even when we achieve satisfaction our pleasure is short-lived, for our experience is ephemeral (*anicca*). Life is characterized as a ceaseless process of change, a transitory and mutable state with no rest in actual being. Time itself is an evil, and our richest enjoyments are tainted by the realization that this too shall pass away. The skull always grins in at the banquet; there is always a worm in the bud.

Third is the Noble Truth of the Cessation of Suffering, which ends with: "the complete cessation of this thirst—a cessation which consists in the absence of every passion . . . with the destruction of desire." That is, sorrow can cease if we eliminate our cravings (*tanha*) and no longer seek to satisfy our desires. This requires a deep knowledge of ourselves so that we can control and then extinguish the bundle of cravings that lie within.

The fourth Noble Truth is the holy Eightfold Path of right behavior that leads to the cessation of suffering: "Right Belief, Right Aspiration, Right Speech, Right Conduct, Right Means of Livelihood, Right Endeavor, Right Mindfulness, Right Meditation."

Right belief pertains to a correct understanding of the world and ourselves, especially as elucidated in the Four Noble Truths. *Right aspiration* means we should strive to conduct ourselves properly, to avoid sensuality and refrain from harming any living thing, and *right speech* refers to clear thinking and expression, not harboring ill-will or saying hurtful things. If our belief, aspiration, and speech are correct, then *right conduct* follows, and this is vital in the Buddhist ethic.

Numerous lists appear in Buddhist writings under this last category. One mandates: (1) not willfully hurting any living creature, a pacifism and a doctrine of non-injury (*ahimsa*) that Buddhists practice more than any other group; (2) not taking what is not given, which is a prohibition against stealing what rightfully belongs to another; and (3) avoiding overindulgence of the senses, which calls for moderation, sobriety, and temperance.

Another list refers to the Ten Fetters which bind us to the wheel of reincarnation and must be overcome: (1) belief in the existence of the self; (2) doubt; (3) trust in good works; (4) lust; (5) anger; (6) desire for rebirth in worlds of form; (7) desire for rebirth in formless worlds; (8) pride; (9) self-righteousness; and (10) ignorance. Three Intoxications and Five Hindrances are also listed, as well as Ten Sins: three of the body—murder, robbery, fornication; four of speech—lying, slander, insult, and frivolity; and three of the mind—coveting, malice, and heresy.

There are numerous lists but they are generally compatible, and the point is to identify right conduct and live in accordance with virtue. *Right means of livelihood* follows as a corollary: we must engage only in that type of work that enables us to practice right conduct. What that might consist of remains rather vague, but it should be an occupation in keeping with Buddhist teaching. *Right effort* also follows because we must convert understanding to behavior, knowledge to actions of the will; in that way, we can achieve virtue. And as we reflect and meditate on our behavior, our wisdom becomes a constant frame of mind called *right mindfulness*, in which we have ingrained and correct habits of thought.

Finally, if we follow each of these steps on the path, *right rapture* is achieved in which we are delivered from earthly sorrow. We slip into a state of trance close to that of a saint (*arahat*), and attain the ecstasy that is called Nirvana. All greed, hatred, and ignorance are erased, and we are enlightened like Gautama.

In brief, the Four Noble Truths state that living is suffering, suffering springs from desire, desire can be overcome, and this is done through behaving rightly. Since desire is the basic cause of suffering, if we extinguish desire through correct behavior, we eliminate life's sorrow.

In speaking of desire, the Buddha does not just mean sensuality but wanting material goods such as land, houses, furniture, and clothing, and loving people such as our parents, spouses, children, and friends. As in the Stoic philosophy, if you want nothing, refusing to depend on things outside yourself, then you become invulnerable. "Therefore let no man love anything; loss of the beloved is evil. Those who love nothing and hate nothing have no fetters." All attachments should be renounced, even attachments to the Buddha himself, because they can be disturbing and prevent the attainment of perfect peace. Oddly enough, Buddhism in its pure form is a religion without gods, including Gautama, so we should only rely upon ourselves and the All within.

Not only does the renunciation of desire give us mastery over our present life, but it breaks the cycle of rebirths. That is, people are reincarnated time after time because of their desire for existence. If people are evil in this way, their evilness pursues them; fresh individualities then come into being because of a craving after existence. Once we no longer desire life and its attractions, we are free from the wheel of reincarnation and will blend with the cosmos at death.

Unlike the Hindus, the Buddhists do not believe in an ironclad Law of Karma according to which our past desires, deeds, and longing for existence automatically produce new incarnations. To the Hindus, karma is an inviolable, mechanical, and just system which ensures that our good actions are rewarded and our bad ones punished. It accounts for our position in our present incarnation—our beauty, intelligence, longevity, wealth, status, and so forth. The Buddhists agree that karma operates in the universe but they claim it can be broken in one's lifetime by a transformation in our approach to life. By being a supremely worthy person, virtually a saint, thinking and acting in terms of the Four Noble Truths, our old karma can be exhausted. Then reincarnations will cease and our individual selves will be extinguished at death like a flame.

Buddhists also reject the caste system of Hinduism that maintains that we are reborn in strict social classes according to the karma amassed from our previous lives. The Buddha taught that there are no castes, and the way to salvation is open to everyone, regardless of their station in life. All that is required is to free ourselves from desires and attachments in the light of our understanding. Then we will seek not existence but extinction.

One important qualification, however, is that we must become monks to attain salvation. In an informal way, that is what anyone becomes who approaches enlightenment. However, the monks as a group must commit themselves to an ascetic life. For clothing they have to wear a simple saffron robe, and have no family or personal property. They must be celibate and beg for their food each day, leaving none left over for tomorrow. In short, they renounce all earthly desires, and in return they earn salvation.

The Buddha did not believe that the soul inhabited a succession of bodies; in fact, he denies the reality of the soul (the doctrine of *anatman* or no soul). Rather, he maintained that our character is reincarnated, continually producing fresh individualities until such time as we no longer desire existence. Between one life and another is a "going" or *gati*. To take some Buddhist analogies, it is not like the passing of a bird from nest to nest but rather like a poem going from a master to a student or one candle being lit by another.

In a deep sense, the self is an illusion to begin with, and once we achieve this understanding we are on the path to salvation. The desire for the self may be the greatest desire, and therefore the source of our deepest sorrow. Once we realize there is no self but only a changing complex of desires, then we are liberated. In the oceanic state, all misery ceases.

An Overall Assessment

1. One criticism frequently leveled against Buddhism is that suffering may not characterize human life. To the Buddhist mind, life is a

trial filled with change, loss, and death, and viewing it as enjoyable is an illusion (*maya*). The state of living is basically an evil condition, so in each new lifetime suffering is simply renewed. It is best, therefore, to lose our individuality and awareness, to escape from the self and merge with the Absolute.

In the West in the twenty-first century, living as suffering does not seem to be a universal truth. Most people's standard of living is adequate, and we enjoy educational benefits, the enrichment of culture, good health care, technological advances, a variety of sports and entertainment, efficient transportation and communication, a multiplicity of products and services, abundant food, and physical comforts of every kind. Life does not appear to be agonizing, and we do not feel the need to escape through renunciation and austerities. Disease, aging, and death add a melancholy note to existence because they entail misery that flesh is heir to, but such suffering may not characterize existence in general. Americans in particular are an optimistic people that have the pursuit of happiness in our founding document; therefore, the belief that life is sorrow is not a congenial notion.

2. If we reject the idea that living entails misery, we could also reject the claim that the extinction of desire is worthwhile. At least some of the time, desire is followed by satisfaction; thirsts are in fact quenched on occasion. Striving can produce achievement and fulfillment, and our longings are not always frustrated. Furthermore, although time destroys some pleasures, it also brings fresh ones; and change does not only mean the passing of pleasures but a relief from pains. The fact that experience is transitory is an encouraging thought when times are bad.

   If we desire nothing we do protect ourselves from disappointment, but we also prevent ourselves from obtaining satisfaction. Attachments to people, for example, certainly make us vulnerable to pain if those we love are injured, but this risk is preferable to not having any human relationships. Surely it is not an ideal life to refuse to love anyone for fear of rejection or disillusionment.

3. As for reincarnation, this is certainly an intriguing idea and one that is quite widespread in the East, but little evidence exists to support it. At various times psychologists or psychics claim to have regressed people to their previous lives, but none of these cases have been verified under scientific conditions. Perhaps when people encounter similar experiences in their lifetime, this gives them a

sense of *déjà vu*, or perhaps there are delays in perception before an experience is mentally registered and this is seen as evidence of a past existence. Whatever the explanation for the reports, reincarnation is a highly questionable concept.

4. We could also question the notion of the unreality of the self, that the soul and personal identity are fictions. To doubt our own existence and individuality as persons runs counter to our deepest feelings. We usually have a strong sense of our reality, and we differentiate between our subjective self and the objective world, refusing to believe we are the same as external objects. In other words, our self-awareness does not seem to be an illusion. In fact, we treat people who have no sense of self as psychotic.

5. Finally, the goal of extinction does not seem particularly attractive as the end of life. As mentioned previously, if conscious living is something desirable, then extinction is not appealing. Most people want a rich existence on earth crowned with life after death in some heavenly realm. The thought that we might be snuffed out is not our highest dream but our worst nightmare.

REVIEW QUESTIONS

1. Describe the principal characteristics of the religious ethic advocated in the Old Testament.
2. Explain the ideal in Christian ethics of agape, as contrasted with eros love. What criticisms can be offered of it?
3. Compare and contrast the concepts of divine and human justice. Which do you think is ethically more defensible?
4. Describe the Five Pillars of Islam. Do you think there is a gap between the religion and the violence in the Muslim world, or is that part of the faith?
5. Explain the concepts of karma, reincarnation, and Nirvana in Buddhist thought.

10

VIRTUE ETHICS

In recent years a number of philosophers have become dissatisfied with attempts to divide ethics into utilitarian and Kantian approaches, or to base ethics on any set of moral principles, categories, or rules. They see ethics as embedded in social situations and the experiences of the individual. For this reason, any effort to extract laws of conduct from the circumstances of life will produce distortion. They maintain that human affairs are too subtle, varied, nuanced, and textured to be reduced to universal moral laws. For the sake of simplifying and unifying our ethical theory we sacrifice the richness of moral experience. Ethics, they claim, concerns the virtuous individual in a historical context, not abstract obligations, rights, or moral imperatives.

These *virtue ethicists* believe that to recommend certain ways of achieving the good life, such as hedonism, self-realization, or naturalism, is a fundamental mistake. Rather, we should focus on what constitutes virtue or character in the individual, the moral traits that would dispose people to behave in commendable ways.

Another way of stating the difference is that most ethical theories have emphasized the rightness or wrongness of *conduct* in terms of some general theory. Virtue ethics stresses whether people are good or bad in terms of their *character*. Instead of speaking of how we should behave according to some objective principles, virtue ethics judges the person performing the action more than the action itself. It is the agent who is called upright, praiseworthy, admirable, and worthwhile, or awful, deplorable, wicked, and blameworthy. Standing at the extremes are the saint and the sinner. On this reading, the moral character of the person becomes more important than the moral quality of the act. A person's motives, disposition, habits, and inner identity take precedence over any theory governing their conduct; being matters much more than doing.

The virtue ethicist points out that correct behavior is not necessarily worthwhile, especially if people behave correctly in order to be admired, to gain some advantage, to win an election, to ensure entrance to heaven, and so forth. Then the motives negate the worth of the actions. On the other hand, if people are outstanding human beings, then we can make allowances for their wrongdoing, attributing the mistake to a moral lapse. We can more easily forgive people for what they do than for what they are.

What's more, having a fine character would naturally lead to correct conduct, with few slips along the way. We would normally expect that the virtuous person would behave virtuously, that his or her character would be expressed in correct conduct, and that this conduct would, in turn, reflect the person's character. Heraclitus recognized this truth when he said "Character is destiny," meaning that we act from what we are.

Seen in historical perspective, the emphasis on the ethics of virtue rather than the ethics of conduct hearkens back to a focus that typified ancient ethics. The Greek word *arête* expressed this notion and means excellence or good character.

A. ANCIENT GREECE

Plato and Aristotle in particular placed great importance on *arête* in their writings; in fact, moral virtue was the pivotal point of their ethical theories.

Plato used a dialogue form in his writings, with his teacher Socrates as the principal spokesman, and the philosophic ideas they offer are therefore indirectly stated. The dialogues are accounts of philosophic conversations between Socrates and other people, and for the most part they are named for the person to whom Socrates is speaking. Thus we have the *Theaetetus, Meno, Parmenides, Gorgias,* and so forth.

Scholars have spilled considerable ink debating whether Plato faithfully reported Socrates's words or whether he used Socrates as a vehicle for the expression of his own ideas. Some scholars claim the early dialogues are Socratic, the later ones Platonic, while others use the subject matter as a dividing line, Socrates being more interested in moral conduct. At this point the consensus seems to be that the dialogues mainly express Plato's philosophy, rendered in dramatic form with Socrates as protagonist.

Wherever the truth lies, virtue is discussed at numerous points in the dialogues, especially in the *Republic*, where Plato sees a correspondence between the just person and the just state. The state is the individual "writ large."

The Noble Person

In Plato's view, human beings are composed of three parts: the appetitive (desires); the spirited (will); and the rational (intellect). Our appetites include the desire for food and drink, sex and power, which are all strong passions. Because of their strength, we sometimes satisfy them in ways that are harmful to ourselves, acting contrary to our best interests. The spirited or willful part of ourselves leads us to action, risk, and adventure, expressions of power and self-assertion, but it can impel us into rash behavior. The rational part is based on intelligence and should control the rest; otherwise the person may function in self-destructive ways.

Reason, therefore, should rule the person, controlling the excesses of both the appetites and the spirit, and producing a well-balanced individual. When that happens, our desires will be harnessed and possess the virtue of *temperance*; the volitional aspect of the person will be channeled into the virtue of *courage*; and the rational faculty will have achieved the virtue of *wisdom*. The ideal person, then, will be temperate, courageous, and wise, under the governance of reason.

Plato, incidentally, applies this same model to his political philosophy, claiming that the ideal state also must be governed by reason in the person of philosopher-kings. They will rule over those who are primarily appetitive and want to obtain wealth so they can indulge their desires; this economic segment of the body politic should be kept moderate. The rational rulers (*guardians*) would also control the spirited segment of the population who had been made into soldiers (*auxiliaries*), ensuring that they are courageous, neither impetuous nor irrationally fearful.

The main point is that Plato regards virtue as the harmonious cooperation of all faculties and functions. They must refrain from encroaching on each other and submit to the guidance of the intellect.[1]

Perhaps even more than Plato, his student Aristotle championed virtue as lying at the heart of ethics, and he is often taken as the founder of this school of thought. As discussed previously, Aristotle endorsed the doctrine of the mean that was prevalent in Greece at the time, giving it a philosophic structure and justification; on the frieze of the Parthenon was inscribed, "Everything in moderation, nothing in excess." To Aristotle, virtue lies in choosing the mean between extremes, such that courage is a mean virtue between the extremes of cowardice and fearlessness; pride is the mean between vanity and humility; and liberality lies between the excess of extravagance and the deficiency of meanness (miserliness). Even anger has a virtue: that of being even-tempered, neither weak-kneed nor hotheaded but appropriately enraged at injustice. The point is to achieve virtue by developing a disposition toward acting in an excellent way, and our guide is the golden mean. Aristotle writes,

> It follows that virtue is a fixed quality of the will, consisting essentially in a middle state—middle in relation to ourselves, and as determined by principle . . . it is a middle state between two vices, one of excess and one of deficiency: and this in view of the fact that vices either exceed or fall short of the right amount in emotions or actions, whereas virtue ascertains the mean and chooses that. Consequently . . . while virtue is a middle state, in point of excellence and rightness it is an extreme.

Rationality, of course, is the means for identifying that middle point. As you will recall from the earlier discussion, reason is man's unique function, that which distinguishes him from plants and animals, so it must be employed to recognize the mean between extremes. Just as Plato seeks to discipline the emotions, especially the passions and will through the dominance of reason, Aristotle wants to disarm the force of the emotions and choose the mean logically. Self-regulation through reason is crucial to both men.

The midpoint or *aurea mediocritas* should be our aim in virtuous living. As the Latin poet Horace said, "Whoever cultivates the golden mean avoids both the poverty of the hovel and the envy of a palace."

Although no cross-fertilization occurred between China and Greece at this time in history, Confucius (551–479 BCE) also had a doctrine of the golden mean or *chungyung*, and his philosophy is a type of virtue ethics. He states, for example, "That virtue is perfect which adheres to a constant mean." Actions and sentiments should be maintained in a balanced way, and the ideal person is one who practices such poise and centeredness. This interpretation is consistent with the Confucian emphasis on equilibrium, proportion, and harmony in one's life, and parallels the Buddhist's Middle Way between indulgence and self-denial. Confucius wanted nothing in excess but everything in due measure, and in that way we establish a oneness between society, earth, and heaven.

For Confucius, "due measure" was expressed mainly through *li* or proper carriage, graciousness, and general decorum, which mirrors the order of the universe. He believed that just as there is an appropriate relation between heaven and earth, and the family and the state, we should assume a proper posture in our dealings with people of various stations. The highly ceremonial and courteous manner of Confucius seems stilted and stylized to Western minds but it was meant as a reflection of the cosmos itself. In any case, his "golden mean" differs significantly from that of Aristotle in that the latter emphasized rationally selecting the path of moderation.

In explaining how to strike the mean, Aristotle uses a metaphor in the *Poetics*, his philosophic writings on art. In this treatise he writes that a work of art is finished when there are no deficiencies and nothing is superfluous. In the same way, we attain the perfection of the mean when we can neither add anything nor take anything away.

One interesting aspect of Aristotle's virtue ethics is his insistence on building a disposition toward virtuous conduct. Instead of agonizing over ethical decisions each time, and being torn between what we want to do and what we ought to do, we should develop habits of virtuous behavior. In that way, acting morally will not require great effort. Desiring things in the right amount should become automatic; when it does, then we will have achieved a fine moral disposition. At that point we will no longer have to deliberate about which action is right in particular situations. Our habitual response will be correct, flowing from a virtuous nature.

In short, good character should always inform our actions, and proper moral action will form good character. They are mutually reinforcing; the virtuous person knows the nature of virtue and therefore behaves virtuously. Differently put, we act from what we are, but we also become what we are through our action.[2]

B. MEDIEVAL PURITY

The medieval theologians, most notably St. Thomas Aquinas, also championed the virtues, although their list differed significantly from that of the Greeks. Instead of such ideals as temperance, courage, wisdom, pride, liberality, and good temper, the medieval thinkers listed justice, prudence, temperance, fortitude, faith, hope, and charity as the cardinal virtues. Corresponding to them were the seven deadly sins of pride, lust, envy, anger, covetousness, gluttony, and sloth.

Notice that temperance is a virtue shared by both cultures, but pride is a vice to the Christians and a virtue to the Greeks. This difference is a significant one in outlook. To Aristotle, for example, vanity and humility were to be avoided, but the mean of pride should be sought; it implied a just satisfaction in our accomplishments. To Aquinas, however, all glory and honor belongs to God, so whatever our achievements, we owe them to God's grace and therefore should be humble.

However, both the Greek philosophers and the medieval theologians emphasized self-mastery, especially regarding the passions and emotions, and our wants and needs—particularly the pursuit of pleasure. All of our natural impulses must be controlled, mainly because they are vulgar and powerful. Virtue consists in directing these forces toward some good. We cannot help wanting money to provide creature comforts, but we can avoid greed and ruthlessness in obtaining it. We cannot help our sexual desires, but we can be respectful and constrained instead of lustful. To the Greeks, mastering our impulses makes us fully human, not part animal like the centaur, minotaur, or sphinx; to medieval Christians, it makes us God's creatures and not instruments of the devil. Both systems of thought prefer an ascetic life ranging from moderation to extreme privation, and both reject a sybaritic life of self-indulgence. A virtuous existence consists in self-control.

C. MODERN PERSPECTIVES

A number of contemporary philosophers have rediscovered virtue ethics following its eclipse after the Middle Ages, and they have brought about a revival of interest in the subject—philosophers such as Alasdair MacIntyre, Bernard Mayo, Philippa Foot, Bernard Williams, Rosalind Hursthouse, Jorge Garcia, Nel Noddings, Richard Taylor, and Christina Hoff Sommers. All of these thinkers share the belief that ethical systems have been too rigid and remote from the persons involved in moral issues, and that the time for a return to an "agent-centered" ethic of virtues is long overdue. They especially reject the highly structured, rigid, and rationalistic approach of Immanuel Kant.

As you will recall, Kant endorsed an ethic based on duty and obligation. Actions that are praiseworthy are grounded in principles, universalizable principles, and do not stem from moral sentiments. Our feelings are too subjective and unstable to furnish the grounds of ethical conduct. Kant writes:

Inclination, be it good-natured or otherwise, is blind and slavish; reason, when it is a question of morality, must not play the part of mere guardian of the inclinations, but, without regard to them . . . must care for its own interests . . . . Even the feeling of sympathy and warm-hearted fellow-feeling, when preceding the consideration of what is duty and serving as a determining ground, is burdensome even to right-thinking persons, confusing their considered maxims and creating the wish to be free from them and subject only to law-giving reason.

For example, giving to charity out of rational duty is commendable, but we should not be charitable because of a momentary sympathy for people's suffering. Such tenderness can betray us into impulsive and unjustified generosity.

Contrary to Kant, the virtue ethicists trust their feelings, especially such moral sentiments as pity, respect, sympathy, protectiveness, fairness, sharing, forgiveness, patience, tolerance, truthfulness, kindness, loyalty, humility, honesty, and caring. Let's explore some of these "governing dispositions of character" and the virtues they might generate.[3]

Character and Moral Sentiments

Forgiveness. The virtue of forgiveness means pardoning someone for an offense they have committed against us. We have been wronged in some way, but we are willing to overlook the offense. In genuine forgiveness, we not only pardon what has been done but we feel no resentment toward the person who did it, purging ourselves of anger and the need for revenge. Generosity and its sister virtues of sympathy, charity, and pity, transcend the wound to our pride; we do not harbor any grudge; we feel no bitterness or ill-will.

If our motivation is Christian, then we believe in forgiving those who sincerely repent, regardless of the enormity of their crime. We hate the sin but love the sinner, believing that all souls are equally precious and that no one is beyond redemption. The model, of course, is Christ, who said of those who persecuted him "Forgive them, Lord, for they know not what they do." Even in a secular ethic, of course, we can practice the virtue of forgiveness, motivated by basic human kindness and a generosity of spirit. Oddly enough, we become psychologically healthier ourselves, while those who keep licking their wounds only prevent them from healing.

One danger in forgiveness lies in forgiving too readily, because this can show a lack of self-respect. It could indicate that we believe ourselves deserving of mistreatment, that the person who harmed us was justified because we merited punishment. Such motivation does not constitute true forgiveness, for it stems from low self-esteem and a weakness of character. It prevents us from recognizing the extent of the harm done to us and our right to fair treatment. An opposite danger lies in forgiving our enemies because they are thought inconsequential and their attack therefore trivial. They do not matter enough to take seriously; and because the person is beneath contempt, forgiving them costs us nothing. Here forgiveness is based on not esteeming the other.

Most virtue ethicists maintain that, before forgiveness is granted, offenders should admit their wrongdoing, show contrition, and promise to mend their ways. If we let them off easily, they will never learn their lesson, have a change of heart, or dedicate themselves to improving. To absolve offenders who have not pledged to reform will only serve to reinforce their behavior; we may be feeding a cancer rather than excising it. Therefore, in order to forgive people, it is important to extract a promise from them to do better in the future.

Fairness. The fair-minded person acts to ensure that everyone receives their just due. This can include benefits, rights, punishment, or rewards, but it must be meted out in an impartial way. Instead of exploiting others for personal gain, the fair individual is even-handed and tries to practice the virtue of justice—even if it entails personal loss.

For example, it would not be playing fair for male legislators to deny the vote to women, even if this might increase their chances of reelection. Similarly, it would be unfair to give black offenders stiffer sentences than whites. It would be unfair to locate toxic dumpsites in low-income areas (ecological discrimination), to pay people on a different scale for doing the same work, or to dismiss employees because of their age or disability when it does not affect their job performance.

Of course, special treatment for certain groups may sometimes be warranted, but such differentials must be consistent with fairness and not a function of bias or self-interest. Treating people equitably does not always mean treating them equally but in accordance with the dictates of fairness. That could mean preferential treatment in hiring for minorities who have been disadvantaged; they are not starting even. In a race we might let a handicapped person start early in order to equalize his chances of winning and make the contest fair.

In general, fairness depends upon a spirit of justice, one that respects other people as equally worthy of regard and does not violate their rights.

Compassion. The compassionate person is one who feels sympathy for those who are suffering as a result of some misfortune. Furthermore, compassion carries with it the desire to ease their pain and to enable them to resume an enjoyable life. Because of tenderness and empathy, people feel sorry for those in need, identifying with their situation.

Some hard-nosed philosophers, such as Thomas Hobbes, claim that we help people in distress in the hope that, if the shoe were on the other foot, they would help us. And some writers claim that we actually enjoy other people's suffering; for example, Edmund Burke (1729–1727) and William Hazlitt (1778–1830):

> I am convinced that we have a degree of delight, and that no small one, in the real misfortunes and pains of others. There is no spectacle we so eagerly pursue, as that of some uncommon and grievous calamity (Burke).

> Why do we always read the accounts in the newspapers of dreadful fires and shocking murders? [Because] love of mischief, love of cruelty is as natural to human beings as is sympathy (Hazlitt).

But compassion seems more deeply rooted in human nature than cruelty or self-interest. As the economic theorist Adam Smith (1723–1790) writes,

> How selfish soever man may be supposed, there are evidently some principles in his nature, which interest him in the fortune of others, and render their happiness necessary to him, though he derive nothing from it than the pleasure of seeing it. Of this kind is pity or compassion, the emotion which we feel for the misery of others, when we either see it, or are made to conceive it in a very lively manner. That we often derive sorrow from the sorrow of others, is a matter of fact too obvious to require any instances to prove it; for this sentiment, like all the other original passions of human nature, is by no means confined to the virtuous and humane, though they perhaps may feel it with the most exquisite sensibility. The greatest ruffian, the most hardened violator of the laws of society, is not altogether without it.[4]

Compassion, then, may be a natural inclination as well as a matter of recognizing a responsibility. Our feelings impel us to help those who are suffering, and our conscience plagues us if we ignore their distress. Its opposite is malice, the desire to deliberately inflict pain on another, and this characterizes the worst of human reactions. At times, all of us have experienced meanness and have felt satisfaction at the suffering of others, especially if they have done us some wrong, but for most people these are passing emotions and not part of their general attitude. The fact that we are ashamed of our malice shows that we regard it as a vice, just as we treat compassion as a moral virtue.

Honesty. Honest people can be characterized as sincere, frank, and genuine, with traits of integrity and trustworthiness; they can be relied upon to keep their word. In their behavior they are not disposed to lie, cheat, or steal, or to practice deception by distorting or withholding the truth. They do not act under false pretenses or in fraudulent ways, they do not mislead people or behave hypocritically, and they avoid all unscrupulous or devious methods, functioning in an open and straightforward manner. In short, honest people are truthful in their social interactions because of a decent character.

Honesty with regard to property is especially important in our society since people are entitled to the goods they have legally acquired. To steal them means appropriating to ourselves someone else's belongings, thereby depriving the owner of the fruits of his labor. The thief did not earn the property, but appropriated what someone else earned, which is what makes theft wrong.

Truthfulness toward others is also a critical part of honesty, since lying harms both the individual and society. People who lie invariably lose a certain self-respect. They have violated their own integrity, which is their internal standard of decency, and they feel ashamed at letting themselves down. Liars are usually afraid to tell the truth, and they cannot help but realize their own weakness. This is why "liar" is such a stinging charge: the person is being called a coward. In addition, the person who is deceived is treated as an obstacle to overcome rather than someone with full human status who deserves to be told the truth. In Kantian terms, the person is being used as a means rather than an end, and therefore becomes an object, deprived of human dignity. For this reason people feel humiliated when they realize they have been lied to.

With regard to society as a whole, lying and deceit tend to break down the fabric of mutual trust that is necessary for social interaction. We expect people to be honest in what they say, and if lying becomes prevalent then society is significantly damaged. Distrust and suspicion can poison relations between people in business, government, the media, politics, and even the family. Advertising is sometimes criticized on just these grounds: that the exaggerated claims, distortions, half-truths, appeals to vanity, small print, misleading free offers, and false images are destructive of social trust. Such advertising is particularly harmful to children, for it is publicly accepted dishonesty.

Lying, incidentally, is not saying what is false but stating the opposite of what we believe to be true. Salman Rushdie in *Satanic Verses* tells of a patient who was due to be released from a psychiatric hospital. However, the doctors still questioned his sanity, so they gave him a lie detector test and asked him whether he was Napoleon. The man answered "No," but the polygraph showed he was lying. That is, although he gave the correct answer, he was lying because he believed he was Napoleon. In the same way, a false statement is not necessarily a lie; it could be an honest mistake.

Many other virtues could be cited—courage, determination, respect, curiosity, tolerance, patience, perseverance, kindness, temperance, industry, ambition, frugality, prudence, gentleness, modesty, sensitivity, trustworthiness, loyalty, friendliness, and so forth—but the four virtues discussed are a fair representation of this approach to ethics.

D. FEMINIST VIRTUE ETHICS

In describing the difference between virtue ethics and most other theories, we discussed the emphasis on rights, obligations, and autonomy that characterizes most traditional approaches. The ethical theories of Plato, Bentham, and Kant in particular apply broad principles and reasoned responses to moral issues. Their schemes were constructed in terms of maxims and rules, using deductions that were strict and sometimes mathematical. Objective judgments were made as to what was worthwhile and what was worthless, and these judgments were tested and defended with proof and logic.

Feminists see these systems as a characteristically male approach to ethics in which correct principles, duties, and moral laws are all-important. By contrast, they see the emphasis on virtue as embodying a more female perspective, especially the values of caring, nurture, relationships, cooperation, love, community, openness, and trust.

Feminist ethics is based not on rational systems of thought, but on more subtle, diffuse, and empathetic modes of understanding. Feminist philosophers prefer a collaborative approach to ethics, hoping for a compromise on ethical differences that all factions can accept. They want mutual agreement, the resolutions of conflict that takes every party's interest into account. Ethics, they maintain, is a matter of finding not the right answer but an acceptable one that everyone can live with. Everyone has a right to representation, so questions of who is correct pale beside the need for cooperative strategies.

In short, the argument goes, men function competitively, women cooperatively; men use rational arguments, women prefer their inner feelings; men operate in terms of general rules, women according to their experience; men talk about their duties, women specific situations; men want action based on logic, women want understanding of their circumstances; and men refer to principles, women to humane values that emerge from personal interaction. Men value culture, women nature; men trust their minds, women their bodies; men are driven by principles, women respond to people; men prefer the mechanical, women the organic; and men function in terms of goals, women earthly satisfaction.

Personal Caring Rather Than Moral Rules

Carol Gilligan, a developmental psychologist, is one of the most influential figures in the feminist movement, and her book *In a Different Voice* describes a more female-centered morality founded on caring, attachment to others, and personal connectedness. She writes,

> The conception of morality as concerned with the activity of care, centers moral development around the understanding of responsibility and relationships, just as the conception of morality as fairness ties moral development to the understanding of rights and rules.[5]

Most feminist writers agree, rejecting the detached, impartial, cerebral ethic in favor of a personal, contextual, emotional approach that allows the free play of moral sentiments in particular circumstances. For example, Nel Noddings rejects objective principles such as truth-telling and promise-keeping in favor of a situation-based compassion; Virginia Held stresses the importance of birthing, caretaking, and family relations; and Annette Baier emphasizes the virtues of sympathy and compromise as particularly female approaches.

Let us examine two major virtues championed by feminist ethics.

Caring and Nurture. The preeminent virtue for many feminist writers is caring about and caring for another person. This is applied particularly to people who are dependent, such as children or the elderly, the sick, the injured, the disabled, and generally the vulnerable members of society. Caring implies that we have genuine concern for other people and want to be supportive of them; we empathize and try to help those in pain. According to feminist ethics, we should respond directly to someone's needs with sympathetic understanding, encouragement, and assistance; our attention demonstrates that the person matters to us.

This means that women's traditional mothering role is honored as well as broadened. For too long women's private function of nurturing has been undervalued because of men's public role of governance; nevertheless, it is at least equally important. This bias may have an economic base because women's labor is largely unpaid, whether as mothers, homemakers, or workers in the fields. A woman's role has been as caregiver, providing physical nourishment and psychological comfort to her family as well as practicing charity in her community. As Peta Bowden states, mothering has "the preeminent role in the creation of new persons, in shaping their language and culture, and developing their morality, as well as providing a stock of memories of caring on which they can draw in their ethical practices." To nurture children so that they are warm and sympathetic in turn is a major ethical accomplishment. Nursing also falls within the context of care-giving, Bowden writes, but "in terms of this reproductive and creative potential, mothering is the most fundamental of caring relations."[6] Nel Noddings and Virginia Held also identify mothering as the central paradigm for the virtue of caring.

Relationships. Personal relationships also hold an important place in feminist ethics, including the relationships of love and friendship, either within or between the sexes. Lesbians point out that we fall in love with people, not genders. Human beings are involved in a myriad of social interactions, many of which involve recognition, attachment, and mutual support based on warm affection. The self, in fact, is largely formed through such interdependent networks within society, rather than developing in an independent way. We depend on one another, and our relationships heavily determine the kind of person we become. Therefore our emotional connections with others must be appreciated and cultivated for the full flowering of the person. Even the development of language, which is a major part of our humanness, depends on social interaction; we become civilized, in fact, through communication within a culture.

Relationships are therefore vital to our well-being, and should be treated with respect as moral values. In both friendship and love we share intimate parts of ourselves, trusting the other not to take advantage of our vulnerability. We rely upon their affection to create a refuge, and within that safe haven, expose our dreams, shameful secrets, and hidden weaknesses. We look for validation and confirmation of ourselves in other people, and we increase our growth and self-understanding once we have discarded the need for self-protection. This can occur through intimate conversation or physical closeness, but as both Plato and Aristotle declare, strong relationships seem essential to our flourishing.

Many feminists claim that women in their friendships are capable of more intense relationships than men. Whether for social or biological reasons, men are protective, competitive, and defensive with each other, while women can be more open, responsive, and supportive. To men, the public display of emotions is viewed as weakness, whereas to women, tears and laughter are socially acceptable. Women find it easier to bond together and relate to communities, whereas men can feel compromised by dependence and are isolated in their independence. Men are concerned with power, will, and self-control, but women can cooperate and share experiences without feeling personally threatened.

Women's relationships are therefore emblematic of the feelings and sentiments that, feminists say, should govern our behavior instead of the masculine ideals of action and reason. Male philosophers have claimed that morality entails impartiality, but feminists prefer a personal engagement that involves our emotions.

A Critical Assessment

1. Virtue ethics has a number of attractive features, but one pervasive criticism has been that virtue may not be sufficient to guarantee ethical behavior.

    For example, by all accounts Lieutenant Colonel George A. Custer was a courageous man who died bravely at the Battle of the Little Bighorn in 1876 along with 264 of his men. Despite his virtue, however, he acted wrongly in trying to crush the Sioux and Cheyenne peoples. His tactics were also poor in deploying his troops for a frontal assault with two flanking columns of cavalry, and he underestimated the Indian forces, which numbered over two thousand warriors. But aside from these mistakes, the justice of Custer's cause is questionable, regardless of the excellence of his character. Should the United States have been trying to destroy Native Americans or should we have shared the land, cohabited with the Indians in a cooperative, mutually beneficial way? As Immanuel Kant remarked, "courage, resolution, and constancy of purpose, as qualities of temperament, are without doubt good and desirable in many respects, but they can also be extremely bad and hurtful." In other words, a great deal depends on the application of the virtue.

Other examples of this point could be found: Although we might admire someone for being ambitious and industrious, that person might be working hard at being a first-rate drug dealer; a sincere and honest person could feel impelled to tell terrorists the truth about building weapons of mass destruction; and a tolerant and generous person could invite serial killers to Thanksgiving dinner, ending up with his family destroyed. That is to say, being a virtuous person is not enough; virtue must be accompanied by practical understanding and moral knowledge as to what is right and wrong—according to rules of conduct.

Some virtue philosophers have tried to answer this charge by saying that the virtues must work in concert. Courage must be accompanied by reflection, honesty by compassion, and generosity by prudence. However, the virtues can conflict when they are combined, and we can still be left without moral guidance as to what action is called for. A courageous and reflective person might still feel, as Custer did, that he has a duty to annihilate the Native Americans.

Various virtues, in fact, can be in conflict. Bravery might be incompatible with caution; loyalty with impartiality and honesty; toughness with sensitivity and kindness. How can we tell which virtue is overriding?

2. A related problem is that the virtues are so broad and abstract that they may not help us in making specific moral decisions. Suppose, for example, that a couple must decide whether a pregnancy should be terminated by abortion. They both have fine characters, sincere, fair, and compassionate, but that may not be enough to make a decision. The mother's health might be at risk if she carried the baby to term, and there are other children to be considered. The father might be burdened already with debt and severe financial problems. On the other hand, the fetus or baby is innocent and utterly defenseless; it should not be harmed and might have a right to life. In this situation, what would sincerity and fairness dictate? The couple is caring, but which parties should they care about most?

Without some moral principles as a guide, no fair solution can be found. Perhaps Kant's moral laws should be invoked, or Mill's consequentialist ethic; but whatever system is used, the couple's virtue alone is not sufficient to solve the dilemma.

Another consequence of the absence of principles is that moral decisions could be made in an arbitrary and capricious way. Instead of using factors such as rights, obligations, justice, merits, and responsibilities, the virtue ethicist considers only the character of the agent. The deciding factor in virtue ethics is how a virtuous person feels about an issue, and that is an unreliable criterion for moral behavior. It certainly could not be used as a basis for legislation.

Perhaps we should not rely on moral feelings if we can be guided by a structure of principles; the risk may not be worth taking. Although ethical systems can be legalistic and fail to capture the texture of decision-making, that does not mean all rules should be discarded. Such an approach would place too much emphasis on sentiments, which do not always guide us correctly.

3. A very different criticism of virtue ethics is made from the standpoint of psychology. Some psychologists contend that what philosophers call virtues embedded in our character are really dispositions of our personality. For example, some people have a tendency toward kindness, others are brave, and still others are truthful by nature. These dispositions can be molded by various circumstances, but the essential elements are present in the person.

If this is true, and traits such as tolerance, patience, and curiosity are essentially characteristics of our personality, similar to shyness, practicality, and warmth, then that is not a moral accomplishment. We cannot praise children who are friendly when they are simply outgoing by nature, or recommend the goal of happiness to those who are naturally cheerful (much less to melancholy people). Aristotle's virtue of moderation may be nothing more than his own tendency to be prudent and cautious. On this interpretation, what we thought were ethical virtues become descriptions of personality types, and virtue ethics only commends those whose traits coincide with virtues.

4. The feminist version of virtue ethics comes in for its share of criticism as well. Serious questions have been raised about the elevation of circumstances, emotion, and personal experience, and the rejection of moral rules and principles, consistency, and impartiality as male bias.

Although ethical theories have tended in the past to neglect the importance of context and feeling, that oversight does not justify rejecting moral standards altogether. No matter how much we try to focus on the particular circumstances, we find the similarities between situations allow them to be grouped under common principles. Regardless of the extent to which we depend on personal feelings, external rules of behavior must also be considered, or our decision will not be fair. Even extreme feminists want rules about equal pay for equal work, suffrage for all citizens, rules against sexual harassment, and so forth. Furthermore, feminists would want impartiality in the law to prevent discrimination, and consistency so civil rights are guaranteed for all people. Relying on the emotions that are generated in a specific context can produce intolerance and injustice, sexism and racism. In short, moral principles seem an indispensable part of any ethical system, protecting it from unfairness.

Some feminists believe so strongly in the contextual nature of moral decisions that they embrace an ethical relativism. As one prominent philosopher Martha Nussbaum puts it,

To many current defenders of an ethical approach based on the virtues, the return to the virtues is connected with a turn toward relativism—toward, that is, the view that the only appropriate criteria of ethical goodness are local ones, internal to the traditions and practices of each local society or group that asks itself questions about the good.

However, once again the feminists themselves would want transcultural norms that condemn such practices as clitoral circumcision, pride killings, compulsory child marriage, the immolation of widows on their husband's funeral pyre, and the general subordination of women. Local traditions should not always be respected. Instead, we might prefer the Universal Declaration of Human Rights adopted by the United Nations General Assembly, which asserts minimal values for all human beings on earth. As stated previously, these rights include the right to life, liberty, and security of person; to family and a political voice; to peaceful assembly and religious expression; to work and the ownership of property; and to privacy, health, and education.

5. Feminist ethics can also be criticized for dismissing a considerable amount of ethics on the grounds that it reflects male attitudes. Such a charge commits the fallacy of *argumentum ad hominem* or argument to the person (circumstantial). In this case the fallacy lies in thinking

that, because men formulated an ethic of principles, it was therefore formulated because they were men; that since a man said it, he must reflect attitudes and biases characteristic of men.

The mistake consists in dismissing a theory because of its origins, and assuming that ideas mirror only the group to which the originator belongs. We would commit this fallacy if we said, for example, that Mary is only concerned with animal rights because she responds to her feminine feelings rather than thinking rationally. Mary may in fact believe that animals should be treated humanely because they are sentient beings, that they have an emotional life and feel pain. We must not confuse the message with the messenger, but judge a theory on its own merits. Even if men or women have something to gain from taking a position, that does not mean they take the position in order to gain something.

Various criticisms can be made of virtue ethics, but it does offer a fresh perspective to the contemporary ethical debate. Perhaps a blend of conduct ethics and character ethics is needed, for right conduct flows from fine character traits, and a virtuous character expresses itself in ethical principles.

REVIEW QUESTIONS

1. What are the differences between virtue ethics and the more customary approaches to ethics?
2. How does Plato's list of virtues differ from that of Aristotle? Do they both favor the use of reason?
3. According to St. Thomas Aquinas, what are the principal virtues and the principal sins? What is the role of self-control?
4. Describe some of the virtues stressed in contemporary virtue ethics, including fairness, honesty, and caring. What other virtues are considered important?
5. Explain some of the criticisms of the feminist version of virtue ethics. What is your own judgment of the feminist position?

11

EXISTENTIALISM

The philosophy of existentialism has had a colorful and contentious history; it is hard to ignore and in fact demands a judgment. From the time of its inception in the nineteenth century to its flowering (like a thistle) in the mid-twentieth century, it has excited a following among the young and acted as a lightning rod for establishment thinkers. Critics have preached against existentialism for promoting moral anarchy and rampant individualism, for making social alienation, malaise, and disaffection something fashionable. It is accused of extolling the perverse and sordid dimension of society, for highlighting the underside of life. Some writers have called it a blend of Nordic melancholy and Parisian pornography. One remarked that the French are not content to let their sewers flow underground; they must rechannel them along the Left Bank.

Yet despite criticism from church pulpits and college lecterns, the impact of existentialism has persisted, and it must be considered one of the major movements of the modern age. The American pragmatist William James may have been right about the classic stages of a theory's career: "First . . . a new theory is attacked as absurd; then it is admitted to be true, but obvious and insignificant; finally it is seen to be so important that its adversaries claim that they themselves discovered it."[1] Existentialism seems to have undergone each stage, and even though the major figures of the movement have died, the ideas permeate the intellectual climate of our times.

The Danish philosopher Sören Kierkegaard is usually taken as the founder of theistic existentialism, although Blaise Pascal prefigured a number of his themes[2] and German philosopher Friedrich Nietzsche is regarded as the founding father of the atheistic branch. In the twentieth century the list of existential philosophers includes Martin Heidegger (1889–1976), Karl

Jaspers (1883–1969), Gabriel Marcel (1889–1973), and, of course, Jean-Paul Sartre (1905–1980), the dean of existentialism. Literary expression in novels, short stories, and essays has always been central to the movement, for example, the writings of Franz Kafka (1883–1924), Fedor Dostoyevsky (1821–1881), Rainer Maria Rilke (1875–1926), André Gide (1869–1951), Jean Genet (1910–1986), and Albert Camus.[3] Together these philosophers, poets, and novelists have altered our notion of what it is to be a human being.

A. THE HUMAN CONDITION

Rather than beginning at the level of abstract theory and deriving the place of man in the total scheme of things, the existentialist prefers to start philosophizing from the perspective of the concrete person in a specific situation. What does it mean to be in existence as a human being, the existentialist asks, or, more specifically, what is the experience of being alive and conscious at this particular time and place? Without reason, we are thrown into the world, and once we realize we exist, we wonder about the condition in which we find ourselves.

This is the proper starting point for understanding human life, not via a materialistic Marxism that views people as economic units, or through Freudian lenses that see Oedipus complexes and symptoms of repressed feelings, or through Platonism that treats the Idea of a human being as more real than any actual person. To the existentialist, the world is not the shadow of ideas; rather, ideas reflect a tangible reality. We must begin with our experience of existence as it presents itself to our awareness and not think of ourselves as detached observers, contemplating life from a remote vantage point. "Existence is not something which can be thought from a distance," Sartre wrote; "it overwhelms you brusquely . . . it weighs heavily on your heart like a fat, loathsome beast."[4]

Anxiety and Alienation

The phenomenon of anxiety can illustrate the point, and explanations of this state are a common feature of existentialism. To understand anxiety both Kierkegaard and Heidegger contrast it with the emotion of fear. When we are afraid, we can specific the source of our fear. We may be afraid of a gun, of falling off a ledge, or of being struck by lightning. "In fear," as Kierkegaard wrote, "we are always in the presence of this or that determinate being which threatens us in this or that determinate manner," and once we are able to name the threat, we gain a certain control over it. In anxiety, however, nothing can be specified as the cause. There does not seem to be any particular reason why we are anxious, yet we feel profoundly uneasy, as if we were living under a sword of Damocles, as though there were some impending doom. Heidegger says that if we are asked what we are anxious about, we will reply that it is really nothing.

But this answer is revealing. Our anxiety may be over nothing; that is, the possibility of nothingness, of no longer being in the world. In anxiety we confront the terror at being extinguished, snuffed out, realizing that the world offers no protection against the void awaiting us. It is the state, as Tillich described it, of a being aware of not being, feeling abandoned and helpless to avert our ultimate annihilation. We become conscious of the emptiness that preceded our birth and that will succeed our death. In short, we acknowledge our mortality.

In facing nothingness, rather than pretending to ourselves that we will live forever, we come to terms with our limited time on earth. Instead of deceiving ourselves and living in "bad faith," people can choose to exist in an authentic way. Although we may lie to others for their good, we should never lie to ourselves, and the cardinal sin to the existentialist is denying the truth of our extinction, for then we deprive ourselves of the chance to be fully alive.

The confrontation with nonexistence can jolt people from their repetitive, routine lives, making them aware of their finite state; they can then utilize the life available to them to become something before they are nothing. Non-being can impel people to maximize their being within the temporal constraints that reality has imposed. Anxiety, nothingness, and existence are, therefore, intimately connected, for as Camus writes, "There is no sun without shadow, and it is essential to know the night."[5]

Alienation refers to a division where formerly there was rapport. In our contemporary mentality we feel a gap between ourselves and various parts of our experience. We feel alienated from government, which is "us" in a democracy and yet seems "them," separate and remote. At the same time we realize that it exercises power over our lives. We also feel alienated from nature, and although we are animals we think of animals as different from us and no longer feel at home in natural surroundings. Whether we go to the woods or the beach, we bring with us the civilized comforts of tents, mosquito repellent, and cell phones. Furthermore, we feel alienated from God. Unlike previous centuries, God seems distant, inaccessible, almost withdrawn, not a vital presence. If we have problems we turn to a friend or therapist, but we are less likely to pray for guidance. We are even alienated from other people, isolated in front of computers, separated in speeding cars, or not eating our meals with others around a table. Once we recognize these forms of alienation, we can act to achieve greater unity and harmony with our surroundings.

The analysis of each of these psychological states yields similar insights concerning the human condition, and the existentialist explores their ramifications, not to wallow in despondency but to stimulate people to a more intense existence.

B. EXISTENCE PRECEDES ESSENCE

By beginning at the level of human beings in the world and confronting our psychological reality, we are led to a central tenet of existential philosophy. Since our mode of being is such that we are aware of our eventual non-being, we are in a position to achieve fulfillment in the time we have; we can act to truly exist.

In fact, we must act because failing to do so means failing to achieve humanness. What makes us human comes about as a result of our concrete decisions and action. We are "the sum of our actions" and "none of our non-actions" as Sartre says, and we create ourselves through the commitments we make. Our actions do not follow from our character but our character follows from our actions. In choosing, we define ourselves and bear responsibility for the type of person we become.

Sartre develops this point by contrasting the mode of being of objects with that of human beings. Objects possess their essential characteristics when they come into existence; the qualities that identify them are fully formed at the moment they come into being, and the objects will not become anything further or different during their lifespan. A paper knife, to use Sartre's example, is present in the craftsman's mind before it is brought into existence, and once it exists it will never develop into anything other than what is meant by a paper knife. Human beings, on the other hand, first exist and then fill out their essence by their choices and actions; their existence precedes their essence. People do not possess any prior, innate qualities but become individuals by what they do once they exist. We can think of the characteristics of a paper knife without it existing, but we cannot conceive of a person's nature until he or she exists and acts to become someone.[6]

In making these assertions, the existentialist presupposes that human beings have the power to decide their lives, that we are creatures with free will; we can choose the kind of person we want to become, and can become the person we choose. They therefore oppose all forms of determinism as applied to people; only objects function according to cause and effect. Existentialists also reject all theories of a fixed human nature, for to regard people as possessing a specific nature when they come into being would render them as objects whose essence precedes its existence. Human beings are nothing other than the ensemble of their actions; we do not manifest the working out of any inherent nature. "Man is the future of man," Sartre declares, and history does not teach us anything about the human race since man is constantly creating himself anew in every age; whatever generalization we make about humankind is contradicted by the "choice of themselves" of the next generation. Collectively, we define human nature at a particular point in time.

Sartre even based his atheism on these grounds, arguing that if God made man then human beings would resemble paper knives with their essence already created in the mind of God. It is only without the notion of God that we can be truly human.

To the existentialist, then, existence precedes essence, and humanness is not a biological fact but a task that is accomplished through decisions and commitments. We achieve humanness by appropriating the freedom to choose our identity and acting to create our own selves. Simone de Beauvoir takes it a step further, maintaining that no one is born a woman but becomes one through accepting a gender role.

In attempting to understand the human situation, and to resolve the various tensions of existence, the existentialists gravely distrust the methods of empiricism and rationalism as well as the conventional morality that is based upon them. In this respect, existentialism resembles virtue ethics. The empiricist, using the techniques of scientific method, is thought to remain outside the events and objects that are being investigated. They are like a person who loses a watch on a dark road and walks to a streetlight to look for it. External attributes are all that can be learned through empirical research and even then, only those external features that can be quantified. The existentialist prefers to seek discovery in a sympathetic way. With this approach one can enter into the *eidos* or quiddity of whatever experience presents itself to consciousness.

Phenomenology

This method carries the formal name of phenomenology, and Edmund Husserl (1859–1938) is generally credited as its founder. Various existentialists have formulated its meaning in different ways: Gabriel Marcel, for example, regards it as concentration on the primacy of experience over pure thought[7]; and Heidegger defines it as the analysis of the way "being" manifests itself to consciousness.[8] In general, the phenomenological method seems to be the intuitive apprehension of the fundamental nature of whatever is encountered by our consciousness. Instead of entertaining dogmatic assumptions about objects we experience, or categorizing them according to their practical function, historical associations, or scientific classification, we plunge directly to the center of phenomena and achieve understanding from within. The inessential layers of use, history, and so forth must be set aside (bracketed) so that the reality of the thing-in-itself is revealed. A landscape, for instance, is not real estate, the site of a decisive battle, or an igneous lava intrusion, but that experiential reality that appears to our consciousness as a self-enclosed phenomenon with its own inner being.

Sartre, in his novel *Nausea*,[9] describes the principal character Roquentin entering a room and feeling something cold and hard in his hand. It is the doorknob, an object we normally do not notice. We habitually treat it as a means for opening a door, but Roquentin regards it as something in itself; he cannot dismiss it as means. He experiences the same reaction to a glass, which is usually ignored, a vessel for carrying liquid to our lips, and to a skimming stone, which suddenly is not a stone but that gritty, dense, moist object in his fingers. All of these objects suddenly demand attention as though they were in picture frames; they are phenomena in themselves with a unique mode of being.

Various insights are thought to accrue from the employment of the phenomenological method. In moral philosophy, for example, contrition was analyzed and found to be more than feeling sorry for doing something wrong, for even after one compensated for the harm, the feeling of contrition remains. More deeply understood, contrition means feeling badly about being the kind of person who could perform an awful action. In a similar manner, Max Scheler (1874–1928) concluded, with regard to human goals, that actions are never directed toward pleasure but toward values. We recognize values in the world and pursue them, with pleasure as an emotional accompaniment. Dietrich von Hildebrand (1889–1977) in his investigation of sexual purity claims it is achieved through sensitivity to sexual attraction; insensitivity to sex is a defect in itself. People who are not moved by sexual desire cannot claim to be pure even if they have not had sexual relations. In all of these cases the phenomenologist attempts to understand experience from within rather than from without. As the poet Gerard Manley Hopkins wrote, we should try to comprehend the "inscape" of things.

The existentialist uses the phenomenological method to understand the various categories of nothingness, being, freedom, authenticity, commitment, and the like. They charge that the empirical approach does not descend within the object and fails to engage the inquirer who is neutral, alienated, and frozen toward the object of inquiry. In the same way, rationalism is superficial because it dismisses emotion, feeling, and the affective states as inferior. The rationalist is like the "poor definition cutter with his logical scissors." We should try to provoke a personal response by using a poetic style, which is why so much of existentialism is cast in literary form, and why existentialists feel contempt for academic philosophy. A professor, Sartre has said, is someone who professes that someone else suffered. In place of rational objectivity, the existentialist wants to stimulate our emotional grasp of the truth through the direct arousal of our feelings.

We also relinquish our freedom if we are ruled by reason, for then we cannot think or do as we please but only as reason dictates. We become intimidated by the need for consistency, reasonableness, and coherent thinking, and believe we must justify our ideas before some imaginary tribunal sitting in judgment inside us. From an existential perspective, we must liberate ourselves from the straitjacket of reason if we are to lead a full existence. In fact, we should be free to behave rationally or irrationally, just as we like. To contradict ourselves is a great relief, so refreshing, as Camus wrote in his play *Caligula*. And as Dostoyevsky said in *Notes from the Underground*: "What sort of free will is left when we come to tables and arithmetic, when it will all be a case of two times two makes four? Two times two makes four even without my will. As if free will meant that!"[10] Reason must always be subordinate to freedom because it is through freely chosen actions that human beings develop their essence and live a full life. If we defer to logic, we become machines not people.

The existential novelist André Gide went so far in his championing of emotion as to advocate unpremeditated, spontaneous action as the highest form of behavior. The "gratuitous act," as Gide called it, is truest to the person and expressive of the genuine self. It does not arise from intellectual considerations as to which alternative is most advantageous, which offers the smallest risk, or even what consequences may follow. Whenever we deliberate, Gide maintains, weighing the pros and cons judiciously, then factors that are not part of our selves begin to dominate our thinking and make the decision for us. Our education, social conventions, prejudices, family beliefs, reading, and so forth are brought into play and become the basis for our choice. For an act to come from us it must be impulsive and spontaneous, without second thoughts, almost without thinking at all; only then are outside influences eliminated. As Gide writes,

> The quickest, the most sudden action seemed to me to be the best. It appeared to me that my action was all the more sincere in that I was sweeping away before it all those considerations with which I attempted to justify it at first. Henceforward, acting haphazardly and without giving myself time to reflect, my slightest actions appear to be more significant since they are no longer reasoned out.[11]

The idea of gratuitous actions is illustrated best in *The Vatican Cellars,* in which Gide portrays a character named Lafcadio who, on an impulse, hurls a fellow passenger out the door of his train compartment. To Gide, even criminal actions are permissible in order to be ourselves; he would not want us to deliberate over the morality of actions any more than we should pause for rational considerations. This would be the extreme position within existentialism, although Dostoyevsky was drawn toward that ultimate assertion of freedom in *Crime and Punishment,* and Nietzsche has told us that "the greatest fruitfulness and the greatest enjoyment of existence is: to live dangerously."[12]

By and large, however, the anti-intellectualism of the existentialists would not be carried that far. Camus's existentialism has a strong humanistic component, Rilke has been compared to St. Francis, and Sartre maintained that we should share our freedom with other people. The existentialists do assert the primacy of emotion over reason, but relatively few would be in favor of total spontaneity, particularly in situations in which harm would result.

The general existential emphasis on the emotions relates to the conviction that the affective part of human beings is the major part and rationality is the outcropping of the mountain of rock. The emotions are also thought to be the medium through which the most essential human communication takes place. It is the way we understand each other, expressing our mutual terrors and profound hopes, and the means by which we project ourselves into the innermost nature of all experience, intuitively grasping its "inscape."

The existentialist, then, favors emotion over reason, subjectivity over objectivity, phenomenology rather than empiricism or rationalism, and the direct experience of human existence instead of abstract theories that deduce man's place in the world. And the existentialist affirms we thereby come to understand the human condition, which is an anguished one, lived with the realization of our impending nonbeing. But the confrontation with nothingness should galvanize us into asserting our freedom and thereby maximize our existence.

C. THE FOUNDING FIGURES

The nineteenth-century origins of existentialism can be traced to Friedrich Nietzsche the iconoclastic German philosopher, and the theologian Sören Kierkegaard, sometimes referred to as a melancholy Dane like Hamlet.

Nietzsche and Kierkegaard

As in the case of Marx, Nietzsche was a philosopher with a hammer who wanted to destroy many of his century's values in order to allow greater achievement for humanity. He deplored mass society, which in his view suppressed the spirit of individuals striving for a higher life; it was a leveling force, imposing mediocre standards upon all people. The tendency of modern society, Nietzsche believed, was to produce an anonymous herd, "one flock and no shepherd," for all independent thought was crushed beneath the weight of public opinion. Outstanding individuals did not dare assume leadership or even speak their minds but were reduced to internal rebellion by the numerical opposition of the masses.

Rather than valuing individual accomplishment, society always prized conformity to the norm, which necessarily means the lowest common denominator, adjustment to the status quo. The goal of mass society is thus to make all the sheep equal, and anyone who is guilty of self-assertion or achieves excellence is stifled. This also suppresses the progress of the human race. If innovative and outstanding individuals were allowed to be heard, the human race would transcend itself; as it was, stagnation and deadness prevailed.

Nietzsche singled out democracy, socialism, and Christianity as destructive forces. Democracy and socialism crushed the vital spirit of humanity because they assume that all people are equal; they should have equal benefits and influence in government. The idea of someone being superior is anathema to their values. Everything must be decided by majority rule, which means that bourgeois morality carries the day. We do not take a vote in order to decide the merits of a work of art or a scientific theory, but oddly enough we allow the masses to decide the social morality under which we live; the conductor does not ask the orchestra whether to have a crescendo but the norms of mediocrity are allowed to rule our daily lives.

Nietzsche criticized Christianity on similar grounds, for it seems in league with everything that is humble. To Nietzsche's mind, Christianity favors humility and self-denial, pacifism, conservatism, and helpfulness. This is a manifestation of "herd morality," founded on weakness rather than strength. Christians are merely excusing their inadequacies, making a virtue of necessity, and transforming faults into virtues. They believe the meek shall inherit the earth because they lack the courage to take the earth. Christianity is the religion of pity, he wrote, and "pity stands opposed to the tonic emotions which heighten our vitality; it has a depressing effect . . . (and) makes suffering contagious. In Christianity the instincts of the subjugated and oppressed come to the fore: here the lowest classes seek their salvation . . . Christian too is mortal enmity against the lords of the earth, against the "noble"—along with a sly, secret rivalry (one leaves them the "body," one wants only the "soul"). Christian, finally, is the hatred of the spirit, of pride, courage, freedom, liberty of the spirit; Christian is the hatred of the senses, of joy in the senses, of joy itself."[13]

Nietzsche thought Christianity is not only anti-vital but diverting in that it drew people's attention away from real issues of human progress. It was a conservative force that asked people to hope for the life to come, not to improve conditions in this life; it was too heavenly-minded to be any earthly good.

In place of the "herd" or "slave morality" promoted by democracy, socialism, and Christianity, Nietzsche advocated a "master morality," at least for the outstanding individuals who had the courage to adopt it. Slave virtues may be fine for the masses who accept their own mediocrity but they must not be allowed to govern the strong, decisive, daring, and creative individuals who are the "masters."

A new ethic must be established, founded on the will to power rather than deference and safety, one that brings about a "transvaluation of all values" or is "beyond good and evil." The masters can transcend conventional morality and, by creating their own code, guide the world out of its lethargy and stagnation.

In effect, Nietzsche advocated a dualistic theory of morals, with one set of values for masters and another for slaves, although he hoped that slaves would eventually be eliminated. For no man is a slave or a master by nature, but only through their cowardice or courage. The master asserts his will and uses his capacity for free action to escape an abject state; he takes the risk of freedom to create himself according to his own lights and raises humanity to a new level.

Master morality was obviously Nietzsche's ideal, and he affirmed it even though turmoil would result. In *The Gay Science* he declares,

> The strongest and most evil spirits have so far advanced humanity the most: they have always rekindled the drowsing passions—all ordered society puts the passions to sleep; they have always reawakened the sense of comparison, of contradiction, of joy in the new, the daring, and the untried. . . . We welcome all signs that a more manly, a warlike, age is about to begin, an age which, above all, will give honor to valor once again. For this age shall prepare the way for one yet higher. To this end we now need many preparatory valorous men who cannot leap into being out of nothing—any more than out of the sand and slime of our present civilization and metropolitanism: men who are bent on seeking for that aspect in all things which must be overcome; men characterized by cheerfulness, patience, unpretentiousness, and contempt for all great vanities . . . men who have their own festivals, their own weekdays, their own periods of mourning, who are accustomed to command with assurance and are no less ready to obey when necessary, in both cases equally proud and serving their own cause; men who are in greater danger, more fruitful, and happier![14]

Nietzsche used the term "*Übermensch*," or "overman," for the perfect master, the true lord of the earth who has overcome his lower self and created a higher mode of being. The overman has drawn strength from man's most basic drive, the will to power, and employing that power, succeeded in reaching a superior state. He is able to elevate humanity to a higher destiny than all previous eras by the force of his efforts and example.

Passages such as these may be inspiring but they have left Nietzsche open to the charge that his doctrines support fascism, and the Nazi party did make use of some of his ideas. By and large, however, Nietzsche's meaning was distorted by the Nazis. For example, he wrote about the "blonde beast," by which he meant lions but it was taken to mean the Nordic, "Aryan" race. Nevertheless, there are parts of Nietzsche's writings that easily lend themselves to a fascist interpretation even though that may not be the main thrust. It is a short step from the notion of a superior class of human beings to the ideal of "the master race."

Nietzsche's notoriety stems from this overemphasis on excellence along with his rejection of God. Religious belief is cowardice and superstition, he thought, which means that we have now killed God by our unbelief. Yet the death of God is not a cause for celebration, because it has been perhaps the greatest dream of mankind. We have killed God, Nietzsche declared in a cryptic metaphor, and we must fill the void created by his absence, assuming responsibility for our own future:

> God is dead. God remains dead. And we have killed him. How shall we, the murderers of all murderers, comfort ourselves? What was holiest and most powerful of all that the world has yet owned has bled to death under our knives . . . Is not the greatness of this deed too great for us? Must not we ourselves become gods simply to seem worthy of it?[15]

The theistic existentialism of Kierkegaard stands in strong contrast to Nietzsche's atheism, but oddly enough the similarities between the two men are more striking than their differences. Nietzsche longed to be a sinner but was an incorrigible saint, and his writing, like that of Kierkegaard, has a decidedly religious tone, especially his *Thus Spake Zarathustra*,[16] and Kierkegaard too criticized his society for its lethargy, conformity, and inauthentic existence. However, Kierkegaard thought the remedy lay in genuine Christian faith rather than in its repudiation.

Kierkegaard's diatribes were directed specifically against the smugness and complacency of his native Denmark, which he considered a microcosm of the world. The religious observance of the people consisted in prosperous membership in an institution, "conventional Churchmanship," as he termed it, rather than an encounter with the living God. The people had substituted the church for religion, and the sense of challenge that Christianity provoked had been lost, for the church itself had become secular and social with little relation to the divine presence.

Kierkegaard had harsh words for the bishop with orders on his chest who urged his followers to renounce the pomp and glory of the world. With this example, we no longer experienced the transcendent behind the temporal, never encountered that fundamental reality on which our lives depend. We are all in the "inescapable presence of God," Kierkegaard wrote, and to confront that fact forces us to a decision as to whether we will lead an authentically Christian life. Being a Christian does not come about automatically at birth, or through baptism, or by church attendance; it is a conscious choice and a lifelong task that calls for spiritual heroism.

Kierkegaard also denounced rational theology as tepid and external, having nothing of the commanding passion of the Gospels. Theology transforms the spiritual impact of Scripture into a network of ideas, casuistic demonstrations of arguments, thereby substituting a detached, technical system for a personal relationship with the Lord. People thus evade their responsibility to decide for or against God; theology intellectualizes the question, leaving it in a limbo of indecision. To Kierkegaard, human beings should live with the constant awareness of being face to face with their maker, naked, guilty, blind, and awaiting judgment. Only then will we come to live an authentic existence.

A central part of Kierkegaard's philosophy involves three stages through which human beings can pass in their ascent toward God. The aesthetic stage is most common; most people remain there all their lives, for it means experiencing a variety of the world's pleasures. Here we just want to enjoy life, and so we repeatedly create cycles of distractions. We adopt a "method of repetition," which consists in changing our jobs, our residences, our friends, our appearance, and so forth in the pursuit of new modes of enjoyment. But we derive less and less satisfaction from our experiences. Our immunity to pleasure grows, so we escalate the pace, becoming frenetic in our search for freshness and variety. We sustain ourselves, Kierkegaard says, like a stone skimming across a pond that must sink beneath the waves once the dance is done.

At this point we descend into despair, and everything then depends on how we despair. If we redouble our efforts to obtain enjoyment, we will inevitably return to a despairing state, and this will become the pattern of our lives. However, we have the ability to leap upward and attain the ethical stage of being.

Here we abandon our self-involved, hedonistic attitude and make an ethical commitment to the welfare of others. We join causes and become involved in movements that promote social progress. Our aim is to improve conditions in the world and to establish freedom and justice for our fellow human beings. We believe in the perfectibility of man, and invest our energies trying to achieve that perfection.

Gradually, however, our enthusiasm begins to wane as we encounter opposition. We discover a perverseness in people that resists being improved, as well as finding a devil sitting inside of us: we resent a life of self-sacrifice. In short, we come to realize the depth of evil in others and in ourselves that makes the moral ideal impossible to attain. And with this realization we experience the debilitating states of penitence, remorse, and guilt that, Kierkegaard says, take the heart out of a person.

Again, everything then depends on our response: whether we throw ourselves into ethical programs with even greater dedication, or decide to risk the higher, religious stage. The first is doomed to repeated failure, the second constitutes our salvation.

In the religious stage, ethical considerations are left behind and we place our trust wholly in God. We no longer look to justify or explain our actions in terms of morality but only want to come into direct relationship with the Lord. Our sole desire is to follow his will without qualification.

In seeking understanding of God, we do not consult the established church or the interpretations of theologians, but strive to experience his immediate presence in our lives. And once we hear the voice of God, that becomes authoritative, transcending our concern for an enjoyable life or any good of humanity. This is the commitment of faith that surpasses the demands of morality or even rationality. The alternatives are to trust in God or rely on the rules of man; it is an either/or choice of this world or the next.

Kierkegaard uses the Abraham and Isaac story as his paradigm of the truly religious life. According to the biblical account, God commands Abraham to sacrifice his son Isaac on Mount Moriah, and without faltering, Abraham prepares to carry out God's wishes. He does not ask himself whether the command is right or reasonable, whether he is hearing imaginary voices or the genuine word of God. He simply acts in accordance with his primary responsibility to God. Rather than thinking that God cannot command an irrational act, thereby lessening God by logic, or claiming that he cannot order anything immoral, thereby limiting God in terms of morality, Abraham accepts the supremacy of God without question.

This, to Kierkegaard, represents the paradoxical nature of faith, that it demands complete trust even in the face of an absurd command such as "Kill your son." For the infinite to come into being in time through the person of Christ is also absurd, as is the doctrine of the Trinity that three persons are one, but each must be accepted if we are to follow faith. To question God's word would be to place reason over religion and betray our faith in God. In order to be a "knight of faith" in the manner of Abraham, we must risk everything and experience the anguish of our commitment, for in this way we overcome despair and lead the fullest existence possible.

D. MODERN EXPRESSION

Nietzsche's philosophy is expressed most fully in *Thus Spake Zarathustra*, Kierkegaard's position in *Concluding Unscientific Postscript*, and these books together with Heidegger's *Being and Time* sound the principal themes of existentialism. The conclusions and recommendations of these existentialists can be markedly different but their style, concerns, and criticisms are much the same. The ideas of Jean-Paul Sartre, on the other hand, are expressed through plays and novels as well as in his philosophic works, especially *Being and Nothingness*. We want to examine some of Sartre's main ideas, although we cannot do justice to the full range of his thought.

Jean-Paul Sartre

As cited previously, Sartre distinguished between the mode of being of objects and that of human beings: the essence of objects precedes their existence, whereas for man the reverse is true. He also separates the two by saying that things exist in an *en-soi* (in itself) state, while human existence is always *pour-soi* (for itself). By these phrases Sartre means that objects are dense and integrated, packed and whole; they are complete in themselves and lack nothing. We can never say that an object should be more than it is, that a rock ought to be a better rock or that a frog lacks something as a frog. However, this can always be said of humans because people have gaps in their being and are less than they could be. Man always exists for himself in that he is perpetually setting projects which will make him more nearly complete.

The main gap within human beings lies between their selves and their awareness of themselves; that is, between people as subject and as object, the "I" and the "me." Nothing really separates us, but it is an everlasting nothing that can never be bridged. There is the self, the self contemplating the self, and worse still, the self that is aware of the self contemplating the self, ad infinitum. The schisms multiply in direct proportion to the individual's awareness. The only way in which this division can be healed is through abandoning self-consciousness, but since that is the main constituent of humanness, a person can become complete only by becoming less than human. Therefore, people will always have fundamental gaps in their being unless they consent to be unconscious objects.

As Sartre says, man is a "futile passion" ("*passion inutile*"), for we long for the impossible and spend our time pursing it. We want to have complete being and at the same time to retain our human consciousness; that is, we desire to be *en-soi–pour-soi*, and all our projects ultimately aim at this self-contradictory goal. Human life is therefore tragic by the very logic of our metaphysical position. We must live out our life in a state inferior to the wholeness of objects, yearning for a completeness that our "ontological status" precludes us from attaining.

But while our consciousness makes us inferior to objects, it also constitutes our superiority, for consciousness enables us to choose the character of our lives, to impose sense on what is otherwise a senseless proliferation of life forms. "Man's freedom is the result of his ontological inferiority," Sartre says, for at least we can decide what we will become and thereby gain greater fullness of being.

To Sartre's mind, there is no God and no reason for the existence of humans or objects. All forms of matter burgeon, buzz, and blossom, ooze and secrete themselves into being without any purpose for existing. There is a "thatness" to things but no "whyness." The universe is empty, devoid of meaning or purpose, and all existence is *de trop*, pointless, unnecessary, excessive, and superfluous. But at least human beings are aware of the senselessness of their existence; and that understanding is significant. It enables people to invest their lives with meaning even though life itself is meaningless. Matter has become self-conscious in human beings only to realize the pointlessness of matter, which is the great cosmic joke. But people can use this knowledge to enrich their existence. "Before you come alive," Sartre wrote, "life is nothing; it's up to you to give it a meaning, and value is nothing else but the meaning you choose."[17]

Our efforts to lead a full life of our own choice naturally produce conflict because each person is striving to do likewise. Sartre devotes considerable space to the analysis of "the other" and the blockages people use to frustrate each other; in fact, in his play *No Exit*, he declares that hell is other people. But we must learn to share our freedom and not frustrate, stymie, or thwart other people's projects, for we are all in the same boat, trying to create a personally meaningful existence. We also have an obligation, Sartre felt, to assume responsibility for our actions because they have been freely chosen by us, in the void and without compulsion. Furthermore, we are nothing but the totality of what we do, so to disavow any action means denying part of ourselves.

Sartre also maintains that we must realize the full extent of our responsibility, for in choosing to act in certain ways and in becoming a particular type of person we are choosing for others; we are presenting a model for all mankind: "If I want to marry, to have children, even if this marriage depends solely on my own circumstances or passion or wish, I am involving all humanity in monogamy and not merely myself. Therefore, I am responsible for myself and for everyone else. I am creating a certain image of man of my own choosing. In choosing myself, I choose man."[18] In order to be human we must act, but we do so without any objective foundation in values now that God has disappeared, and we experience anguish and forlornness in the realization that our actions "fashion an image" that is "valid for everybody and for our whole age."[19]

To exist as a human being, then, means to Sartre acting in good faith, with a clear awareness of our existential condition. The completeness of objects is impossible for human beings, as well as undesirable, for we would then lose awareness (which is the condition for choosing our lives), but we must commit ourselves to courses of action so as to fulfill ourselves to the greatest extent. Our capacity for freely chosen action must be engaged for the maximization of our being, and in acting we should not interfere with other people's freedom or evade responsibility for our choices. Without illusions, with a lucid recognition of our solitary state, we must decide upon the meaning of our lives and thereby achieve authentic existence.

A Critical Assessment

1. The subjective and personal tone of a great deal of existential writing is extremely worrisome to a number of critics. The existentialists are thought to rely too heavily on their private emotions to the exclusion of the more general experience of humankind. As Bertrand Russell (1872–1970) remarked, "Subjective certainty is inversely proportional to objective certainty." The fact that we have strong feelings, therefore, cannot be taken as a criterion for truth. Quite often the preoccupation with such states as anxiety, dread, forlornness, and alienation also borders on the pathological. The existentialists claim they are only uncovering those psychological states that are endemic to the human condition, but perhaps they are merely reflecting their own, rather morbid personalities.

    By stressing subjectivity so strongly, the existentialists are also led to a wholesale rejection of reason and empiricism as valid means of knowledge. This position is extremely dangerous, for then subjective impressions cannot be challenged by rational argument or scientific proof which are publicly verifiable. For example, there is no way to adjudicate between an existentialist's claim that existence precedes essence and an essentialist's contention (such as Plato's) that essence precedes existence. Both cannot be right, but the issue cannot be resolved once reason is disqualified. Similarly, Heidegger supported Nazism, but this becomes as defensible as the humanism of Albert Camus since each is founded on private sentiments. A position of this kind does not have sufficient safeguards against error and lacks appropriate means of distinguishing between the genuine and the bogus.

2. Another set of criticisms has to do with the existential view of the human mode of being. The existentialist claims that there is no such thing as human nature, that we create our essence through our actions, but this is contradicted by the claim that we possess an innate capacity for free actions. The ability to act freely, then, must be part of our essential nature. Furthermore, theistic existentialists such as Kierkegaard claim that human beings are born with original sin and are inherently depraved, and Marcel and Jaspers spoke about the human need to establish social communication. These are assertions about human nature. All of the existentialists appear to have some notion of humanness apart from what people make of themselves, if only the assumption that we strive to maximize our being.

The existentialist also seems to carry the concept of freedom too far in maintaining that we are wholly responsible for our lives and our character. We do act to form ourselves, but we also act from ourselves. Also, common sense tells us that circumstances affect what we become, at least to some extent; we may have diminished responsibility because of our upbringing. It also seems extreme to hold people responsible for what others do because of their example.

The term "freedom," like many other key existentialist concepts, is used in such an ambiguous way that it is often difficult to determine what the existentialist means by it. And it seems paradoxical that in order to be human we are compelled to be free, which means that, qua human beings, we are not free to refrain from exercising our freedom.

3. Another difficulty with the existentialist position has to do with the harshness of its values. Nietzsche's hard code of master morality makes a virtue of warlike behavior, if not war itself; divides people into masters and slaves; and condemns Christian pity and compassion. André Gide carries gratuitous acts to the point where he approves of spontaneous murder. Kierkegaard, for his part, would have us kill our children if we thought we heard God telling us to do so, which makes one wonder whether people should not stop at the ethical stage rather than going on to the religious one. In good conscience, we wonder if we can adopt such a doctrine, especially in an age of suicide bombers.

Apart from criticisms of specific values, the existentialists generally maintain that values are created, not discovered, and that an action becomes valuable by virtue of the fact that we choose it. Sartre, as a prime example, quoted with approval Dostoyevsky's statement that "If God did not exist, everything would be permitted"; and since Sartre himself rejected belief in God, he could not see any ultimate justification for principles. We have previously seen that the loss of God need not entail the loss of values, but passing over that difficulty for the moment, it hardly seems correct to say that whatever type of life we lead is valuable because we chose it. Mass murderers or political tyrants may have chosen their lives, but that does not absolve them of blame. There do seem to be better and worse ways to live, otherwise the existentialists would not try to persuade us to adopt their ideas. Yet Sartre wrote that "all human activities are equivalent. . . . Thus it amounts to the same thing whether one gets drunk alone or is a leader of nations."[20] This consequence of existential thinking may point up the inherent weakness of the ethic.

Despite these criticisms, the existential attitude carries resonance and weight, demanding a judgment. In a sense, existentialism is not so much a philosophy as an orientation, a mood, a setting in which philosophy is done. It is hostile to theories about life's purpose, which they believe only reflects the need to find meaning even in a set of random numbers. By and large, existentialists want people to be treated decently out of compassion for humankind, despite the lack of foundation for decency. It sees us as insects on a ball of mud, but insects that realize the absurdity of our lives and the pointlessness of our deaths. The knowing allows us choice and functions as the basis of our dignity. We are then in a position to maximize our existence during our brief moment in time.

REVIEW QUESTIONS

1. Describe the starting point of existential philosophy, and illustrate it by citing various psychological states that have philosophic significance.
2. Explain the meaning of "existence precedes essence" and the way in which it impacts the existential ethic.

3. What did Nietzsche mean by master and slave morality, and by "God is dead"?
4. Describe the three stages through which human beings can pass in their ascent toward God, according to Sören Kierkegaard. What are the dangers inherent in the religious stage?
5. Explain Jean-Paul Sartre's distinction between the *en-soi* and the *pour-soi*, and his notion of what constitutes "good faith."

A DICTIONARY OF ETHICAL TERMS

Absolutism. The affirmation of absolute moral principles that are universally binding. For example: Never treat people as a means only, but as an end as well (Kant).

Act-deontologism. The theory that we should choose those actions that are right in themselves. *Compare with* **Rule-deontologism**.

Act-utilitarianism. The theory that we should choose those actions that will produce the greatest good or happiness for the greatest number of people. *Compare with* **Rule-utilitarianism**.

Aesthetics. That branch of philosophy dealing with taste and standards in judging art and nature, especially the canons of beauty.

Agape. Selfless love, as endorsed by Christian ethics, in which one is dedicated to what is best for the object beloved rather than for oneself.

Akrasia. Knowing what is right but lacking the will to do it; a weakness in self-discipline. The presence of a moral struggle indicated to Aristotle an imperfection in character.

Altruism. The position that one should always act for the welfare of others. *Compare with* **Egoism**.

Antithesis. An opposing or contrasting idea. In the Marxist and Hegelian dialectic, a contrary proposition that is equally strong. *Compare with* **Thesis and Synthesis**.

Anxiety. Acute apprehension and distress due to impending danger. In existentialism, a basic dread of our ultimate non-being.

Apatheia. A Stoic state of tranquility and emotional detachment regarding external events, including disasters and misfortunes. The Stoic will play his part in human affairs but will remain aloof and untouched by them.

Arete. Excellence or virtue. In Aristotle's system, the arete of our function of rationality would be to reason well, choosing appropriate means and ends.

Argumentum ad hominem. An argument to the person whereby the character or status of the individual is attacked rather than the position presented.

Aristotelianism. The philosophic position advocated by Aristotle. In ethics, Aristotle emphasized using our function of reason to choose moderate actions that are then virtuous.

Atheism. The doctrine or belief that God does not exist.

Aurea mediocritas (meden agan). The so-called golden mean of Aristotle's ethics, whereby virtue consists in acting and feeling neither too much nor too little but just the right amount in all circumstances.

Axiology. A division of philosophy dealing with value in ethics, aesthetics, politics, and religion.

Behaviorism. The theory that human (or animal) psychology can only be studied scientifically through objectively observable and quantifiable events.

"Be natural" theory. The view that the good life consists in living naturally, emulating primitive and animal ways that are harmonious with the natural order.

Biographical fallacy. The mistake of assuming that the value of a person's actions or creations can be determined by understanding the person's life.

Calculus of pleasures. *See Hedonic calculus.*

Calvinism. The doctrine of John Calvin that emphasizes predestination, the authority of Scriptures, the supremacy of grace over works, and the sovereignty of God.

Caritas. Charity, tenderness, affection, esteem. Equivalent to the Greek *agape,* meaning selfless love that desires the other's well-being above one's own.

Carpe diem philosophy. Seize the day. The philosophic view that stresses the enjoyment of the present moment without regard for the future.

Categorical imperative. Immanuel Kant's formulation of the unconditional moral rule, usually expressed as only acting on those principles that we could endorse as universal law.

Censor. Sigmund Freud's concept of a psychic force that guards the gateway to consciousness, prohibiting entry to traumatic thoughts or emotions.

Christian ethics. The position that divine commands should furnish the basis for human conduct, especially the principles of love, forgiveness, brotherhood, and mercy contained in the teachings of Christ.

Christian Science. A religion, founded by Mary Baker Eddy, that strongly emphasizes spiritual healing based on Scriptures.

Communism. A political system based on Marxism that favors common ownership of property, a classless society, and the ultimate "withering away" of the state.

Confucianism. A religious and philosophic tradition, beginning in the sixth century BCE, with Confucius, that emphasizes love for humanity, reverence for parents and ancestors, and the moral perfection of the individual.

Consequentialism. The ethical view that the result or outcome of actions is most important in judging their value.

Contextual ethics. *See Situation ethics.*

Cost-benefit analysis. An approach to economics and social issues in which the ratio of costs to benefits is used to determine the desirability of decisions.

Cultural relativism. The view that ethical judgments are relative to society; right actions are those approved of by the culture.

Cyrenaic. An ethical view, originating in Cyrene in ancient Greece, that pleasure alone should be sought.

Daimon. A spirit, supernatural power, "genius" of a family, or "demon" said by Socrates to stop him from wrongdoing. It has been interpreted as a divine voice or sign, perhaps the prohibitions of conscience.

Deconstructionism. A critical movement, originating in France in the 1960s, that questions the ability of language to diagram reality.

Deduction. Along with induction, one of the two main forms of logic; in deduction, the conclusion follows necessarily from the premises.

Deontological theory. The ethical position (also called *formalism*) that actions are inherently right or wrong.

Determinism. The doctrine that all events and actions are the result of natural law, so that causal conditions necessitate the occurrence of every happening exactly as it happened.

Dialectic. In Plato, a process of question and answer to elicit a fundamental philosophic idea. In G. W. F. Hegel and Karl Marx, a process of reaching a higher truth through the confrontation between a thesis and its antithesis.

Divine justice. The notion in Christian ethics that, following Christ's example, people should be given what they need, not what they deserve.

Duration. One of the seven "marks" in Jeremy Bentham's hedonic calculus, referring to the length of time that a pleasurable experience continues.

Eidos. A metaphysical concept referring to the essence or core of a phenomenon.

Ego. An energy system in Freudian psychology that is the conscious rational component of the psyche, mediating between the id and superego.

Egoism. The doctrine that one ought always to act for one's own self-interest.

Empiricism. The epistemological view that all knowledge is based on sense-perception.

En-soi. A concept used by Jean-Paul Sartre to indicate the unity and completeness of objects as compared to the dividedness of human existence. *Compare with* **Pour-soi.**

Epicureanism. The ethical view of Epicurus and his disciples that mental happiness or the absence of pain is the goal in living, far surpassing physical pleasure in value. *Compare with* **Cyrenaic.**

Epistemology. A branch of philosophy concerned with the nature, scope, origins, and limits of valid ways of knowing, with the definition of truth, and with knowledge.

Eros. In Christian ethics, a form of love that desires possession of the object beloved for the sake of personal enrichment; it is contrasted unfavorably with agape.

Ethical hedonism. The ethical theory that happiness or pleasure, for the individual or society, is the aim of life.

Ethics. The branch of philosophy that investigates ideals in living (a good life) and morally correct conduct (right actions) as well as virtuous character.

Eudaimonia. Vital well-being or happiness, which for Aristotle consists in using the unique function of reason to choose the mean between extremes and to engage in contemplation.

Evolutionary ethics. The theory that a good life is one in which we support and further the evolutionary development of nature.

Existentialism. A twentieth-century philosophic theory with roots in the nineteenth century that stresses the maximization of human existence in a fortuitous world in which the exercise of our freedom provides meaning.

Extent. One of Jeremy Bentham's seven "marks" in his hedonic calculus, referring to the number of people to whom an act extends.

Fallacy of composition. An informal fallacy of assuming that what is true of the part is true of the whole; for example, since a feather is light, a truckload of feathers is light.

Fecundity. Another of Jeremy Bentham's "marks" in his hedonic calculus, referring to the tendency of a pleasure to be followed by similar pleasures.

Feminist theology. A revisionist theological movement that stresses the importance of the goddess in religious history, the feminine aspects of the godhead, and the role of women within institutional religion.

Formalism. *See Deontologic theory.*

Formal logic. The rules and application of strict, rigorous, and systematic reasoning in argumentation.

Free will. The doctrine that human decisions are not causally determined by prior factors but emanate from an autonomous self.

Freedom. The ability to do what one wills.

Freudian psychology. The theory of personality and psychoanalytic view of Sigmund Freud that emphasize the force of the unconscious in motivating behavior.

Function. The philosophic notion, originating with Aristotle and formally called *teleologism*, that every object including human beings has a unique or distinctive function in being.

Genetic fallacy. Also called the *fallacy of origins* and *biographical fallacy*, the mistake of assuming that the source of an idea is the measure of its worth. For example, since Nietzsche went insane, his ideas can be dismissed.

Golden mean. *See Aurea mediocritas.*

Good. That which is postulated as the ideal goal, end, aim, or purpose to human existence.

Grace. In Christian theology, the freely given, undeserved favor and love of God.

Gratuitous act. In existentialism, and in the writings of André Gide in particular, the unmotivated act that arises spontaneously from the individual.

Hard determinism. The view that, since every event is caused in accordance with natural law, people are not responsible for their actions. *Compare with* **Soft determinism.**

Hedon. A pleasure unit in Jeremy Bentham's hedonic calculus.

Hedonic calculus. The system devised by Jeremy Bentham to measure scientifically the number of hedons to be derived from any given action.

Hedonism. The ethical theory that pleasure or happiness alone is the only intrinsic good, and unpleasant consciousness the only intrinsic evil. Pleasure is therefore the goal in life, and pain should be avoided.

Hedonistic paradox. The apparent contradiction that when we pursue pleasure, we are least likely to attain it; but when we seek some other goal, pleasure can occur as a byproduct or accompaniment.

Hermeneutics. The science of interpretation, especially of Scripture, as in Biblical exegesis.

Highest good (summum bonum). Often synonymous with "the good," it is the ultimate end or aim of life.

Homeostasis. The tendency of a system, whether animal, institutional, or cosmic, to maintain its equilibrium and internal stability.

Human nature. The psychological, physical, and social qualities that constitute the essence of human beings.

Hypothetical imperative. A moral prescription of a conditional kind, for example, treat people with respect if you want to be treated with respect in turn. Usually contrasted with categorical imperatives, which state unconditional moral duties, for example, treat human beings as worthy of respect.

Id. The basic energy system in the Freudian theory of psychology, standing, above all, for constant and inextinguishable sexual desire.

Inchallah. The Muslim notion that all events are preordained by Allah.

Individualistic hedonism. A variety of ethical hedonism which recommends that each individual should pursue his or her own pleasure.

Induction. Along with deduction, one of the two main forms of logic; in induction, the premises provide proof of the probability of the conclusion.

Intensity. One of Jeremy Bentham's factors in his hedonic calculus, referring to the strength of the pleasure to be derived from an experience.

Intentionalism. The view that the intention or motive of the agent is the most important factor in judging the ethical worth of action.

Kantianism. The philosophic position advocated by Immanuel Kant. In ethics, Kant stressed our obligation to act in accordance with universal principles.

Karma. In Hinduism and Buddhism, actions that incur inevitable rewards or punishment in this life or in a reincarnation.

Kismet. The Islamic concept of fate or destiny.

Laissez-faire. The economic doctrine that the market should operate freely, without government regulation.

Law of non-contradiction. The basic law in logic, first articulated by Aristotle, that two contradictory propositions cannot both be true.

Law of parsimony. A rule of thought, first presented by William of Occam (and sometimes called *Occam's razor*) that the simplest explanation is best or that explanations should not be compounded beyond what is required.

Lazy argument. A standard criticism against Stoicism that if all events are inevitable, then human effort is futile and laziness is justified.

Libertarian. In ethics, an individual who affirms a free-will position.

Linguistic analysis. A twentieth-century movement maintaining that the clarifying analysis of language can solve, resolve, or dissolve many philosophic problems.

Logic. One of the main branches of philosophy, concerned with the principles governing correct inference in deductive and inductive reasoning.

Logos. Reason, proportion, word, definition, or faculty. Socrates used *logos* to mean a distinguishing characteristic; Plato, to mean a true account; and Aristotle to mean rationality, right, reason, or ratio. To the Stoic, it was the bond of the universe or the mind of God.

Major premise. In logic, the first premise in a deductive syllogism, usually the most general statement in the argument.

Marxism. The philosophy of Karl Marx and Friedrich Engels. *See **Communism**.*

Meden agan. *See **Aurea mediocritas**.*

Metaphysics. One of the major branches of philosophy, concerned with the nature of ultimate reality, its features, processes, and structure.

Method of repetition. In the philosophy of Kierkegaard, the futile process of varying one's occupations, entertainments, residences, etc., in an effort to escape boredom and despair.

Moira. The Greek concept of fate or destiny that circumscribed even the will of the gods.

Multiculturalism. The modern movement to recognize and include the diverse array of world cultures when deciding political, social, religious, educational, psychological, and intellectual questions.

Naturalism. In ethics, the view that we should conform to the natural order in living the good life, whether as the "be natural" movement, transcendentalism, Stoicism, or even evolutionism.

Naturalistic fallacy. The logical mistake of deriving values from facts, the evaluative from the descriptive, "ought" from "is."

Natural selection. A key feature of Darwin's theory of evolution whereby those creatures possessing the requisite attributes called for by the environment survive and produce offspring, whereas the unfavored creatures perish in the struggle for survival.

New morality. Situation ethics that rejects general moral principles and affirms the uniqueness of each circumstance and a particular morality appropriate to it.

Objectivism. The ethical position which maintains that moral principles can have objective validity whereby certain actions are right or wrong in themselves. *Contrast with **Relativism**.*

Occam's razor. *See* **Law *of parsimony*.**

Oedipus complex. The Freudian notion that a complex can develop from the developmental phenomenon whereby boys desire union with their mothers and the death of their fathers.

Overman. Friedrich Nietzsche's ideal of the perfect master, who is courageous, innovative, strong-willed, joyful, and powerful.

Phenomenology. A twentieth-century Continental philosophic movement that attempts to describe scientifically the structure of phenomena as they appear to consciousness.

Philia. The Greek prefix meaning *love of*; philosophy, therefore, is literally, the love of wisdom.

Philosophy. The field of knowledge that tries to understand the nature of human existence at its most fundamental level.

Phronesis. Practical wisdom in conduct that, in Aristotle's system, enables an individual to choose virtuous actions prior to virtue becoming habitual common sense.

Political philosophy. The study of the ideal form of government, the grounds for the authority of the state, the concepts of justice, freedom, and equality, and the rights and obligations of citizens.

Post hoc, ergo propter hoc. Literally, after this, therefore caused by this. The mistake in thinking that because event *A* preceded event *B*, event *A* is necessarily the cause of *B*.

Pour-soi. Jean-Paul Sartre's notion of the "for itself," the mode of being of humans whereby consciousness enables us to choose the type of life we want to live. *Compare with* **En-soi.**

Pre-determinism. In contrast to social scientific determinism, pre-determinism is the theory that a cosmic destiny controls all events.

Prima facie obligations. Duties that are apparent, perhaps self-evident, and that we ought to honor unless overridden by another *prima facie* duty.

Principle of entropy. The view that energy is constantly being transformed into unusable forms or that it is being progressively lost to human beings or less available for use.

Principle of utility. In utilitarianism, the moral principle that we should seek the greatest amount of happiness for the greatest number of people.

Projection. A defense mechanism in Freudian psychology in which the psyche protects itself from guilt by assigning blame for shameful conduct to outside forces or other people.

Prophetic tradition. The series of Hebrew prophets, in the second of the three divisions of the Old Testament, who are believed to speak for God or to prophesy by divine inspiration.

Psychoanalysis. The method of treating psychological disorders, devised by Sigmund Freud, that seeks to draw repressed material to the level of consciousness and thereby effect a cure.

Psychological egoism. The view that all people seek their own advantage or self-interest, whether they acknowledge it or not.

Psychological hedonism. The view that everyone pursues his or her own pleasure in life; sometimes referred to as the *pleasure principle.*

Psychology. The study of the human mind, and mental states and processes, or the study of human and animal behavior for the sake of deriving principles of understanding and methods of control.

Purity. Another of the "marks" in Jeremy Bentham's hedonic calculus, referring to the degree of pleasure and pain in a given action.

Quiddity. The core, essence, or *eidos* of a phenomenon.

Rationalization. A term sometimes used as synonymous with reasoning but more properly, finding a plausible excuse for what we want to do anyway.

Realpolitik. Political realism or practicality in public affairs, especially the belief that power, not ideals, always proves decisive.

Relativism. *See Cultural relativism.*

Religious ethics. Ethical theories in which the basic principles are grounded in divine commands, usually as contained in sacred writings and interpreted by institutions.

Retributive theory of justice. The doctrine that justice should be meted out according to people's deserts, not their needs, that a system of proportionality should operate whereby rewards or punishment are commensurate with the individual's praiseworthiness or blameworthiness.

Right. Morally correct conduct, actions, or behavior.

Rule–deontologism. The theory that we should choose those moral principles that are right in themselves. *Compare with* **Act–deontologism.**

Rule–utilitarianism. The theory that we should choose those rules that would promote the greatest good (especially happiness) for the majority. *Compare with* **Act–utilitarianism.**

Sadism. The view, associated with the Marquis de Sade, that advocates sexual gratification through inflicting pain or causing degradation to others.

Sadomasochism. Sexual gratification through inflicting pain or receiving pain or psychological humiliation.

Sapir-Whorf hypothesis. The sociological theory that language determines thought much more than thought determines language.

Second law of thermodynamics. *See **Principle of entropy**.*

Self. The individual person that exists as the same continuous being from birth to death, underlying consciousness and experience.

Self-realization. The ethical theory that advocates the maximum development of one's self or one's humanness.

Sine qua non. A necessary or indispensable condition or factor; for example, freedom as a *sine qua non* of democracy.

Situation ethics. *See **New morality**.*

Social Darwinism. The doctrine, prominent in the nineteenth century, that the survival of the fittest principle and natural selection should apply to human life.

Soft determinism. The view that, although events occur according to natural law, rational beings are responsible for their actions insofar as they act voluntarily. *Compare with **Hard determinism**.*

Stoicism. The philosophic theory that advocates the acceptance of the natural and inevitable order of events as a way of achieving independence and tranquility.

Subjectivism. The ethical view that moral judgments simply reflect the personal beliefs, attitudes, or feelings of the person rendering the judgment. *Contrast with **Objectivism**.*

Sublimation. The Freudian concept of diverting sexual energy from an unacceptable goal to one that is socially approved.

Summum bonum. *See **Highest good**.*

Superego. In Freudian psychology, the energy system that embodies social rules and prohibitions as instilled in us by our parents acting as society's agents.

Syllogism. A formally structured argument in deductive logic containing a major premise, a minor premise, and a conclusion.

Synthesis. In the philosophies of G. W. F. Hegel and Karl Marx, a new and higher level of development of an idea, institution, or phenomenon produced by the reconciliation of a thesis and its antithesis.

Talion. The Hebrew law of talion whereby one reaps what one sows; people receive what they deserve in a universe governed by a just God.

Teleological argument. One of the principal proofs for the existence of God, which argues that since the world exhibits evidence of design, there must be an intelligent cosmic designer.

Teleologism. The view that the universe and human existence is purposive in nature and contains ends and goals rather than being random and purposeless. *See Function.*

Theistic existentialism. The branch of existential philosophy that assumes human existence can only be maximized through non-rational devotion to God.

Theology. The study of the nature of God, his attributes, and his relation to human beings.

Theoria. Aristotle's concept of the highest employment of reason, which is pure contemplation.

Thesis. In the Marxist and Hegelian systems, an ascertainable proposition that is opposed by an apparent opposite, and is reconciled in the higher unity of a synthesis. *See Antithesis and Synthesis.*

Transcendentalism. The American philosophic movement that affirms the intuitive and spiritual realm above or within the natural world.

Übermensch. *See Overman.*

Universalistic hedonism. The hedonistic view that pleasure or happiness should be sought not just for oneself but for humankind. The individual agent is to count for one and only one in the moral equation. *Compare with Individualistic hedonism.*

Utilitarianism. The form of universalistic hedonism that seeks the greatest happiness for the greatest number.

Utilitarian theory of justice. The doctrine that justice consists in giving people what they need, not what they deserve. Punishment therefore should be forward-looking, designed to improve the individual, deter potential wrongdoers, and protect society. *Compare with Retributive theory of justice.*

Valid argument. A train of reasoning that is formally correct, such that the conclusion is entailed by the premises.

Weltanschauung. A worldview that encompasses a conception of the universe and humanity's relation to it.

Zen Buddhism. A form of Chinese Buddhism that later spread to Japan and Korea in which meditation and intuition, rather than sacred writings or rational teaching, are used to receive enlightenment.

NOTES

CHAPTER 1: THE NATURE OF ETHICS

1. Aristotle, *Categoriae*, in *The Basic Work of Aristotle*, ed. R. McKeon (New York: Random House, 1941), 8–28.

2. See S. Kierkegaard, *Fear and Trembling* and *The Sickness unto Death*, trans. W. Lowrie (New York: Doubleday and Co., 1954), passim; and St. Augustine, *The City of God*, trans. M. Dods (Buffalo: 1887), Vol. I, 391. For modern treatments see S. Cahn, ed., *Philosophical Explorations: Freedom, God, and Goodness* (New York: Prometheus Books, 1989), and R. Swinburne, *Providence and the Problem of Evil* (Oxford: Oxford University Press, 1999).

3. Even the fact of our mortality may make us wonder what crime we have committed to deserve a sentence of death. The Biblical story of the Fall trades upon this type of thinking, offering an explanation for death in terms of the sin of Adam and Eve, which all of humankind inherited. Also included would be the belief that Christ died for our sins, and through belief in him we can gain eternal life.

4. B. Pascal, *Thoughts*, trans. W. F. Trotter (New York: P. F. Collier, 1910), Sec. IV, No. 277.

5. D. Hume, *Treatise of Human Nature* (Oxford, England: Clarendon Press, 1896), 469; G. E. Moore, *Principia Ethica* (Cambridge, England: Cambridge University Press 1919), 73.

6. Some contemporary philosophers believe that the descriptive/evaluative distinction has been overstated; they try to show that values can, in some way, be derived from descriptive facts. See W. D. Hudson, ed., *The Is/Ought Question* (New York: Macmillan, 1969); and D. A. Rohatyn, *Naturalism and Deontology* (Paris: Mouton, 1975). See also R. Crisp, "Naturalism and Non-Naturalism in Ethics," in S. Lovibond and S. G. Williams, eds., *Identity, Truth and Value* (Malden, MA: Blackwell, 1996); and R. Shafer-Landau, *Moral Realism: A Defense* (Oxford: Oxford University Press, 2003).

7. St. Thomas Aquinas *Summa Theologica* (London: Burns, Oates and Washbourne, 1927–1935), Part I, Question 2, Article 3.

8. Plato, *Euthyphro* in *The Dialogues of Plato*, trans. B. Jowett (New York: Random House, 1920), Vol. I, 391.

9. Plato, *Euthyphro* in *The Dialogues of Plato*.

10. B. Blanshard, "Morality and Politics," in *Ethics and Society*, ed. R. T. deGeorge (New York: Doubleday, 1966), 19. See also Kai Nielsen, *Ethics without God* (Buffalo, NY: Prometheus Books, 1990).

11. W. James, *Varieties of Religions Experience* (New York: Longmans Green, 1923), 20.

CHAPTER 2: FREE WILL AND DETERMINISM

1. The problems of determinism and relativism were mentioned at the beginning of the book in discussing how ethical theories may be justified, and chapter 1 referred to psychological egoism, which is a determinist doctrine.

2. W. Shakespeare, *King Lear*, in *William Shakespeare: Complete Works*, ed. Peter Alexander (New York: Random House, 1952), Act. 1, Scene II.

3. See W. H. Sheldon, *The Varieties of Human Physique* (New York: Harper and Brothers, 1940).

4. A. Toynbee, *A Study of History* (New York: Oxford University Press, 1935). Toynbee believed that societies succeed or fail depending upon their response to the challenges of the environment. This environmental determinism can also be found in the writings of Ellen Semple, Ellsworth Huntington, and Thomas Taylor.

5. One proposed explanation given by theologians for the existence of natural evil and human suffering (in a world governed by a benevolent God) trades upon these facts of psychology. That is, theologians will sometimes argue that human development depends upon there being obstacles to struggle against. If the world were a paradise, they say, people would not be challenged and their character would lack the stimulus to improve. God provides sufficient incentives on earth in the form of disease, illness, volcanic eruptions, floods, earthquakes, tigers, scorpions, deserts, jungles, and so forth for the human race to develop medicine, engineering, science, and all the other means of controlling the environment. In addition, combating these evils encourages individuals to build strength of character.

6. R. Benedict, *Patterns of Culture* (London: Routledge and Sons, 1935), 2–3; see also A. Montagu, *The Biosocial Nature of Man* (New York: Grove Press, 1956), 74–76.

7. See E. Sapir, *Culture, Language and Personality* (Berkeley: University of California Press, 1970).

8. For an exposition of this idea, see A. Flew, ed., *Logic and Language*, Vol. II (Oxford: Basil Blackwell, 1961), especially the papers by G. Ryle, F. Waismann, J. Austin, and J. O. Urmson.

9. It should be mentioned that the theory of sociobiology claims that all human behavior is a function of our genes in their drive to perpetuate their group strain. Human organisms are the housing the genes require, and their continued existence is our reason for being. It is as though an egg were using a chicken to produce another egg. See the writings of Edward O. Wilson and Robert Trivers, especially Wilson's book *Sociobiology: The New Synthesis* (Cambridge, MA: Harvard University Press, 1975).

10. See I. Pavlov, *Conditioned Reflexes* (New York: Dover Publications, 1957); J. B. Watson, *Behaviorism* (Chicago: University of Chicago Press, 1930); and B. F. Skinner, *Science and Human Behavior* (New York: Macmillan, 1953), and *Beyond Freedom and Dignity* (New York: Knopf, 1971).

11. For some provocative discussions on determinism see D. Dennett, *Elbow Room: The Varieties of Free Will Worth Wanting* (Cambridge, MA: MIT Press, 1984); James Rachels, *Problems from Philosophy* (New York: McGraw Hill, 2005); and Manuel Vargas, ed., *Four Views on Free Will: A Debate* (Malden, MA: Blackwell, 2007).

CHAPTER 3: THE CHALLENGE OF RELATIVISM

1. W. G. Sumner, *Folkways* (Boston: Ginn and Co., 1907), Chap. XI.

2. W. Shakespeare, *Hamlet*, in *William Shakespeare: The Complete Works*, ed. Peter Alexander (New York: Random House, 1952), Act 2, Scene II, 142.

3. Deconstruction and postmodernism reject the "centralized power" that decides essential truth, including moral truth, in favor of the multiplicity of individual experience. Associated with Jacques Derrida and Paul de Man, it criticizes the unquestioned assumptions of important texts on which Western culture is based. Evaluation will only reflect the subjective or relative opinions of the evaluator.

4. Sumner, *Folkways* (Boston: Ginn and Co., 1907).

5. V. Pareto, *Mind and Society* (New York: Harcourt Brace and Co., 1915).

6. R. Benedict, *Patterns of Culture* (London: Routledge and Sons, 1935). Compare M. J. Herskovits, *Man and his Works* (New York.: Alfred A. Knopf, 1948).

7. See D. Hume, *An Enquiry Concerning the Principles of Morals* in *Philosophical Works of David Hume* (Boston: Little Brown, 1854). See also C. L. Stevenson, *Ethics and Language* (New Haven: Yale University Press, 1969), and A. J. Ayer, *Language, Truth and Logic* (Oxford, England: Oxford University Press, 1916).

8. Freud's theory of ethics is contained in a series of works that have been published under the title *Collected Papers* (New York: Basic Books, 1959), and *The Standard Edition of the Complete Psychological Works of Sigmund Freud* (London: Hogarth Press, 1966). See especially Volumes 13 and 21 of the latter.

9. Karl Marx, *Capital* (New York: Modern Library, 1936), and with Friedrich Engels, *The Communist Manifesto* (Chicago: H. Regnery Co., 1954).

10. Karl Marx, *Theses on Feuerbach*, in *The German Ideology*, ed. C. J. Arthur (New York: International Publishers, 1970), 123.

11. The dialectic development of biological forms was stressed more by Hegel, who wrote of the bud being negated by the blossom and the two being "resolved" in the growing fruit. Marx obtained the idea of the dialectic from Hegel but, as is frequently pointed out, Hegel conceived of spiritual forces developing in a dialectic pattern, whereas Marx considered the essential forces to be material in nature.

12. For classic studies of the relationship between Christianity and capitalism see R. H. Tawney, *Religion and the Rise of Capitalism* (London: John Murray, 1926), and Max Weber, *The Protestant Ethic and the Spirit of Capitalism* (New York: Routledge, 2001).

13. Marxists would also analyze Hinduism as a case in point because it stresses that a person's socioeconomic caste in his or her current life is determined by the moral quality of his or her previous incarnation; it is therefore justified. One cannot change caste in one's lifetime but can only hope to be reincarnated into a higher caste sometime in a future life. According to the Marxist view, this suits the rulers perfectly for it sanctions their power and wealth.

14. See Louis Pojman, "Who's to Judge" in *Vice and Virtue in Everyday Life*, Christina Sommers and Fred Sommers, eds. (Fort Worth: Harcourt Brace, 2001).

15. Bertrand Russell attempted to resolve this paradox with his *theory of types*, according to which a class statement cannot be considered a member of its own class. Thus, the proposition "all reasoning is really rationalization" is not itself a member of the class of rationalizations. But many logicians have been dissatisfied with Russell's reasons for exempting class statements from their own categories.

16. Plato, *Theaetetus*, in *The Dialogues of Plato*, trans. B. Jowett (New York: Scribner, Armstrong and Co., 1874), Vol. III, 373.

17. Plato, *The Republic*, in *The Dialogues of Plato*, trans. B. Jowett (New York: Scribner, Armstrong and Co., 1874), Vol. II, 159ff.

18. See Raymond Boudon, *The Poverty of Relativism* (Oxford: Bardwell Press, 2006), and William Gardner, *The Book of Absolutes: A Critique of Relativism* (Montreal: McGill Queens University Press, 2008).

19. See Charles Taylor, *Multiculturalism and "The Politics of Recognition"* (Princeton: Princeton University Press, 1992), and Simon Caney and Peter Jones, eds., *Human Rights and Global Diversity* (London: Portland, 2001).

CHAPTER 4: HEDONISM AS THE GOOD

1. These are Aristotle's points, and although he is not technically regarded as a hedonist, his ethic of self-realization does contain hedonistic elements. He regarded pleasure as the natural accompaniment of virtuous activities, and these activities constitute both our self-realization and our happiness. Pleasure, therefore, is a good but not *the* good.

2. See Diogenes Laertius, *Lives of Eminent Philosophers*, trans. R. D. Hicks (Cambridge, MA: Harvard University Press, 1950), Vol. 1, Chapter II, 65–93.

3. See Howard Jones, *The Epicurean Tradition* (London: Routledge, 1989).

4. See also Ernest Albee, *A History of English Utilitarianism* (New York: Routledge, 2004).

5. John Stuart Mill, *Autobiography*, in *The Harvard Classics* (New York: P. F. Collier and Son, 1909), Vol. XXV, 94.

6. Pierre Gassendi (1592–1655) and Francis Hutcheson (1694–1747) also modified hedonism in interesting ways but they are not among the major philosophers.

7. For a complete presentation of Bentham's views, see his book *An Introduction to the Principles of Morals and Legislation* (London: Athlone Press, 1970). See especially Chapter IV for a description of the calculus. In attempting to make philosophy scientific, Bentham was in company with philosophers such as Descartes, Leibniz, Spencer, Comte, Bradley, Ayer, and Russell.

8. In addition, it is uncertain whether it would be better to provide diluted pleasures to more people or greater pleasure to fewer people.

9. Aristotle, *The Nicomachean Ethics*, (London: Routledge and Kegan Paul, 1969), Vol. X, 211. See F. Rosen, *Classical Utilitarianism from Hume to Mill* (New York: Routledge, 1989).

10. A problem exists in what constitutes "the greatest number." Mill defined it as "the whole sentient creation," but that could include animal life as well as future generations of people, in which case people alive today could be asked to sacrifice their happiness for the sake of the larger group of animals and future human beings. See Fred Feldman, *Utilitarianism, Hedonism, and Desert* (New York: Cambridge, 1997).

11. Aristotle, *The Nicomachean Ethics*, 234

12. Mill did mention two "sanctions" that he believed would keep people from pursuing their own happiness at the expense of others: the external sanctions of law, public opinion, and religious belief, and the internal sanction which is "the feeling of unity with our fellow creatures"; the latter supposedly makes it impossible for us to be happy unless we make others happy also. But not only are these points rather weak but they would allow immoral pleasures provided they were shared. See C. I. Sheng, *Defense of Utilitarianism* (Lanham, MD: University Press, 2004).

CHAPTER 5: SELF-REALIZATION

1. T. H. Green, *Prolegomena to Ethics* (Oxford: Clarendon Press, 1883); and F. H. Bradley, *Ethical Studies* (Oxford: Clarendon Press, 1927).

2. W. F. Hocking, *The Self, its Body and Freedom* (New Haven: Yale University Press, 1928), and *Human Nature and its Remaking* (New Haven: Yale University Press, 1918); J. Royce, *The World and the Individual* (New York: Macmillan Publishing Co., 1904).

3. See A. Maslow, *Motivation and Personality* (New York: Harper, 1970); C. Rogers, *On Becoming a Person* (Boston: Houghton Mifflin, 1961); and E. Fromm, *Man for Himself* (New York: Rinehart, 1947).

4. G. Santayana, *Three Philosophical Poets* (Cambridge, MA: Harvard University Press,1910), Chapter IV.

5. In the play *Peer Gynt* by Henrik Ibsen the same idea is expressed through the figure of the Button Molder who melts down all souls who, instead of being true to their essential selves, have sought diverse experiences.

6. See A. Tennyson, *Poetical Works* (Boston: Ticknor and Fields, 1864), Vol. I, 90–96.

7. O. Wilde, *The Picture of Dorian Gray* (London: Oxford University Press, 1974).

8. At the time of writing humans have been successful cloned as have fish, rabbits, sheep, pigs, mules, horses, deer, cats, dogs, and cattle, the last commercially. Clones are identical to their parents and the problem of differentiation is greater than that of identical twins.

9. For a subtle contemporary discussion of personal identity see Derek Parfit, *Reasons and Persons* (Oxford: Oxford University Press, 1984).

10. Fromm, *Man for Himself* 19–20.

11. It has been claimed that we should develop every *real* aspect of ourselves, and that negative traits are not real in themselves but are the lack of something positive. This view can be traced to the medieval notion of evil as the absence of good, just as cold is the absence of heat, dark is the absence of light.

12. An account of the recent research in primatology can be found in Christina J. Campbell, *Primates in Perspective* (Oxford: Oxford University Press, 2006), and Jane Goodall, *Through a Window* (Boston Houghton Mifflin, 1990. See also D. Premack, *Intelligence in Ape and Man* (New York: Erlbaum Assoc., 1976); and A. J. Premack, *Why Chimps Can Read* (New York: Harper and Row, 1976). It was formerly believed that apes could not use language because they did not speak, but now it is known that they possess the capability for language but lack the vocal apparatus for speech. Some gorillas and chimpanzees have been taught sign language and have progressed to a relatively high level, using abstract terms.

13. Perhaps we are unique in having religious feelings, but one intriguing suggestion regarding our belief is that we long for God as herd animals seeking the lost pack leaders, essentially wolves baying at the moon when we offer up prayers.

14. J. J. Rousseau, *The Social Contract and Discourses* (London: J. M. Dent, 1913).

15. T. Hobbes, *Leviathan* (London: J. M. Dent, 1914).

16. The other three are Plato's *Republic*, Immanuel Kant's *Foundations of the Metaphysics of Morals*, and John Stuart Mill's *Utilitarianism*. See Nancy Sherman, ed., *Aristotle's Ethics: Critical Essays* (Lanham, MD: Rowman and Littlefield, 1999).

17. Aristotle, *The Nicomachean Ethics*, trans. F. H. Peters (London: Kegan Paul, Trench, Trubner, 1901), Book II, 6. The problem of means and ends is an interesting one in philosophy. If, for example, we were to climb a mountain, would we regard scaling a cliff as a means toward climbing the mountain or the end of climbing the mountain?

18. Aristotle, *The Nicomachean Ethics*. Aristotle never actually used the word "golden"; that was added later by neo-Aristotelians. For a good, contemporary analysis of Aristotle see Kelvin Knight, *Aristotelian Philosophy* (Cambridge: Polity Press, 2007).

19. Aristotle, *The Nicomachean Ethics*.

20. Aristotle's teleological theory is a metaphysical one which holds that the universe as a whole and every object in it is arranged according to ends and purposes. Events are therefore explained not by their prior or "efficient" causes but by their purpose or "final" causes. The metaphysical theory of "mechanism" maintains the former, teleologism the latter. Christianity has adopted this teleological theory in the thought of St. Thomas Aquinas by conceiving of God as the being responsible for the purpose behind all life. See J. Barnes, *Cambridge Companion to Aristotle* (Cambridge: Cambridge University Press, 2007).

21. It should be noted that Aristotle addressed this point through the concept of *phronesis* (practical wisdom) in Book VI of the *Nichomachean Ethics*, but it is arguable whether he solved the problem.

CHAPTER 6: FOLLOWING NATURE

1. We will not discuss the special types of naturalism of John Dewey or George Santayana. Neither will we cover the ethical naturalism of following one's own nature, doing what is natural to oneself, nor being true to one's real self, which is actually closer to a self-realization ethic. A philosophic naturalism of a technical kind, which is also excluded, is the claim that all moral judgments are about some natural quality in actions rather than being based on some non-natural (or spiritual) quality.

2. H. D. *Thoreau*, Walden (London: Walter Scott, 1886) 88–89.

3. In addition to Wordsworth, Byron, and Keats, we could also list Shelley and Coleridge as having a strong naturalism at the heart of their poetic works.

4. J. S. Mill, *Nature, The Utility of Religion, and Theism* (London: Longmans Green, 1874), 28–29.

5. A comparable criticism can be made of aesthetic naturalism. A good work of art is not good because it is a naturalistic representation of the world, faithfully mirroring a natural object. Some aspects of nature are not worth copying, and everything depends on the dialogue between the subject and the artist.

6. For excellent expositions of the philosophy of transcendentalism see Philip Gura, *American Transcendentalism* (New York: Hill and Wang, 2007); B. I. Packer, *The Transcendentalists* (Athens, GA: University of Georgia Press, 2007); G. Hicks, *The Great Tradition* (New York: The Macmillan Co., 1933): and W. G. Muelder, L. Sears, and V. Schlabach, *The Development of American Philosophy* (Boston: Houghton Mifflin, 1960). See also the primary works of Ralph Waldo Emerson and Walt Whitman as well as Theodore Parker, Amos Bronson Alcott and William Ellery Channing.

7. See Lucretius (97?–54 BCE) in *De Rerum Natura*.

8. Epictetus, *The Works of Epictetus*, trans. E. Carter (Boston. Little Brown, 1865), Chapter I, 6.

9. Diogenes Laertius, *Lives of Eminent Philosophers*, trans. R. D. Hicks (Cambridge, MA: Harvard University Press, 1950), Chapter VII, 88.

10. Epictetus, *Works*, Chapter II, 10.

11. Marcus Aurelius Antoninus, *The Meditations of the Emperor Marcus Aurelias Antoninus*, trans. George Long (New York: A. L. Burt, 1864), Chapter VII, 55 and Chapter V, 2.

12. Several of the Eastern religions contain basic ideas which parallel those of Stoicism, including the Hindu and Buddhist belief that we must free ourselves from desire; the Confucian ideal of "*li*" or equanimity, poise, and decorum; and the Taoist notion of passivity, quietism, and receptivity to the harmonious flow of the universe. The *Tao Te Ching*, for example, says, "There is no greater calamity than not to be contented."

13. Epictetus, *Works*, Chapter I, 6. *Cf.* the following statement by the Roman Stoic and Platonist Boethius (c. 480 – c. 524) from his famous hook *The Consolation of Philosophy*. Boethius was wrongly imprisoned by Theodoric the Great after a life of outstanding public service. He wrote the following words in prison one year before he was executed: "He who has calmly reconciled his life to fate, and set proud death beneath his feet, can look fortune in the face, unbending both to good and bad . . . Why then stand wretched and aghast when fierce tyrants rage in impotence? Fear naught, and hope naught: thus shall you have a weak man's rage disarmed. But whoso fears with trembling, or desires aught from them, he stands not firmly rooted, but dependent: he has thrown away his shield; he can be rooted up, and he links for himself the very chain whereby he maybe dragged." (Boethius, *The Consolation of Philosophy*, trans. W. V. Cooper (New York: Modern Library, 1943), 8.

14. Another Stoic argument for pre-determinism is that statements about events are either true or false; they do not become true or false relative to future happenings. We may know in the future whether a statement is true or false but the statement is not made true or false by subsequent events. The proposition "There will be a world war" does not become true when war breaks out but is verified as being true at that time. Therefore, the Stoic would argue, a true proposition about the future states an unavoidable event, a false proposition, an impossibility.

This problem, of whether there can be true propositions about the future has been extensively debated among logicians. Aristotle, for example, took the position that truth refers to reality, which encompasses only the past and the present. The future is not real and therefore no proposition about the future can be true now; it can only become true as the future passes into the present.

CHAPTER 7: EVOLUTIONISM

1. W. Paley, *Natural Theology* (London: J. Faulder, 1809), 3, 11. See also Chapters VIII to X, and XIX to XXII.

2. Certain biologists such as J. B. de Lamarck (1744–1829) and T. D. Lysenko (1898–1977) proposed an unusual interpretation of the way in which evolution operates. They argued that species can acquire new characteristics through interaction with their environment and genetically transmit these changes to their offspring. Giraffes that stretched their necks reaching for leaves would have offspring with longer necks. The orthodox Darwinian interpretation is that those species that already possessed favorable variations were able to compete successfully.

3. See William Behe's *Darwin's Black Box*; William Demski's *Intelligent Design*; and the work of physicists such as Paul Davies, John Polkinghorn, and John Barrow.

4. The concept of the fittest is also subject to the criticisms that it is circular, for an organism is called "fit" because it survives, and it survives because it is fit.

5. H. Spencer, *The Data of Ethics* (New York: A. L. Burt, 1897), 26.

6. H. Spencer, *The Principles of Ethics* (New York: D. Appleton and Co., 1895), Vol.1, 15.

7. C. Darwin, *The Descent of Man* (New York: D. Appleton and Co., 1876), 612.

8. Still further, the integrative complexity that Spencer regarded as evolutionary progress may not always be worthwhile. A simple, good-hearted person, the honest uncomplicated soul, can be far more admirable than the complex one. Even though complexity may be a later development in evolution, it is not necessarily better.

CHAPTER 8: THE ETHIC OF DUTY

1. This utilitarian view of punishment should not be confused with the theory of utilitarianism discussed in chapter 4, which advocates providing the greatest amount of happiness for the greatest number of people. They are distinct but related theories, and both would advocate this view of punishment.

2. To reform someone means to ensure that he or she will not commit the offense again; it usually involves counseling and perhaps religious instruction. To rehabilitate means to provide that individual with the means to lead a law-abiding life, such as providing education or teaching someone a trade.

3. As a representative of act-deontologism see E. F. Carritt, *Theory of Morals*. Also included under this heading are situation moralists such as Rudolf Bultmann, John A. T. Robinson, and Joseph Fletcher, as well as most existentialists such as Jean-Paul Sartre.

4. Among rule-deontologists could be listed R. H. Price, W. D. Ross, Samuel Clarke, Thomas Reid, and, of course, Immanuel Kant.

5. Whether or not we are blameworthy depends upon the degree of wrong in the consequence we allow. In Catholic ethics, for example, if we merely foresee but do not intend a harmful result in an essentially worthwhile act, then it is still right. If, for example, in trying to save the life of a baby, the mother is allowed to die this is an unwilled, foreseen side effect and therefore permissible in Catholic ethics. The mother is not killed intentionally; rather, the baby is being saved.

6. Immanuel Kant, *Foundations of the Metaphysics of Morals* (New York: Bobbs-Merrill, 1959), 9. See also H. Paton, *The Moral Law; Kant's (Groundwork of the Metaphysics of Morals* (London: Hutchinson University Library, 1965). Paton offers an excellent textual analysis.

7. Kant, *Foundations*, Chapter 1.

8. One question that has been raised in this connection is whether it is preferable for a person to behave well on principle or by inclination. Many moralists conclude that they would he better off living among those who are naturally kind instead of those who control their malice in accordance with proper rules of conduct.

9. Kant, *Foundations*, 17

10. Kant, *Foundations*, 18. For a good analysis of the Categorical Imperative see Allen Wood, *Kant's Ethical Thought* (Cambridge: Cambridge University Press, 1999).

11. Kant, *Foundations*, 47. John Rawls discusses the Kantian ethic with great insight in his *Lectures on the History of Moral Philosophy* (Cambridge: Cambridge University Press, 2000).

12. See F. M. Kamm, *Intricate Ethics: Rights, Responsibilities and Permissible Harms* (Oxford: Oxford University Press, 2007.

13. See Gary Banham, *Kant's Practical Philosophy* (New York: Palgrave Macmillan, 2003.

14. W. D. Ross, *The Right and the Good* (Oxford: Clarendon Press, 1930).

15. See the discussion on "right," "ought," and imperatives in R. M. Hare, *The Language of Morals* (New York: Oxford University Press, 1952), Chapters 10 and 11.

CHAPTER 9: THE TEACHINGS OF RELIGION

1. In the New Testament, for example, the earliest Gospels, Matthew and Mark, were written about 75 BCE, some forty-five years after the death of Christ, and the latest, John, around 95 BCE. A gap of time of this magnitude would necessarily produce inaccuracies; it is therefore problematic to treat the Bible as literal truth.

2. For a contemporary study on acting as if the sin had never been committed see Vladimir Jankelevitch, *Forgiveness* (Chicago: University of Chicago Press, 2005).

3. See M. Buber, *I and Thou* (New York: Charles Scribner's Sons, 1958).

4. St. Thomas Aquinas, *Summa Theologica*, trans. the English Dominican Fathers (London: Burns, Oates, and Washbourne, Ltd., 1912–1936), First Part of the Second Part, A.62, A.4.

5. Although God's love is freely given to human beings, the Christian view is that a person can only come into relation with that love through faith in Christ. In this way humanity's sinful nature is redeemed and people are drawn into the realm of divine grace.

6. The Christian idea of eternal damnation in Hell sometimes causes embarrassment to theologians because of the difficulty in reconciling this idea with the general concept of forgiveness. The notion of a temporary Hell has been proposed, and Catholic theology includes belief in Purgatory, which is an intermediary stage where souls are punished and purified of sin; but even these mild ideas appear to contradict a non-retaliatory system. If Christians are obliged to help even unrepentant sinners, it is difficult to see why God would give people the punishment they deserve.

7. Socrates predated Jesus in this idea, for Plato reported Socrates as saving "we ought not to retaliate or render evil for evil to anyone, whatever evil we may have suffered from him," and again, "a man ought to do what be admits to be right. Neither injury nor retaliation nor warding off evil by evil is ever right." Plato, *The Works of Plato*, trans. B. Jowett (New York: Dial Press, 1936), Vol. 3, 150–51.

8. Christians have differed in their adherence to a pacifist view. Some, such as Leo Tolstoy in *A Confession, The Gospel in Brief,* and *What I Believe,* trans. Maude, Aylmer (Oxford: Oxford University Press, 1948), have taken nonviolence as a primary Christian principle, whereas others have accepted the "church militant" and justified the Inquisition and the Crusades. There is Biblical precedent for both views, for Christ not only advocated turning the other cheek but also whipped the moneylenders out of the temple.

9. Joseph Fletcher, "Six Propositions: The New Look in "Christian Ethics," *Harvard Divinity Bulletin* (October 1959), 14.

10. Joseph Fletcher, *Situation Ethics: The New Morality* (Philadelphia: Westminster Press, 1964), 158.

11. Emil Brunner may be taken as representative of this approach, claiming that whatever God wills becomes good or right. "God's will controls absolutely everything," he wrote, and "What God does and wills is good; all that opposes the will of God is bad." E. Brunner, *The Divine Imperative, A Study in Christian Ethics,* trans. Olive Wyon (Philadelphia: Westminster Press, 1947), 119 and 53, respectively.

12. R. Niebuhr, *Moral Man and Immoral Society* (New York: Scribner's Sons, 1953). See also Garth Kasimu Baker-Fletcher, *Dirty Hands: Christian Ethics in a Morally Ambiguous World* (Minneapolis, MN: Augsburg Fortress, 1999).

13. Scientists have identified the black stone as a meteorite, which to the believer means that it fell from heaven. For a general description of Islamic thought see C. T. R. Heuver, *Understanding Islam* (Indianapolis: Augsburg Fortress Press, 2006).

14. See Jarret Brachman, *Global Jihadism* (London: Routledge, 2009).

15. Jonathan Brockopp, ed., *Islamic Ethics of Life: Abortion, War, and Euthanasia* (Columbia: University of South Carolina Press, 2002).

CHAPTER 10: VIRTUE ETHICS

1. Gail Fine, ed., *The Oxford Handbook of Plato* (New York: Oxford University Press, 2008).

2. See Timothy Chappell, *Values and Virtues: Aristotelianism in Contemporary Ethics* (New York: Oxford University Press, 2006).

3. See Roger Crisp and Michael Slote, eds., *Virtue Ethics* (New York: Oxford, 1997).

4. Adam Smith, *Theory of the Moral Sentiments*, Part I, Chapter 1 (New York: Cambridge University Press, 2002).

5. Carol Gilligan, *In a Different Voice* (Cambridge: Harvard University Press, 1993). See also Philippa Foot, *Virtues and Vices* (Berkeley: University of California Press, 1978); Nel Noddings, *Caring: A Feminine Approach to Ethics and Moral Education* (Berkeley: University of California Press, 1999); Virginia Held, *The Ethics of Care* (Oxford: University of Oxford Press, 2006); and Annette Baier, *Postures of the Mind* (Minneapolis: University of Minnesota Press, 1985).

6. Peta Bowden, *Caring: Gender-Sensitive Ethics* (London: Routledge, 1997).

CHAPTER 11: EXISTENTIALISM

1. William James, *Essays in Pragmatism* (New York: Haffner Publishing Co., 1948), 159.

2. Blaise Pascal, *Thoughts*, trans. W. F. Trotter (New York: P. F. Collier, 1910).

3. Also numbered among the existentialists is Nicholas Berdyaev (1874–1948), Miguel de Unamuno (1864–1936), Jose Ortega y Gasset (1883–1955), Jacques Maritain (1882–1973), Martin Buber (1878–1965), Paul Tillich (1886–1965), and Simone de Beauvoir (1908–1986).

4. Jean-Paul Sartre, *Nausea*, trans. J. Alexander (Norfolk, CT: New Directions, 1964).

Once we become aware of ourselves as existent beings, we also become aware of certain psychological states that have philosophic significance. The catalog of these states include anxiety, anguish (*angst*), dread, forlornness, boredom, alienation, estrangement, despair, and melancholy. Such states cannot be eliminated but they can function as catalysts, enlivening human beings to the possibilities that life presents. They can rouse us from our customary slumber, and move us toward a richer existence.

5. A. Camus, *The Myth of Sisyphus* (New York: Alfred A. Knopf, Inc., 1955), 91.

6. Jean-Paul Sartre, *Existentialism*, trans. B. Frechtman (New York: Philosophical Library, 1947).

7. G. Marcel, *The Existential Background of Human Dignity* (Cambridge, MA: Harvard University Press, 1963), 96.

8. M. Heidegger, *Being and Time*, trans. Macquarrie and E. Robinson (New York: Harper and Bros., 1962), 62.

9. Jean-Paul Sartre, *Nausea*, 7–20.

10. F. Dostoyevsky, *Notes from the Underground*, trans. R. E. Matlaw (New York: E. P. Dutton, 1960).

11. A. Gide, *Prometheus Illbound*, trans. L. Rothermere (London: Chatto and Windus, 1919).

12. F. Nietzsche, *The Gay Science*, in *the Portable Nietzsche*, ed. W. Kaufmann (New York: Viking Press, 1954), 97. See also F. Dostoyevsky, *Crime and Punishment*, trans. S. Monas (New York: Signet, 1968), especially Part 3, (Chapter 5, 255ff, and Part 8, Chapter 4, 400ff.)

13. F. Nietzsche, *The Anti-Christ*, in *The Portable Nietzsche*, 572–73, 589.

14. F. Nietzsche, *The Gay Science*, in *The Portable Nietzsche*, 93, 97.

15. F. Nietzsche, *The Gay Science*, in *The Portable Nietzsche*, 95, 96.

16. F. Nietzsche, *Thus Spake Zarathustra*, trans. M. Cowan (Chicago: H. Regnery Co., 1957).

17. J.-P. Sartre, *Existentialism*, 58.

18. J.-P. Sartre, "The Humanism of Existentialism" in *Existentialism* (New York: Citadel Press, 1968), 37.

19. Jean-Paul Sartre, "The Humanism of Existentialism" in *Existentialism*.

20. Jean-Paul Sartre, *Being and Nothingness*, trans. Hazel Barnes (New York: Philosophical Library, 1956), 627. For a general introduction to existentialism see D. Cooper, *Existentialism* (Oxford: Blackwell, 1999) and Richard Appignanesi, *Introducing Existentialism* (Cambridge: Icon, 2001).

INDEX

.

ABOUT THE AUTHOR

Burton Porter is the author and/or editor of numerous books on philosophy including *The Head and the Heart, Philosophy Through Fiction and Film, The Voice of Reason, Religion and Reason, Personal Philosophy, Reasons for Living, Philosophy: A Literary and Conceptual Approach, Deity and Morality,* and the present 4th edition of *The Good Life.*

Dr. Porter received his Bachelor's degree from the University of Maryland and his Ph.D. from St. Andrews University, Scotland, with graduate study at Oxford University, England. He has taught at various institutions such as Russell Sage College and Drexel University, and has served as a Department Chair and as Dean of Arts and Sciences. At present, Dr. Porter is on the faculty at Western New England College in Springfield, Massachusetts, and is visiting professor at Mount Holyoke College in South Hadley, Massachusetts. He received the award of Outstanding Educator of America.